Stephen King

The First Decade,
Carrie to *Pet Sematary*

Twayne's United States Authors Series

Warren French, Editor

University College of Swansea, Wales

TUSAS 531

STEPHEN KING
(1947–   )
Photograph reprinted by permission of WORLD WIDE PHOTOS.

Stephen King
The First Decade,
Carrie to *Pet Sematary*

By Joseph Reino

Villanova University

Twayne Publishers
A Division of G. K. Hall & Co. · Boston

Stephen King: The First Decade, Carrie to Pet Sematary
Joseph Reino

Copyright 1988 by G.K. Hall & Co.
All rights reserved.
Published by Twayne Publishers
A Division of G.K. Hall & Co.
70 Lincoln Street
Boston, Massachusetts 02111

Copyediting supervised by Lewis DeSimone
Book production by Gabrielle B. McDonald
Book design by Barbara Anderson

Typeset in 11 pt. Garamond
by r/tsi typografic company, inc.
Hamden, Connecticut

Printed on permanent/durable acid-free paper
and bound in the United States of America

Library of Congress Cataloging-in-Publication Data

Reino, Joseph.
  Stephen King: the first decade, Carrie to Pet sematary.

  (Twayne's United States authors series; TUSAS 531)
  Bibliography: p.
  Includes index.
  1. King, Stephen, 1947–   —Criticism and
interpretation.   2. Horror tales, American—History
and criticism.   I. Title.   II. Series.
PS3561.I483Z84   1988   813'.54   87-19247
ISBN 0-8057-7512-9 (alk. paper)

For

S. M. G.
S. G.
A. R.

Contents

About the Author

Joseph Reino was born in Queen Village, Pennsylvania. A graduate of Temple University, where he specialized in modern British and American literature, he earned his doctorate on a teaching fellowship at the University of Pennsylvania. Since then, he has taught both in the graduate school and the honors program of Villanova University. He delivered a series of eighty television lectures on modern literature on Philadelphia's "WFIL-TV University of the Air." His earlier volume in Twayne's United States Authors Series, *Karl Shapiro*, was an outgrowth of these popular television lectures. Dr. Reino has also conducted seminars at the annual meetings of the *Modern Language Association* and has recently published a lengthy article on the Scottish poet-novelist George Mackay Brown in the *Dictionary of Literary Biography: Poets of Great Britain and Ireland, 1945–1960*. He has authored three volumes of poetry: *Half-Remembered Outcries* (1972), *Who Would Dare Dream It Again?* (1984), and *Kol Nidre for a Cast-Off* (1987). An undergraduate course entitled "Tales of Terror and the Supernatural," introduced into the curriculum of the English department of Villanova University in 1980, led to the writing of the present book on Stephen King.

Preface

What is surprising about Stephen King is less his prodigious popularity and productivity—although this has been the subject of considerable comment and controversy—than the fact that an author who encourages a public fun-and-games self-image should, in much of his creative work, have so grim a view of himself, his readers, his state (Maine), his nation, and the malevolent universe into which he had the misfortune to be born. It is not unusual to come across a newspaper or magazine photograph of King in a hairy bear wig, or with grinning vampire teeth in his mouth—seeming to be playfully strangling his wife, sticking out his tongue at a photographer, or giggling at an interviewer like an unstable adolescent—behaving in public as if he wrote nothing that was to be taken seriously. The comic book edition of *Creepshow*, containing cartoon versions of "Father's Day," "The Lonesome Death of Jordy Verrill," "The Crate," "Something to Tide You Over," and "They're Creeping Up on You," is filled with what are supposed to be horror sketches of King himself as a half-lunatic boy reading *Creepshow* comics (on the front cover), or skeletal guide making supposedly scary introductions to successive comic strips, always preceding his brief comments with a corny "heh, heh, heh."

Obviously, this kind of constant clowning sells books and is no detriment to King's popularity among American teenagers. But whether such giggling self-abuse in public is part of a deliberate publicity ploy (motivated by a need ever to increase and multiply sales), or is prompted by an inner urge to create the image of a brainless adolescent (ultimately motivated by a compulsive need to conceal painful sensitivities and malevolences), cannot be ascertained. Be that as it may, this process of acting out the role of a public clown is a kind of "image-mutilation" that differs only in degree of popular awareness from that of such distinguished Harvard figures as Robert Lowell, who deliberately exposed his mental and sexual problems in the prose and poetry of *Life Studies* (1960). Significantly however, Lowell, relatively unknown to the average American, was trying to tear away a "mask"; whereas King, who is capable of producing such a brilliant novel as *'Salem's Lot*, such sensitive novellas as "The Body" and "Apt Pupil," and such poetic short stories as "Night Surf" and "The Last Rung on the Ladder" (and sustaining his remarkable popularity at the same time), seems bent on imposing on the public a diverting persona. The phrase used by the dramatist Pirandello to explain the psychology of his characters to an uncomprehending drama public back in the 1920s seems appropriate here: "naked masks."

Perhaps closer to a darker "Stephen King" is the front cover of the New English Library edition of the novel *Rage* (1977/1983), pseudoanonymously authored by a fictitious Richard Bachman, that pictures a seated, sullen-looking boy of twelve (the bizarre Charlie Decker of the novel) holding a pistol close to his crotch. The face has been made to look suspiciously like that of a boyish Stephen King. The blurb next to the figure intriguingly states that "The problem was complex," that is, the problem of the boy's psyche, but the "solution killingly simple"—one of the words ("kill*ing*ly") containing the four letters of King's last name. Such masochistic wordplay is hardly accidental, for throughout his narratives, King toys with himself (his name, career, and personal relationships) in a now-you-see-it / now-you-don't way. Not only does one come across characters called Steve, Stevie, Stephens, Stevenson, etc.—characters that tend to be consistently sinister, like the never-aging Stevens of "The Breathing Method"—but bits and pieces of King's personal life crop up in a variety of out-of-the-way places. As *Danse Macabre* observes in another connection, "You will find the autobiographical element constantly creeping in" (12). In its fireplace motto, "The Breathing Method" may make the objective and repeated claim that "IT IS THE TALE NOT HE WHO TELLS IT" (*DS*, 442), but the frequency of autobiographical teasers in novels and novellas seems to suggest, as in "The Reaper's Image," that King himself is sometimes "half sick" of distorted revelations—or Tennysonian "shadows" as he poetically calls them (*SK*, 369). Whether the reader is supposed to recognize these odd scraps of autobiography, or indeed know at what point "revelation" leaves off and high fantasy enters in, is a subject for endless conjecture and beyond the limited scope of this book. In this connection, one is reminded of the "three-dimensional" magic mirror of same "Reaper's Image," possessing a "faint magnifying effect" that "added an almost fourth-dimensional distortion"— sometimes reflecting a "black splotch," a "pearly patch," a "blind eye," a "moth-eaten buffalo head," a "hooded figure," and sometimes nothing at all. Sometimes, one suspects that King suspects his ever-avid horror fans may think of him in the phrase that a prostitute shouts to the back of her rock-star sex partner in *The Stand* as he permanently abandons her bedroom, "You ain't no nice guy" (75–77); and this may, perhaps, explain all the compensating giggling and public horsing around in which King so much likes to engage. To paraphrase an astute observation in Herman Melville's *Billy Budd* (chapter 11)—as will be repeatedly implied, and sometimes stated directly throughout the chapters of this book—to try and enter into King's imagination and personality, without a clue derived from some source other than what is known as "knowledge of the world," is hardly possible.

From time to time, this study will note certain formulas, conscious or unconscious, upon which, or around which, King weaves his countless tales of terror and the dark supernatural. But none is more devastating than the inescapable conclusion one must reluctantly draw from the incisive and psychologically penetrating "Apt Pupil," that subtly moves beyond mere storytelling into contemporary gothic parable (*DS*, 109–286). The typical All-American boy who likes to hear horror tales of Nazi tortures has to stand for none other than horror fans themselves (especially horror-hungry teenagers), and the disreputable old ex-Nazi who fills the boy's ears with an endless supply of unspeakable and sometimes revolting Teutonic terrors is yet another symbolic mutilation of—*mirabile dictu*—none other than King himself, or any skillful terror master for that matter. In "Apt Pupil," the corrupt boy-listener and old tale-teller so intertwine and eventually externalize their mutually encouraged criminality—at first only verbally—that one is led thoughtfully to ponder the rationale of the entire gothic genre. The eternal ethical/aesthetic question—one of the imponderables of literature—that "Apt Pupil" seems to compel upon a reflective reader is simply this: what is the difference between the avid fan who "loves horror" and the ancient Romans who went to the amphitheater to be entertained by bloodshed and mayhem, or bestial dictators and terrorists of the twentieth century who bash and brutalize their victims with serenely untroubled consciences? "Apt Pupil" takes dim delight in an American civilization that claims Nazism was "bad," but certain American manly magazines all too willingly advertise "German flags emblazoned with swastikas and Nazi Lugars and a game called Panzer Attack." King appears to turn his critical knife both inward and outward when he points out that while those same magazines' "words" were saying that Nazism was "bad," the advertisements seem to suggest that "a lot of people must not mind" (DS, 119). Among this "lot of people" one must find—willingly or unwillingly—both horror-reader and horror-author. As with the gothic genre in general, "Apt Pupil" blandly observes that "what the Germans did exercises a deadly fascination over us, something that opens up the catacombs of the imagination" (DS, 279)—precisely what Stephen King's terrors do to the minds of some readers who themselves turn into, or perhaps already are, "apt pupils."

Philosophic reflections such as these, coupled with psychological penetrations, deceptive appearances, tantalizing vanishings, a remarkable talent for multileveled gothic symbolism, and an ability to pass beyond public horseplay into a kind of literary comedy that is sometimes almost Chaucerian in its hilarity, raise the stories that Stephen King has published during his first decade as a best-selling author above the current level of terror-claptrap, the traditional penny-dreadfuls that trash the marketplace of popular paperback fiction. Stories like "Night Surf" and "Last Rung on the Ladder"—and passages like the haunting evocation of the vanished "twenty-year-old blueberry bucket" of a dead boy in "The Body" (holding it, reading it, feeling it, looking at "my own face in whatever reflection might be left" [DS, 419–20])—are sheer prose poems, here and there limned with delicate touches of pathos. In certain respects, these are not easily overmatched.

Analysis in this present study is limited to twelve important publications that appeared between 1973 and 1983: nine major novels (Carrie, 'Salem's Lot, The Shining, Firestarter, The Stand, Cujo, Dead Zone, Christine, and Pet Sematary—that already constitute the classic King), two volumes of short fiction (Night Shift and Different Seasons), and one book of movie criticism, Danse Macabre. Conjoined with a brief outline of King's personal life, chapter 1 explores the Cinderella motif in both Carrie and King's personal life. Bound together in chapter 2, "Jerusalem's Lot" and 'Salem's Lot delve into darker fantasies of vampirism and personal isolation in two similarly named towns. Because some young innocents are entrapped by compulsive supernal forces over which they have little understanding and almost no rational control, The Shining and Firestarter are taken together in chapter 3. Some impressive and unusual themes of universal destruction in the epic-apocalyptic Stand, King's longest and too uncomfortably massive novel, are discussed in chapter 4. Cujo and Dead Zone in chapter 5 and Christine and Pet Sematary in chapter 6 are taken together because of important similarities: adolescent psychology in the first instance, and the despair of the dark philosopher in the second. The critical *Danse Macabre* and the poetic novella *Cycle of the Werewolf*, works of considerable importance in a serious study of King, are frequently used as support points. Primarily thematic and favorable, this book strives for critical objectivity, highlighting in-depth examinations of psychology, symbolism, imaginative wordplay, and mythic and current cultural analogies.

This is a preliminary study of the early works that lifted King to celebrity status and moved him to the very forefront of gothic fiction, and as such, is not intended to be definitive. Comic books, privately printed volumes, high-priced collector's items, incomplete works, memorabilia, and motion picture scripts and films (most of which are quite forgettable) are not included. Whenever possible, King's works are referred to by abbreviated titles; and because of their importance in explaining King's point of view, citations from six in particular are identified within parentheses after references and quotations according to the following pattern of abbreviations:. *'Salem's Lot (SL), Danse Macabre (DM), Night Shift (NS), Skeleton Crew (SK), Different Seasons (DS)*, and *Cycle of the Werewolf (CW)*. Abbreviations limited to one chapter alone are so designated in the respective notes. Unless otherwise indicated, all page references are to paperback editions.

One cannot conclude this introduction without acknowledging an important reference volume, *Horror Literature*, edited by Marshall B. Tymn, indispensable for the study of the gothic genre, and the basic work in analysis and interpretation of Stephen King by such editors and commentators as Douglas E. Winter, Darrell Schweitzer, Tim Underwood, and Chuck Miller. Their respective volumes are listed in the bibliography. Worthy of special commendation is the extensive work of Michael R. Collings in an important series of recent and continuing publications: *The Many Facets of Stephen King* (1985), *The Shorter Works of Stephen King* (1985), *Stephen King as Richard Bachman*, and *The Films of Stephen King* (1986). These scholarly contributions to an understanding of King's fiction are impressive, and their impact upon the present study, despite occasions of interpretive disagreement, is considerable. The present volume would have been much the poorer without them.

Joseph Reino

Villanova University

Chronology

Residence at Stanley Hotel in Estes Park suggests basic plot and symbolism for "The Shine," eventually expanded and retitled *The Shining. Carrie.*

1975 Purchases house in Bridgton, Maine. Completes *The Stand. 'Salem's Lot.*

1976 *'Salem's Lot* nominated to best-novel category in World Fantasy Award. Release of film version of *Carrie*, directed by Brian DePalma.

1977 Meets Peter Straub on a trip to England; upon return, purchases a new home in Center Lovell, Maine. *The Shining; Rage*, first novel to appear under pseudonym Richard Bachman.

1978 Moves to Orrington, Maine, to serve as writer-in-residence in the English Department of the University of Maine at Orono. Theories developed while teaching creative writing eventually mature into a book-length analysis of horror movies, *Danse Macabre*. Signs major book contract with New American Library. Serves as judge for the 1977 World Fantasy Awards. *The Stand* and *Night Shift.*

1979 Moves back to Center Lovell. *Night Shift* nominated to best collection/anthology, and *The Stand* to the best novel categories of World Fantasy Awards. Release of television mini-series version of *'Salem's Lot*, directed by Tobe Hooper. *The Dead Zone; The Long Walk* (second novel under pseudonym Richard Bachman). Guest of honor at World Fantasy Convention, Providence, Rhode Island.

1980 Purchases winter home in Bangor, Maine, retaining Center Lovell as summer residence. Receives World Fantasy best novel nomination for *The Dead Zone*, but withdraws the book from the final ballot. Receives a special World Fantasy Award for contributions in the genre; Baltrop Award in best anthology/collection category for *Night Shift*. Named *People* magazine's Writer of the Year. Film version of *The Shining*, directed by Stanley Kubrick.

1981 *Danse Macabre. Roadwork* (third Richard Bachman novel). Receives special British Fantasy Award for contributions to the field, Career Alumni Award from the University of Maine, World Fantasy *Award* nomination for "The Mist," and best short story nomination for "The Way Station" in Nebula Awards.

1982   *The Dark Tower: The Gunslinger; Different Seasons*; *The Running Man* (fourth Richard Bachman novel). Release of film *Creepshow*, directed by George A. Romero. Receives British Fantasy Award in best novel category for *Cujo*, Hugo Award in best nonfiction category for *Danse Macabre*. "Do the Dead Sing" receives World Fantasy Award in best short story category.

1983   *Christine* and *Pet Sematary*. Film versions of *Cujo*, directed by Lewis Teague; *Dead Zone*, directed by David Cronenberg; and *Christine*, directed by John Carpenter.

1984   *The Talisman* (coauthored with Peter Straub). Film versions of *Children of the Corn*, directed by Fritz Kiersch; and *Firestarter*, directed by Mark Lester. World Fantasy Award nominations for *Different Seasons* and "The Breathing Method."

1985   9 February, interview appearing in *Bangor Times* reveals for the first time that King has been publishing novels under the pseudonym Richard Bachman. *Thinner* (fifth Bachman novel) and *The Bachman Books* (containing *Rage, The Long Walk, Roadwork*, and *The Running Man*). Release of film *Silver Bullet*, directed by Danial Attias. *Skeleton Crew*.

1986   *Maximum Overdrive*; *Bare Bones*; *It*.

1987   *The Eyes of the Dragon*.

Chapter One
Cinderella Hero/
Cinderella Heroine

Father, Friend, and Dream

The first specific in just about every biographical sketch of Stephen (Edwin) King is the separation of his father and mother when the author-to-be was about two years old (1949).[1] A merchant mariner during World War II, the father Donald King walked out of the lives of wife Nellie Pillsbury (presumably from a lesser New England branch of the famous Pillsbury Flour family), natural son Steve, and adopted son David—never to be heard from again (*DM*, 93). A typical literary echo of the lost father appears in the short story "The Monkey," one of countless instances in which narrative details parallel the private life of the author: the "vanished father" of the fate-obsessed Hal Shelburn is a "merchant mariner with a navigator's certificate" (*SK*, 150).

In a mysterious manner, befitting the heritage of America's most famous contemporary writer of terror and the supernatural, Donald King did manage to communicate with his sons, especially the younger Steve, by way of a shipboard film, a paperback collection, some unpublished manuscripts, and a batch of rejection slips from publishers of weird fiction. Like some of the overcurious youngsters in his narratives (Mark Petrie in *'Salem's Lot*, Marty Coslaw in *Cycle of the Werewolf*, Charlie Decker in *Rage*, and Gordie Lachance in "The Body"), Steve and his adopted brother found a home movie that once belonged to their father. Pooling their savings to rent a movie projector, they watched "over and over again in fascinated silence" as the filmed father, leaning against the deck rail of an unnamed ship, raised his hand, smiled, and—as young King liked to imagine— appeared to be waving to sons Dave and Steve, who were as yet not even conceived when the film was originally made (*DM*, 95).

The discovery of the shipboard film, which the boys "watched" and "rewound" and "watched again," occurred in a kind of "family museum," an attic over the garage of an aunt's house in Durham, Maine, an attic with "just [enough] room for a small boy to twist and turn his way along narrow aisles, ducking under the arm of a standing lamp or stepping over a crate of old wallpaper samples" (*DM*, 94). In "The Monkey," a similar closet is a "storage space that ran the length of the second floor on the left side, extra space that had never been finished off . . . chilly in winter and hot enough in summer to wring a bucketful of sweat out of your pores" (*SK*, 150). In addition to the father-revealing movie, young Steve found a "treasure trove" of his father's old Avon paperbacks of horror stories and weird fiction, as well as—most surprising of all—discarded manuscripts of horror stories that Donald King had unsuccessfully attempted to publish. In "The Monkey," the closet houses stacks of charts, twenty volumes of Barron's *Guide to Navigation*, a set of cockeyed binoculars, "touristy things," a glass globe with a "tiny Eiffel Tower" inside, funny records in foreign languages, etc. (*SK*, 151). According to Nellie King, her husband "would go around with a paperback western stuffed in his back pocket." But apparently Donald King's "real interest" was science fiction and horror stories (*DM*, 95). Delving into this abandoned box of the elder King's "real interest" was the young King's first introduction to such masters of weird fiction as Robert Bloch, Clark Ashton Smith, Frank Belknap Long, Ray Bradbury, Fritz Leiber, Zelia Bishop, and Abraham Merritt. What King now refers to as the "pick of the litter," however, were works of the often controversial but nevertheless widely acknowledged master of fantasy-horror, Howard Phillips Lovecraft— whose shadow, according to King, "so long and gaunt, and his eyes, so dark and puritanical . . . overlie almost all of the important horror fiction that has come since." In photographs of Lovecraft, it was the eyes that King especially remembered, "eyes like those in the old portraits which still hang in many New England houses, black eyes which seem to look inward as well as outward" (*DM*, 97).

Steve's vanished father may have posthumously introduced his son to horror fiction; but his aunt thoroughly disapproved of such readings, suspecting, like Danny and Ralphie Glick's mother in *'Salem's Lot*, that "all that stuff was bad news, rotted your brains or something" (69). A short while after the attic adventure of the stepbrothers, the entire paternal collection of paperbacks disappeared and, like Donald King himself, was never found again. Steve has always suspected his aunt "might have been an unindicted co-conspirator in

[this] case . . . not that it mattered in the long run" (*DM*, 97). Though unknown and unpublished, Donald King had opened for his son imaginative horror-doors that would never again be closed—doors that became, in future stories, the mysterious trap door in the subbasement of the rat-filled factory of "Graveyeard Shift"—the forbidden door to Room 217 about which Danny Torrance is so curious in *The Shining*—the door of Hubie Marsten's upper room that young Ben opens to his everlasting regret in *'Salem's Lot*. In "The Monkey," it is a down-the-rabbit-hole door—metaphorically, the same hole in which the huge and shaggy St. Bernard Cujo is bitten by rabid bats. Whether the loss of his father in early years is the ultimate cause, the theme of a father lost and strangely regained was to be one of the identifying hallmarks of King's fiction. The opening line of *'Salem's Lot* reads, "Almost everyone thought the man and the boy were father and son"; and the opening line of *Pet Sematary*, some eight years later, states: "Louis Creed, who had lost his father at three and who had never known a grandfather, never expected to find a father as he entered his middle age, but that was exactly what happened." Instances of this obsession, too numerous to catalog here, are referred to as the "lost-father motif" throughout this study. Interesting ramifications, both dramatic and psychological, are explored in considerable depth in subsequent chapters.

Quite by accident, the disappearance of yet another person was revealed in March 1979—this one more sudden and savage than the father's and characterized by an unexpected ambivalence. This traumatic loss might be regarded as a second major specific in a King biography. King had been invited to be one of three speakers in a panel discussion of horror sponsored by a mystery-and-detective bookshop in Manhattan. The other two panelists were fellow writers Janet Jeppson and Robert Marasco. Rather inevitably—and King should surely have expected it, considering the kind of fiction he produces and the gothic orientation of the audience of writers and fans—the panelists were asked whether they could remember anything from childhood that was "particularly terrible." Robert Marasco wisely said that he could not. Perhaps unfortunately, King quickly snapped at the bait by offering what he calls a "train story" so that the questioner would not be "totally disappointed": "According to Mom, I had gone off to play at a neighbor's house—a house that was near a railroad line. About an hour after I left I came back (she said), as white as a ghost. I would not speak for the rest of that day; I would not tell her . . . why my chum's mom hadn't walked me back, but allowed me to come home alone. It turned out that the kid I had been playing with had been run over by a freight train while playing or crossing the tracks. Years later, my mother told me they had picked up the pieces in a wicker basket . . ." (*DM*, 83).

When King revealed to the audience that he could not actually recall the childhood incident, psychiatrist-novelist Janet Jeppson remarked, "But you've been writing about it ever since"—to which the audience gave its "murmuring approval." Ironically, though King is astute in dealing with the psychology of his characters, especially in pinpointing interrelationships between traumatic childhood experiences and subsequent adult behavior, he expressed strong objection to Jeppson's innocuous remark, calling it a "by-God *motive*" and "jumped-up astrology." In his understandable but not-too-thoughtful reaction, King seemed to have ignored the objective accuracy of what was said. He interpreted the retort to mean that Jeppson was pointing to the ultimate cause of his writing gothic fiction. But according to King's own recording of the comment, all Jeppson appears to have noted was that King had been writing about trains and train accidents all his life—in such stories as "The Body," where an accidental train killing is the chief motif of the story—or in "Sometimes They Come Back," where the murder of a brother occurs in an underpass while a train roars overhead—or in "Apt Pupil," where hoboes are entrapped by the railroad tracks by two psychopathic killers—or in "The Breathing Method," where the inhale-exhale method of giving birth is called "locomotive" breathing—or even in 'Salem's Lot, where Mark Petrie's plastic *Aurora Monster Set* is covertly referred to as "electric trains" in order to deceive some overanxious parents. "The Monkey" narrates an incident that is an imaginative duplicate of the unremembered trauma, here involving a mother, a friend, and a car (instead of a train) accident (*SK*, 157).

Obviously, as with the lost-father obsession, one cannot draw infallible connections between the traumatic loss of a playmate by a train accident (assuming, of course, that the accident with the "slow train" really happened) and King's subsequent tendency to associate trains, railroad tracks, and train stations (and ultimately diabolical vehicles, as in "Trucks" "Uncle Otto's Truck," and *Christine*) with terror and the supernatural. But that psychological and literary interconnections might exist is not exactly improbable. Indeed, in the astute and penetrating "Sometimes They Come Back"—a title that has several implications as applied to King's creative mind—the sound of a roaring train ("thrumming vibration" and "shaking road" in the "horrible sludgy slowness of dreams") seems to "fill the world" at the very moment when twelve-year-old Wayne Norman is slashed by switchblades—a terrifying, repetitive dreamworld, as it were, unconsciously symbolizing King's gothic imagination (*NS*, 149).

Having tried to negate the Jeppson comment, King proceeded to affirm the very obvious—that the past does indeed supply "grist for the writer's mill." *Danse Macabre* records an instance of an intensely vivid dream experienced at the age of eight: "I saw the body of a hanged man dangling from the arm of a scaffold on a hill. Rocks perched on the shoulders of the corpse, and behind it was a noxious green sky, boiling with clouds. This corpse bore a sign: ROBERT BURNS. But when wind caused the corpse to turn in the air, I saw that it was my face—rotted and picked by the birds, but obviously mine. And then the corpse opened its eyes and looked at me. I woke up screaming" (*DM*, 84). Purporting to believe that dreams are merely "scraps and remnants of waking life woven into curious little subconscious quilts by the thrifty human mind" (85), King reveals that he used the dream as one of the central images in *'Salem's Lot* and merely changed the name of the corpse to Hubie Marsten.

But by carefully rearranging the psychology of a personal dream-experience into the deep self-doubts and dark self-questionings of one of the main characters (Ben Mears, significantly also a novelist), King has done more than merely change dream-names, as the following brief dialogue from *'Salem's Lot* illustrates:

"And there was Hubie, hanging from the beam with his body silhouetted against the light from the window."

"Oh, Ben, don't—" [Susan] said nervously.

"No, I'm telling you the truth," he insisted. "The truth of what a nine-year-old boy saw and what the man remembers. . . . [Hubie's] face was not black at all. It was green. The eyes were puffed shut. His hands were livid . . . ghastly. And then he opened his eyes."

Ben took a huge drag on his cigarette and pitched it out his window into the dark.

"I let out a scream that probably could have been heard for two miles. And then I ran." (29)

With a "jag of old bitterness" buried in his voice, and in the context of wanting to prove himself at being "straight," novelist Ben Mears

reveals to his prospective girl friend Susan Norton (with whom he
will soon have intimate relations), the remembered hanging. Braving
the haunted Marsten House was part of a brotherhood-initiation that
was supposed to earn young Ben a much-desired membership in the
"Bloody Pirates," a macho boy's club so exclusive that only members
with "at least three references" (a phrase with not-too-subtle genital
implications) were permitted to apply for admission (28).

Ben's only "reference" is a "glass snow globe" from a "table in the
front hall" that he still had in his hand when he ran from the
Marsten House. At the very end of 'Salem's Lot, an older Ben holds
the stolen snow globe before his eyes (tangible, but highly fragile,
proof of his masculinity), as if trying hard to understand the glass
globe and penetrate its snowy mystery.[2] He is both fascinated and
terrified to see emerge from an open-shuttered window of a little
Lovecraft-like house encased in the globe:

a palid face . . . looking out at you, grinning with long teeth, inviting you
into this house beyond the world in its slow and endless fantasyland of false
snow, where time was a myth. The face was looking out at him now, pallid
and hungry, a face that would never look on daylight or blue skies again.
It was his own face. (418)

Ben tosses the glass paperweight onto the floor where his proof of
masculinity shatters into a thousand pieces. Then, in one of his many
provocative final lines, King points out that novelist Ben Mears,
perhaps out of an unconcious fear of having to face some unbearable
realities, runs away without waiting to see what might have
"leak[ed] out" of the broken snow globe.

Danse Macabre offers the bland cliché that a writer's "success" is
being "in the right place at the right time"; but takes quick refuge
in some not very meaningful images: that the "right time" is in the
"lap of the gods" and the "right place" is one of the "amiable
mysteries of human experience" (85–86). One cannot help adding
that the relationship between dreams and creative use of dreams is
also one of art's "amiable mysteries"—a labyrinthine relationship that
psychologists and literary critics cannot be forbidden endlessly to
explore. Even though King makes every attempt to appear rational
about his creative process—as if it were always in his total imaginative control—his novels and short stories take every opportunity to
proclaim the exact opposite. In 'Salem's Lot, the theory is offered that
"humans manufacture evil just as they manufacture snot or excrement

or fingernail parings—that it doesn't go away—specifically that the Marsten House may have become a kind of evil dry-cell, a malign storage battery" (201).

This philosophy is considered the "old parapsychological wheeze" and part of Ben Mears' psychological baggage, but it is counteracted by the speaker (Susan Norton) when she offers her own rational belief that "houses are only houses" and that "evil dies with the perpetuation of evil acts." Yet Susan and the one to whom she is speaking (Matt Burke) are both going to be devoured by the evil powers of the very house about which Ben has such bizarre ideas; and Susan's common sense explanations (that a house is only a house) are thus rendered utterly null and void. This psychological balancing act—in which rationality consistently tends to lose and irrationality insidiously tends to win out—is exploited in every gothic work that King creates. In its better moments *Danse Macabre* confirms reason's defeat when King acknowledges that (like his "Uncle Clayt" attempting to dowse a well with an applewood "wishbone")—"I have tried again and again to lull the readers of my stories into that state of believability where the ossified shield of 'rationality' has been temporarily laid aside" and "the suspension of disbelief is at hand, and the sense of wonder is again within reach" (89).

As a symbol of the gothic imagination, encased in a globe of protective glass, impenetrable until finally bashed onto a floor, the paperweight image at the beginning and conclusion of *'Salem's Lot* is stunningly effective. Its counterparts are the endless impenetrable doors, corridors, and Kafka-like upper rooms of the brownstone house that stands at 249B East Thirty-third Street that the Eliot-like protagonist of "Breathing Method" is afraid to pursue too far (he is called "Adley," as though he was the uncertain namesake of the 1952–56 Democratic candidate for president, Adlai Stevenson):

[Adley] opened [his] mouth. And the question that came out was: "Are there many more rooms upstairs?"

"Oh, yes sir," [Stevens] said, his eyes never leaving mine. "A great many. A man could become lost. In fact many *have* become lost. Sometimes it seems to me that they go on for miles. Rooms and corridors."

"And entrances and exits?"

[Stevens's] eyebrows went up slightly. "Oh yes. Entrances and exits."

[Adley] waited, but [he] had asked enough—thought . . . [he] had come to the very edge of something that would, perhaps, drive [him] mad. (*DS*, 496)[3]

King may claim that "writers are made, not born out of dreams nor childhood trauma—that becoming a writer . . . is the direct result of conscious will" (DM, 85)—but by the frequent, and indeed what appears to be uncontrollable, expression of private experiences, such as the above-mentioned nightmares, father-losses, and unremembered train-traumas, King often hurls both himself and his ever-eager followers through the "rooms and corridors" and past the "entrances and exits" (i.e., births and deaths) over the very edges of imaginative chaos, sometimes into madness itself. Like Todd Bowden's mind in "Apt Pupil" (an insidiously designed mirror-image of the contemporary horror-enthusiast, especially the young), King's fiction simply "turns and turns." But so often—in spite of its brilliance, or perhaps because of it—these gothic tales "turn on nothing," and, sometimes, "everything inside" a reader becomes deathlike "shades of black on black" (DS, 203). Judging by the sales records of both hard and paperback editions of King's work, American readers must relish these cosmic nihilisms that verge on madness—must indeed enjoy being repeatedly and helplessly engulfed in King's psycho-philosophic black hole.

Early Failures and Successes

Stephen King has been writing from so early an age that it is difficult to pinpoint the precise beginning of his literary career; but if one were to follow the chronology of his essay, "On Becoming a Brand Name," one must assume that his first novel, what he considers his book #1, was written when he was a freshman at the University of Maine. Once his career was established, this early novel was to emerge under the Richard Bachman pseudonym as The Long Walk; but when he wrote it, he submitted it to a Bennett Cerf First Novel competition in the fall of 1967. The novel was promptly rejected with a form letter, and King reports that he was "too crushed" to submit the book to anyone else for consideration (FI, 16). As a sophomore (aged twenty), he composed what would then be his book #2, a 500-page race-riot novel; and through the influence of a creative writing professor, he was fortunate to obtain an agent who recommended the book to some twelve publishers, including Doubleday, who later published his first five books (FI, 17). Throughout his junior and senior years, he wrote book #3.

Upon graduation from the University of Maine, he married Tabitha Spruce, was unable to find a teaching position—a profession for which his abilities were as circumscribed as the teacher's in the short story, "Sometimes They Come Back"—and worked in a laundromat for sixty dollars a week while his wife Tabby worked nights in a Bangor Dunkin' Donuts. Quite by accident, he came across Loren Singer's *The Parallax View* (1970) in the Bangor Public Library and was attracted to its "slightly surrealistic flavor that reminded me of my own work" (*FI*, 17). Because the Singer novel had been published by Doubleday, he was prompted to direct an inquiry there, "fairly confident that I would be invited to send the novel for a reading, and I felt that it was at least possible that they might publish it." He thus came into contact with editor William G. Thompson, who liked the second book and tried to get Doubleday to publish it. Unfortunately, the book was rejected, "a painful blow for me, because I had been allowed to entertain some hope for an extraordinarily long time, and had rewritten the book a third time, trying to bring it into line with what Doubleday's publishing board would accept" (18).

The year 1972, when he and his wife were living in a trailer in Hermon, Maine, was unsatisfactory, or, to use his own elemental slang, the "pits." He obtained a teaching position in a local high school, Hampton Academy; but the salary was only $6,400 a year, and his workload (allowing precious little time for creative writing) consisted of six periods of English teaching with stacks of themes to be corrected at home in the evening. For an hour and half a day, King wrote publishable short stories, but unfortunately unpublishable novels, on his wife's typewriter perched on a child's desk in a furnace room of the trailer. Despite these nagging inconveniences, he managed to produce book #4. King remembers the writing of this fourth book as a "fantastic, white-hot experience," but the book itself was hardly "fantastic." After a quick review for possible Doubleday publication, Bill Thompson returned it and told him to try again. The rejection caused a depression as deep as the publication failures of his first book, and "I began to have long talks with myself at night about whether or not I was chasing a fool's dream" (*FI*, 19). Excessive drinking ensued, as well as a creative dry spell in which he searched in vain for story ideas. The latter, however, turned out to be the proverbial blessing in disguise since it encouraged King to reevaluate—successfully—the type of fiction he had been producing.

Thus far his four rejected novels had been either suspense stories or science fiction. Despite the fact that he had written and successfully sold seven short horror-stories—two to *Startling Mystery Stories* ("Glass Floor" and "The Reaper's Image"), and five to *Cavalier* magazine ("Graveyard Shift," "I Am the Doorway," "Suffer the Little Children," "Battleground," and "The Mangler")—he had not seriously considered writing novel-length horror. The previous summer, he had begun a short story, "Carrie," intending it for *Cavalier*, but under the influence of Ira Levin's *Rosemary's Baby* (1968), Thomas Tryon's *The Other* (1971), and William Blatty's *The Exorcist* (1971)—three novels he considers to have initiated the 1970s vogue in horror fiction (*FI*, 20; *DM*, 253)—he decided in December 1971 to turn the short story into a novel. Because he was in a "dry period," he worked on *Carrie* in the absence of anything better to do, and indeed remained uninspired during its composition and numerous revisions. He had been teased about an apparent inability to write about girls and so took up both the original short story and subsequent novel partly as a challenge. Rather like the lady who protests too much, King goes out of his way needlessly to explain his discomfort with the female subject matter of *Carrie*:

The opening scene revolves around the unexpected (and late) arrival of Carrie White's first menstrual period, and as I arrived at this—on page two—I suddenly realized that I (1) had never been a girl, (2) had never had a menstrual cramp or a menstrual period, (3) had absolutely no idea how I'd react to one. On top of that, the entire geography of that first scene was misty to me. I had been in a girl's shower room exactly once—as part of a college summer job as janitor in a largish Maine high school—and I was aware that there were sanitary napkin dispensers, but I could not recall if the napkins were a dime each, a quarter each, or possibly a freebie supplied by the school as are paper towels and toilet tissue. (*FI*, 21)

Because of his being ill at ease about the physiological and psychological ramifications of his female subject matter, he crumpled up the already written pages and hurled them into a kitchen wastebasket. Some time later, his wife rescued the rejected pages out of the wastebasket and coaxed her husband into continuing. He claims to have completed the novel partly to please Tabby, "who was amused to find her husband hopelessly mired in the sociological peer-dance of the adolescent girl" (*FI*, 20), and partly because "I was dry and had no better ideas" (23). Unlike the "fantastic, white-hot experience" of creating the rejected fourth novel, he "detested" *Carrie* and suspected—in total contradiction to subsequent publishing developments—that he was writing the "world's all-time loser." Completely convinced of the novel's inadequacies, he felt it a complete waste of time and effort to send out what he considered a "certified loser." By chance his Doubleday friend Bill Thompson dropped him a note in early January 1973 asking whether he was writing anything; and to show that he was "still in there pitching, if only in the bullpen," King decided to send him *Carrie*.

Cautionary but optimistic, Thompson's response suggested that *Carrie* might be publishable if the last quarter of the book, some fifty pages of the original draft, "could be brought into line with the rather low-key development of what had gone before" (*FI*, 24). King promptly rewrote the latter part of the novel along the lines that Thompson had recommended and for the first time experienced a sense of exhilaration at the "ease with which his suggestions reinforced the book's main thrust" (24). Thompson's response to the rewrite was immediate and encouraging; and in February 1973 he borrowed $75 from his wife's grandmother and traveled to New York City on a Greyhound bus to meet Bill Thompson and his secretary for a "publishing lunch." King's self-satiric description of his awkwardness in the restaurant is worthy of inclusion in any of his novels:

I had blisters on both feet because I had foolishly worn a new pair of shoes purchased especially for the trip. My neck hurt from doing the famous out-of-town country-boy, my-look-at-them-tall-buildings crane. I had not slept on the bus the night before, ordered two gin-and-tonics and was almost immediately struck drunk. I had never been so determined to make no glaring social *gaffe* and never so convinced (at least since the night of my high school junior prom) that I would make one. To top it off, I ordered fettucini, a dish bearded young men should avoid. (25)

The rest is publication history. At the luncheon, King was informed that the publication possibilities of *Carrie* were at least 60/40 in his favor, and a month later he learned by telegram that Doubleday was indeed going to publish the book and was offering an advance of $2,500. "After about 1,500 pages of unpublished manuscripts," King observes, "I was a bona fide first novelist." The book was published some two months after the February publication of Peter Benchley's *Jaws* and hit the best-seller lists immediately. King was beginning to suspect that he could leave teaching, and that, if the financial bonanza was properly and carefully managed, could spend his full time writing. Both he and his wife were "flabbergasted" shortly thereafter to learn that New American Library had read the book and made a preemptive bid of $400,000. King records: "Thompson called me with the news on Mother's Day of 1973, and I called him back that night, at his home, convinced that what he had actually said was [a mere] $40,000. And for the next two or three weeks"—like an insecure character in one of his own terror novels—"I lived with a constant, nagging fear that somebody would call and tell me it had all been a mistake or a misunderstanding" (FI, 28).

After so many disappointments and living at virtually a poverty level as both a teacher and laundry worker, King went through one of his most prolific six-month periods, producing books #5, #6, and #7, this last becoming the graceful and highly literate 'Salem's Lot, one of his most finely honed novels and his favorite (FI, 28–29). Thereafter, every novel, collection of short stories, or volume of criticism, or pseudonymed collection (as with the Bachman novels) rose to best-seller heights immediately upon publication, making Stephen King the first living horror writer consistently to place novel after successful novel on best-seller lists.

Considering the intensity of King's work—his lopsided popularity—his ability to appeal to huge uncritical audiences (especially teenagers)—his unabashed candor on matters of race, nationality, politics, and sex—the inevitable stock situations he must employ in so confining a genre as the gothic tale—considering too, the massive personal fortune that accrues from so many commercially successful novels and motion pictures, and the inevitable envy that such repeated successes must arouse—it was inevitable that reactions to, and evaluations of, his work range from the openly hostile to the thoughtlessly ecstatic. Hostile critics, by no means few in number, have called King's writings immature, adolescent, puerile, lacking in taste and elemental good sense, styleless, subservient to pop culture—and King himself a helpless victim of logorrhea. However, what impresses Fritz Leiber, himself a distinguished author of science fiction and horror, about King's work is the "all-out, no holds barred imaginings" that do not hinge merely on supernatural explanations but on a special kind of gothic supernatural: "highly energetic," "mostly unstoppable," and "outrageous in one way or another" (FI, 109). Friend Peter Straub, with whom King eventually coauthored

The Talisman (1984), considers King generous, magnanimous, monogamous, eccentric, mutually silly, and "great," and unblushingly asserts that "I love him and don't know what I would do without him" (*FI*, 13).

The Ultimate Blasphemy

Since King was himself a Cinderella hero living in a rags-to-riches Cinderella society, where the commonest sentiment is that "in America you can be anything you want to be," one should not be surprised that his first financially successful novel is based on everybody's favorite fairy tale. One critic asserts that "to say that Stephen King deliberately set out to do a modernday Cinderella story with a nasty end would be both silly and misleading" (*FI*, 65). Yet King's popular *Carrie*, based on a popular fairy tale, differs markedly from James Joyce's intellectual *Ulysses*, in which a detailed knowledge of the ancient Greek epic is necessary for an understanding of the novel. Whereas Joyce's use of ancient lore is academic, King's use of the fairy tale is elemental and even simplistic. Of his own novel, *The Stand*, King is capable of saying, "I was doing a fast, happy tapdance on the grave of the whole world" (*DM*, 400). "Yes, folks, in *The Stand* I got a chance to scrub the whole human race, and *it was fun!*" (402). If King enjoyed scrubbing out the whole human race and doing a tap dance over it in his fourth novel, he would hardly have thought twice about scrubbing a mere Jacob Grimm fairy tale and tap dancing over it. He does similar things elsewhere. In *'Salem's Lot*, images of Fred Astaire and Ginger Rogers dance, in fairy tale fashion, all over Father Callahan's concept of twentieth century Christianity (148–49). But from *Carrie* alone, of course, it is impossible to guess at precisely what point the author determined to draw the fateful fairy tale analogy, and at precisely what point readers are supposed to recognize it, if indeed such recognition is necessary to enjoy the novel.

But that the Cinderella analogy was intended can hardly be denied, what with the motifs of cruel stepmother (Margaret White, Carrie's mother), Prince Charming (Tommy Ross, Carrie's escort), the fairy godmother who arranges for Cinderella to go to the ball (Susan Snell, Carrie's noble-motived friend), the cruel stepsisters (the school companions in the gym who cruelly mock Carrie's sexual innocence), the ball at which Cinderella's beauty is acknowledged (the high school prom), etc. The very name itself, the four-syllable *Carietta* echoes the four-syllable *Cinderella*, the accent in both instances on the penultimate syllables. Incidentally, Carrie's name appears to pun on "caring," since she lives in a world where (like Cinderella) few people care about her. For example, Mrs. White's "care" is misdirected; and later on, Susan Snell's "care" misfires.[4] However, to enjoy *Carrie* without being aware of the Cinderella analogy is one thing, but to comment critically on the novel without recognizing the importance of the analogy would indeed be "silly and misleading."

In and of themselves, the Cinderella analogies are admittedly not all that interesting, though certain baroque modifications are unusual. The opening scene of the novel, with which King had so much psychological difficulty, roars and stabs into the reader's consciousness. In a girl's high school shower room an unpopular and despised teenager (Carrie White) experiences her first menstruation, not realizing what she is undergoing, since she was raised in total sexual and biological ignorance by a puritanical mother. Concerning misguided intentions of parents, one is reminded of the mother of the medieval Perceval, who attempted to raise her son in ignorance of his masculinity in order to save him from early death; or of the mother of Achilles in Greek mythology, who attempted to hide her son from his military—and hence masculine—obligations. But those were legends of gentler days. In King's twentieth-century tale, one is dealing with blunt biology, a "Blood Sport," as King names it. Innocent and ignorant little Carrie White thinks she is bleeding to death.

The insensitivity of the other girls in the locker-room in King's twentieth-century novel is brutal enough: "then the laughter, disgusted, contemptuous, horrified, seemed to rise and bloom into something jagged and ugly, and the girls were bombarding her with tampons and sanitary napkins, some from purses, some from the broken dispenser on the wall" (8). Their shouts of "Plug it up, plug it up, plug it up" will certainly strike some readers as crude and insensitive, but the "ultimate blasphemies" are the bizarre beliefs and practices of Carrie's mother. Margaret White gave birth to her daughter without assistance—brave enough perhaps—but "it staggers both imagination and belief to advance the hypothesis that [even in the final stages] Mrs. Margaret White did not know she was pregnant" (14). The mythical mother of Achilles and the legendary mother of Perceval attempted to save their sons from certain early death and, though misguided in their relationships with their sons, had benign motives. But Carrie's mother was a religious psychopath who drew around her daughter a "redplague circle" from the "first day she had left the controlled environment"—a red plague circle that was "like blood itself—you could scrub and scrub and scrub and still it would be there, not erased, not clean" (22–23). Like antisexual fanaticism of the Cathari or Abigensian sects of the twelfth century, Momma White believed that all sexual relations, even those within marriage, belonged to the "kingdom of whoredoms and pestilences" (55).

Her pseudo-Miltonic theology was simply that "Eve was weak and loosed the raven on the world . . . and the raven was called Sin, and the first Sin was Intercourse" (54). Momma White's surrealist living room was dominated by a huge plaster crucifix, the impaled Christ-image "frozen in a grotesque, muscle-straining rictus of pain, mouth drawn down in a groaning curve" (39)—an image that draws from Carrie a touching little free-verse poem to her seventh grade teacher: "Jesus watches from the wall, / But his face is cold as stone, / And if he loves me / As she tells me / Why do I feel so all alone?" (72). Also in the living room, dully illuminated by a "hideous blue bulb that was always lit," was "Derrault's conception of Jonathan Edward's famous [eighteenth-century] sermon, *Sinners in the Hands of an Angry God*" (54). Jacob Grimm's Cinderella swept up the ashes of a cruel household of stepmother and stepsisters, but King's Carietta lived among the ashes of a moribund Christianity and the threatening hell fire of a Calvinist Satan, who perpetually "grinned at her with his jackal mouth, and his scarlet eyes [that] knew all the secrets of woman-blood" (57). This secret knowing is a theme that shows up in other King stories, a kind of seeing through when it appears in Barlow ('*Salem's Lot*), Danny Torrance (*The Shining*), or Randall Flagg (*The Stand*), or the one who walks behind the rows ("Children of the Corn").

The unfortunate incident in the locker room has two consequences: one good (temporary), the other bad (permanent). The good thing is that one of the girls (Susan Snell), who had participated in the tormenting and mockery of Carrie White, has a bout of conscience and repents. Playing the role of fairy godmother, she asks her boy friend (handsome and sensitive Tommy Ross) to take Carrie to the senior prom, thereby bravely exposing herself to the loss of Tommy, who might fall in love with Carrie (and indeed almost does), and relinquishing her chance to be elected queen of the prom. She does this in order to give Carrie social compensation for the excruciating embarrassment she had previously endured in the locker room. Susan's little plan of atonement succeeds, although the consequences—unlike those in the Cinderella story—are disastrous. Tommy is a perfect Prince Charming, and Carrie is beautifully transformed in her lovely new gown. Without benefit of magic wand, magic mice, magic pumpkin, and midnight curfew, the handsome couple attend the Senior Class Spring Ball and are, surprisingly, elected king and queen. The Cinderella fairy tale that is the American Dream of happiness is about to have its fulfillment, climaxing in the cuteness of a sentimental Judy Garland/Mickie Rooney movie—precisely what Stephen King appears to despise. Appropriately reflecting this in her memoirs, *My Name Is Susan Snell*, Susan is supposed to have observed: "Whenever anything important happens in America, they have to gold-plate it, like baby shoes" (98).

When she had seen Carrie's new gown prior to the prom, Carrie's psychopathic mother (who at one point almost killed her baby Carrie) had warned: "Be sure your sin will find you out. Burn it, Carrie! Cast that devil's red from you and burn it! Burn it! Burn it! *Burn* it!" (121). This hysterical command is fulfilled in totally unexpected ways. Some of the teenagers of the town, nourishing their dislikes and resentments, arrange to have two buckets of pig's blood crash upon Carrie and her escort, 'crowning' them, at the very moment of the announcement of their election (by one vote—Tommy's) as king and queen. Carrie is dowsed with animal blood to the general merriment of just about everyone at the prom, including the usually sympathetic gym teacher, Miss Desjardin, who had been one of Carrie's defenders in the embarrassing locker room episode. Gales of laughter follow before anyone has a chance to realize that, struck on the head by one of the buckets, Tommy Ross is lying dead.

Carrie takes telekinetic revenge. As the sentimental part of the fairy tale ends, the supernatural part begins. As King summarily observes, the "fairy tale was [already] green with corruption and evil" (183). Like the resounding laughter at Carrie's "blood bath," Carrie's psychic revenge is so excessive as to strain credulity and enter the realm of absurd apocalytic fantasy, the kind of massive, quasi-mythological destruction that one would come to expect at the end of King's novels. Assuming almost Wagnerian dimensions, Carrie's revenge is one of the most all-encompassing in Western literature since the bloody revenge of Siegfried's wife Kriemhild for the treacherous murder of her husband in the twelfth-century Middle High German epic-romance *Das Nibelungenlied*. Thus, because of Momma White's cold Calvinist Christianity, Carrie White's menstrual rite of passage becomes a bloody progression from biological ignorance through sentimental fairy tales to massive myth; and Stephen King's career as a popular writer of gothic fiction is launched.

Chapter Two

The Dracula Myth: Shadow and Substance

Blundering Ghosts in the Dark

The first short story in *Night Shift*, "Jerusalem's Lot," contains all the traditional gothic paraphernalia that derive from Horace Walpole's "gothick tale," *The Castle of Otranto* (1765). In Howard P. Lovecraft's *Supernatural Horror in Literature*, a valuable though unfortunately brief analysis by one of the horror-masters, he catalogs these literary trappings as follows: exotic names, moldy manuscripts, rattling chains, moving curtains, extinguished candles, appalling legends, subterranean passageways, obscure languages, mysterious noises and knockings, strange lights from unknown sources, etc.[1] To this list must be added the epistolary technique exploited in Bram Stoker's *Dracula* (1897). "Jerusalem's Lot" consists of thirty-four pages of letters and journal entries, the latter occupying a one-month period from 2 October 1850 to 4 November 1850 and turning out to have been forged by the protagonist to reinforce "paranoid delusions" (*NS*, 33).

"Jerusalem's Lot" does not use exotic names in the manner of *The Castle of Otranto*;[2] but King does indeed play New England name-games with persons and places, a technique he frequently employs with considerable ingenuity and subtlety. In the gracefully shaped *'Salem's Lot*, for example, the name of the vampire (*Barlow*) is dimly but deliberately echoed in the name of the young bully (*Boddin*) with whom teenager Mark Petrie has a school fight (45–49) and in the name of the young adulterer (*Bryant*) with whom the vampire is going to have one of his most successful confrontations (233–36). Both "Salem" and "Lot" in the title have the biblical resonances of the Book of Genesis, and the Salem in King's Maine inevitably recalls as the unfolding plot with its endless vampiric perversions seems to suggest, the notorious Salem, Massachusetts, witch trials and burnings of 1692. Covertly, Salem is also a punning reminder of Sodom.

In "Jerusalem's Lot," name resemblances are less shadowy than those of *'Salem's Lot*. A forty-year-old widower in uncertain physical and mental health (Charles Boone), who has just fallen heir to, and moved into, an ancient ancestral home (sinister, mildewed, bizarrely furnished, and pseudoreligiously named Chapelwaite),[3] corresponds in depth with an "ailing abolitionist" friend recuperating in Florida. The friend, whose real name is Everett Granson, is nicknamed "Bones." The Boone/Bones name resemblance, seemingly less subtle than the Barlow/Boddin/Bryant interconnections of *'Salem's Lot*, is nevertheless important to an understanding of the psychic and symbolic implications of the story. For, while Boone, ostensibly, may be addressing letters to his far-off Florida friend "Bones," he is—in his brain-fevered condition—unconsciously addressing the unfriendly "bones" that haunt both the walls and basement of Chapelwaite, as well as the walls of the desecrated church. In a basement, for example, Boone confronts the terrifying "bones" that have been channeling their way through Chapelwaite, the "hideous tenants" within his walls: a "face with eyes as ebon as the Styx itself"; a "mouth yawned in a toothless, agonized grin"; a hand, "yellow, rotted" that "stretched itself out to us"; and a girl with "palid, moldering face and a corpse-like grin," whose head "lolled at a lunatic angle" (*NS*, 20).[4] In addressing a geographically distant friend, Boone is—symbolically, at least—addressing Chapelwaite's ancestral dead, death itself, and ultimately the demise of his own diseased mind: "twisted shapes that lurk in the nightmare corridors of [his own] delirium." Charles's own bony features, resulting from his not having eaten for about a week (27 October to 4 November), merge him into those walled-up and hideous ancestors who are ghostily reflected in the window-glass, "palid as any vampire's." Charles himself describes these as "pipestem arms and skull face" (29). Intriguingly, the slang use of "bones" for "dice," with the inevitable suggestion of "fate" or "lot" in life, connects the salutation, "Dear Bones," with the name of the bedeviled town itself, Jerusalem's Lot, "lot" here having its secondary meaning of "fate" or "fortune." That Charles should be responsible for the murder of his "companion and long time friend," the significantly named Calvin[5]—who presumably accompanies the letter writer through subterranean vaults and an apparently desecrated chapel,[6] but whose journal jottings are forged to cover up his

having been, in fact, murdered—simply adds deeper dimensions of
horror to the already multilayered implications of the name "Bones."[7]

"Jerusalem's Lot" is not only the name of the short story, but
served as one of several temporary titles of *'Salem's Lot*, before the
final title of the novel was settled upon. As a matter of fact, except
for passing references to vampires in the short story (*NS*, 21, 29),
the two tales have little in common. Readers looking for nineteenth-
century family history of Ben Mears, Susan Norton, Mark Petrie,
Jimmy Cody, and Matt Burke (the generally positive protagonists of
an otherwise negative *'Salem's Lot*) might find themselves disappointed. Characters and time-frames are entirely different. In "Jerusalem's Lot," King is setting up a pseudohistorical Maine, "blundering"
and "thudding" its "hideous shadow-life" in walls, basements, and
abandoned chapels, over which there is a curse that "refuses to be
buried" (*NS*, 27), a "tenebrous village" of potential religious horror
from its initial pseudo-Puritan foundations (20). Thus the appearance
of the satanish Barlow in the later *'Salem's Lot* is made the more
inevitable in an historically demon-oriented town that "became an
anomaly which could only have existed in those isolated and queer
days when belief in witches and the *Virgin Birth* existed hand in
hand: an interbred, rather degenerate religious village controlled by a
half-mad preacher [a "dour religious fanatic named James Boon"]
whose twin gospels were the Bible and de Goudge's sinister *Demon
Dwellings* . . . a community of incest and the insanity and physical
defects which so often accompany that sin" (*NS*, 22–23).

Basic to the philosophy of "Jerusalem's Lot," and indeed of virtually all of King's narratives, is Lovecraft's concept of cosmic fear,
terror, or horror, defined as a "certain atmosphere of breathless and
unexplainable dread" that expresses a malign and peculiar suspension
or defeat of those fixed laws of Nature that are our only safeguard
against the assaults of chaos and the daemons of unplumbed space.[8]
In the demon-shambled church, Charles Boone (accompanied by the
about-to-be-murdered Calvin) comes across, among other bloody
abominations, the noisome words of his devil-worshipping ancestor
concerning the *magna vermis*: "words [that] shuddered and writhed on
the page before me . . . prize of a creature that shambles beyond the
stars" (*NS*, 31). In his final stupor (probably at the moment when he
kills Calvin), Charles sees the eyes of his ancestor—eyes that, in a
Lovecraftian manner, "glared with the empty life of the pathless
wastes beyond the edges of the universe" (*NS*, 33).

While universal and/or divine malevolence is not harped upon
with Lovecraft's psychopathic insistence, a God-hostile point of view
permeates much of King's work. Universal pessimism also seethes
beneath King's second commercially successful novel, *'Salem's Lot*,
whose protagonist (novelist Ben Mears) is, like protagonist Johnny
Smith in *Dead Zone*, "a man lost in a great and grinding nightmare
where clockwork ran on endlessly, unseen, but just below the surface
of things" (401). However, as successsful counterbalances to the Marsten House horrors, King often uses (to paraphrase Walt Whitman's
"Song of Myself") the "cool hand" of literary and religious conven-
tions to "control what would master him" in *'Salem's Lot*, that is, the
artifacts of Catholicism (crucifix, Christopher medal, holy water,
confessions, etc.) and the folklore remedies against vampires (stakes
through the heart, garlic in the mouth of the undead, etc.). Most
interesting and unusual, both here and in all of King's work, is the
psychological interpenetration of the characters (the presumed father/
son relationship of Ben Mears and Mark Petrie, for instance)—
extensive in-depth explorations of the conscious and unconscious
mind—that turns virtually all of King's novels and many of his short
stories into psychological studies. Thus, what goes on behind the
doors and shutters of the Marsten House reflects what goes on behind
the doors and shutters of all the houses of the morally doomed "Lot."
In one form or another, therefore, every house is a Marsten House in
miniature, neatly symbolized by the previously mentioned little
house in the haunted snow globe that a young Ben Mears once
grabbed or stole as a first proof of his advance beyond boyhood into
manhood. After some four hundred pages of thorough exploration of
machismo problems in a mature Ben and puberty problems in a
teenage Mark, *'Salem's Lot* yields at last to cosmic horror and satanic
malevolence, always King's ultimate compulsion. To paraphrase and
reverse Van Helsing's speech to Arthur Holmwood in *Dracula*: the
two male protagonists of *'Salem's Lot* must go through the "sweet
waters" of endless explanation of their friendship before they reach
the "bitter waters" of ultimate gothic confrontation—"horror" revealed for what it really is (338–39).

What Is Past Is Prologue

King regards Bram Stoker's *Dracula*, which derives its symbolism,
at least in part, from John Polidori's *The Vampyre* (1819) and J.

Sheridan LeFanu's "Carmilla" (1870), as a "frankly palpitating melodrama," a "remarkable achievement," one of English literature's most
engaging tricks, a *trompe l'oeil* that has rarely been matched (*DM*, 49,
64). Stoker devotes two lengthy passages in chapters 16 and 18, from
Dr. Seward's diary, to an explanation of the powers, limitations, and
accoutrements of Dracula-like creatures. Of the vampire's many associations, *'Salem's Lot* makes interesting use of four: animals, blood-
sucking, moonlight, and time itself. A Romanian word meaning
"not dead," "undead," or "walking dead" (a term, incidentally, made
popular by a 1922 German film *Nosferatu: Eine Symphonie des Grauens*
and fleetingly adopted by King in "Jerusalem's Lot" [*NS*, 21]), the
"nosferatu" are associates of rats, bats, owls, moths, foxes, and
wolves—animals of stealth, cunning, darkness, and decay. Dr. Seward, the physician whose diary entries constitute a considerable
portion of Stoker's epistolary novel, notes that on one occasion, in
order to "tidy up" the room before the entrance of a female visitor,
the vampirized patient (Renfield) simply swallowed up all the spiders
and flies in the box, becoming, like Beelzebub, a kind of "lord of the
flies." On another occasion the zoophagous Renfield disgusted Dr.
Seward by catching a horrid blow-fly, holding it "exultantly for a few
moments between his finger and thumb, and before I knew what he
was going to do, put it into his mouth and ate it." Less disgustingly,
this fly tradition from *Dracula* finds its way into the haunted kitchen
of the Marsten House in *'Salem's Lot*—full of flies, always "buzzing
around," contaminating what is to be eaten.

Most important among the animal associates, obviously, are the rat
and the bat. In one of his most popular short stories, "Graveyard
Shift," which narrates the terrors of a rat-filled factory in which the
rodents grow larger and larger as the challenged workers (Warwick
and Hall) descend to the lowest and most grisly depths, King manipulates an unstated formula: rat equals bat equals vampire. In the
subbasement of the factory, huge and repulsive creatures have undergone "some hideous [Darwinian] mutation that never could have
survived under the eye of the sun." Their "rear legs were gone and
they were blind as moles, like their flying cousins." The queen-rat, a
magna mater (the Cybele of ancient times), is a "huge pulsating grey
. . . whose progeny might someday develop wings." In the standard
vampire story the human metamorphoses into the vampire, but in
"Graveyard Shift"—in a kind of parody of biological evolution—it is
the rat itself that is in the process of gradually transforming into the

vampire. By this symbolic pattern, the belly-crawling rodent (losing
its limbs) eventually evolves into the flying rodent (blind and black),
which then infernally encases and encloses the soul of the nosferatu.
There is a certain tongue-in-cheek quality, often bordering on the
hilarious, about these transmutations of Stephen King, much more of
the pagan spirit of Ovid's *Metamorphoses* or Lucan's *Pharsalia* than
scientific spirit of Darwin's *Origin of the Species*. Since vampires are—
according to one of King's pointed observations—"apparently dead
from the waist down" and "can make love with their mouths alone"
(*DM*, 66), the sexual specifics of their victims becomes a matter of
little consequence.[9] It is hardly surprising, therefore, that the vampires of *'Salem's Lot* are bisexual. The victims of the vampire (Kurt
Barlow) are indifferently male (Ralphie and Dannie Glick, Corey
Bryant, Dud Rogers, etc.), or female (Susan and Anne Norton,
Ruthie Crockett, Eva Miller, etc.). More than traditional vampire
ritualism is involved when Matt Burke informs Ben Mears that, in
order to destroy the power of the bisexual vampire, he must "pound
the stake [symbolically, the phallus]—first into Barlow, then into her
[Susan Norton]" (321). Appropriately enough, both vampire Barlow
and his assistant (Richard Throckett Straker), the recently arrived
tenants of Marsten House, are considered "queer for each other" by
one of the town's furniture movers (86). Were one to combine the
metamorphic implications of both "Graveyard Shift" and *'Salem's Lot*,
the above-stated symbolic formula would flow as follows: rat equals
bat equals vampire equals androgyny.

According to Bram Stoker's *Dracula*, the nosferatu need no normal
food to survive: fresh human blood keeps them alive, if indeed these
undead can in any sense be considered alive. Blood rites are per-
formed upon the necks (the numerous pulsing veins in *'Salem's Lot*) of
sleeping or hypnotized persons—either male or female, as indicated
above—according them a kind of kinship with the blood-oriented
creatures of myth and folklore. The monster Grendel in the Anglo-
Saxon epic *Beowulf* is conspicuously a flesh-eater and bone-cruncher,
but since it is only mentioned in one half line of poetry, it is
sometimes forgotten that he is also a voracious blood-drinker, gorg-
ing himself on the blood of flayed and dismembered warriors
(*Beowulf*, 742b). In Homer's *Odyssey*, the spirits of the dead, like
animals, lap up the blood of two throat-slit sheep spilled into a
trench (the blood mixing with honey, milk, wine, and water) so that
the dismal spirits of the dead might acquire the strength to advise

and prophesy (book 11). In fact, this Hellenic ghost rite is widely believed to be the ultimate origin of the blood-sucking portion of Western European vampire legends.

Despite the excesses that such a topic as horror is likely to produce—and King has been often and deservedly criticized for such excesses—he deliberately observes strict Apollonian restraints in portions of this novel, especially in earlier sections. *'Salem's Lot*, for example, avoids the bloodier grotesqueries of vampire behavior by sometimes reducing ghoulish blood-lettings to metaphoric, albeit highly effective, statements. This is especially noticeable in the close-out of chapter sections. When the Lot's first youthful victims (Ralphie and Danny Glick) are captured and supposedly vampirized, the scene abruptly ends with a vague phrase—hardly more than a cliché yet producing the suspenseful effect of a terrifying night-embrace as the "darkness enfolded them" (71). When a school bus driver (Charlie Rhodes) becomes the frightened victim of a busload of vampirized children, they come grinning toward Charlie and, in the final line, simply "fell on him" (370). When a guilty and humiliated lover (Corey Bryant) is accosted and hypnotized by the town's vampire, he sinks into a poetic blend of the infernal rivers Lethe and Phlegethon, the "great forgetful river" whose "waters were red" (236). When a faith-weakened Catholic priest (Father Callahan) is trapped by the town's vampire, even though he holds his breath for "what seemed like aeons," before he partakes of Barlow's blasphemous communion, "Yet at last, he drank" (355).

According to Stoker, however, these nosferatu neither live nor die in conventional patterns. The normal passage of time that, in all other living things, results in death, produces in these undead a highly refined and insidious cunning, according them a kind of timeless malevolence. Though they are in a sense free of time, they are nevertheless boxed or bound in by the diurnal motions of the earth. Their special hours are four: *sundown* and *sun-up* (the dark hours of human sleep when they batten on fears and nightmares), *noon* (when they have the power to shift shapes),[10] and *midnight* (when they offer up their dark prey). Full moon superstitions are also important for the ultimate expression of their powers, especially evident in *The Stand*, when the Dracula-like Randall Flagg sexually annihilates a supposedly virginal Nadine Cross, while the text keeps reminding readers that "the moon is full," or that the "bloated" moon stares down "blankly," or that Nadine actually "look[s] up at the moon" during her sexual demonization (675).

Dr. Seward, the physician in *Dracula*, wonders why the behavior of his disturbed patient is linked to astronomical events. For three nights, Seward observes, his patient is "violent all day then quiet from moonrise to sunrise," and Seward tries to determine why the patient's paroxysms come on only at "high noon and at sunset" (chapter 9). In *'Salem's Lot*, precisely at noon, a cunning real estate agent receives an ominous visit by an as yet unidentified vampire agent (52–58); and precisely at 11:59 P.M. (73), a "dark figure," later identified as Straker himself (320), "stood meditatively inside the gate" of a cemetery, waiting for midnight to offer up the "figure of a child in his arms." At 7:02 P.M., in another part of town, later identified, as the moment of Sunday-sunset, 5 October 1975 (309), the vampirized mother (Margarie Glick) of the vampirized boys (Ralphie and Danny) starts to come back to life in a funeral parlor (265–66). At the same 7:02 P.M., in another part of town, a prospective vampire victim (the twelve-year-old Mark Petrie) saves himself by bashing in the brains of Straker, melodramatically escaping from the sexual advances of the sunset-arising Barlow just in the nick of time (291–92).

In the clock and calendar orientations of *'Salem's Lot*, "time" sometimes overlaps—as in the preceding incident when Ben Mears looks at the clock at exactly the moment when his young friend Mark is making his successful escape. Time sometimes moves backward in numerous remembrances and flashbacks—as in Ben's ghostly remembrances of the motorcycle death of his wife, or the horrible hanging of Hubie Marsten, remembrances rendered so realistically that time present is virtually absorbed into the terrors of time past (e.g., 28–31). Indeed, time in *'Salem's Lot* seems to carry through the philosophy of the opening lines of T. S. Eliot's "Burnt Norton" (1936): "Time present and time past / Are both perhaps present in time future, / And time future contained in time past." The consequence of this philosophy is a curious time suspension or time elasticity—as when "day trembled on the edge of extinction" (73); or when Mark Petrie seems to have "minutes rather than bare seconds" to aim at the skull of Straker (291), or, when, at the same moment, Ben Mears watches the clock as the hands "hesitated" between 7:01 and 7:02 (292). In Milt Crossen's agricultural store, immediately following an ominous appearance of Straker, the futile conversation of the town's old codgers "progress[ed] more in the silences than in the speeches, like a chess game played by mail," and the day seemed to "stand still and stretch into eternity" (95). Mark's brilliant, though perhaps not quite believable, escape from the binding cords that are to hold him captive until Barlow's sunset arousal is to bring him castration and death, is filled with time references ("the knot defied him for what seemed an endless time") and also offers striking psychedelic images that interconnect time and space: "his vision began to fade under the onslaught of large black flowers that burst into soundless bloom before his eyes" (290).

One Step Beyond

'Salem's Lot is characterized by a curious love triangle, involving Susan Norton, Ben Mears, and twelve-year-old Mark Petrie. The relationship of Ben and Susan seems, at least on a superficial level, to be obvious enough; but the attractions between Ben and Mark are difficult to gauge with any degree of precision. Simplistic explanations of what is going on beneath the psychological surface are of little value and suggest, perhaps, an insensitivity to the kind of haunted nuance at which King is most skillful—to take what the novel initially seems to propose—namely, that they were "like" father and son. The opening line of 'Salem's Lot observes that this is what "almost everyone thought," words that have various resonances as the novel progresses. Obviously grosser observers, even if only few in number, might have suspected a relationship less familial. Readers concerned only with rapid story and not with subtle characterization are likely to notice only "father and son," but readers would have to be dense indeed not to be jolted by a bit of dialogue only a few pages later. Admittedly under an as yet unexplained emotional strain, the boy asks, "Do you love me?" And the anonymous "tall man" (Ben Mears), also under considerable emotional stress, responds with "Yes—God, yes" (xix). King knows very well that this brief two-line exchange is not the kind that Americans generally, and the suspicious Maine residents of 'salem's Lot in particular (Eva Miller and Mabel Werts, for example [316]), would regard as normal or natural—especially when followed by a desperate embrace.

A similar dialogue, equally sharp and brief, occurs much later, when the hands of Ben Mears ("as if wreathed in ghost gloves" [406]) turn luminous as a result of the supernatural holy water with which they have been splashed. Ben holds out his hand to Mark saying, "I love you"; and though the boy "flinched," the two of them nevertheless "clasped hands" (409). Mark's sensitive evaluation of the luminosity that surrounds Ben's hands and face—Ben seemed to be a "column of fire," a "man taken over, possessed" by an "eldritch fairylight"—applies subsurfacely to the affectionate fairy-feelings between them, not quite sexual, but something well beyond "father and son," something elemental, unrefined, "coughed up out of the ground in naked chunks." Mark saw this "without knowing, or having to know" what deeper psychological dispositions both in Ben and perhaps even in himself he was basically "seeing." Mark understood that the "possession was not in the least Christian," though it seemed somehow "good" (408). The "naked" chunks in the above quotation refer to something underground, but deliberately suggest something in the unconscious, and are echoed when Ben says, "I want you with me"— a "truth" that is "pure" and significantly "naked." On the plot level, Ben is obviously referring to his return visit to the vampire-haunted Marsten House; yet this "wanting" is said "more softly" and more than once. Even though described as sounding like a macho "football coach before the big game," Ben felt an inexplicable "germ of self-disgust" (never again alluded to) and seems to be talking about something else (398). Readers of this passage should hardly be surprised if, like Vic Trenton innocently engaging in a conversation with his unfaithful wife in the later novel *Cujo*, they have the "curious, unpleasant feeling" that Ben Mears, at this and other places in *'Salem's Lot*, seems to be "talking about several things at once— again (56).

Ben and Mark are approximates of one another, and at certain points (despite age differences) almost exact duplicates. Mark is "delicate looking," moving with grace and litheness that is not the common lot of boys his age," possessing an almost "milky complexion" with features that "would be considered aquiline later in life, but at the age of twelve were a trifle feminine" (136). Physically, Ben is never completely sketched out in any one section of the novel; but from bits and pieces one understands that he is tall (in fact, referred to as the anonymous "tall man" for several pages in the prologue and epilogue), having black hair that is not always properly combed, and looks like a none-too-masculine college professor, etc.

Mark is called "four eyes queer boy" by the teenage bully Richie

Boddin but, through wit and sheer intelligence, triumphs in an elementary school yard fight (46–49). Ben is called similar names, "sissy boy" (191), behind his back by Ann Norton, Susan's mother, who pointedly brings to her daughter's attention that Ben's novel has "lurid scenes . . . with boys getting together with boys." Ben gets into a fight with Susan's rejected boy friend (Floyd Tibbets), and—in this respect differing from the more astute Mark—is severely beaten and ends up in the hospital. Yet even Susan, perhaps annoyed at this obvious proof of Ben's male inadequacies, and in an unwanted way influenced by her mother's bigotries ("a seed of doubt had been planted" [193]), meticulously inspects the physiognomy of her new-found lover for the first time as he lies unconscious on a hospital bed. She "looked at his face slowly, hardly noticing the way it had been marked.[11] Sissy boy, her mother had called him, and Susan could see how she might have gotten that idea. His features were strong but sensitive. She wished there was a better word than sensitive. That was the word you used to describe the local librarian who wrote stilted Spenserian stanzas to daffodils in his spare time. But it was the only word that fit" (195). Rather regretfully, Susan observes that Ben's hair seemed to be the only "virile" thing about him, yet even that "seemed almost to float above his face."

Literate Ben Mears writes a novel with a homosexual rape scene in the prison section, perhaps like a similar scene in "Rita Hayworth and Shawshank Redemption" (DS, 32–34). Nevertheless, to Susan, Ben seemed healthy and normal. Imaginative Mark Petrie has a plastic collection of Aurora horror monsters (Dracula, the Mad Doctor, Mr. Hyde, etc.), but nevertheless—despite Richie Boddin's superficial accusation—seems, according to his father, to have his feet "pretty solidly planted on the ground," got along with his peers, and in general wanted the "same things" they wanted (137–38). Both Ben and Mark are "bookish," prone to attract unflattering attention, and because of their respective sensitive, delicate, or even feminine appearances are magnets for masculine troubles. One is reminded of what is said of the androgynous vampire when first encountered by one of his unlikely victims, the supersexed Corey Bryant: "The shadow had a manlike form, but there was something . . . something" (234).

The first meeting of Ben and Mark does not occur until page 314 and is more appropriate for the heterosexual encounters of Ben and Susan (8–10), with which it is deliberately compared, than a first-time meeting between a mature man and a twelve-year-old boy, neither known to the other:

> They looked at each other for no great space of time, but for Ben the moment seemed to undergo a queer stretching, and a feeling of unreality swept him. The boy reminded him physically of the boy he himself had been, but it was more than that. He seemed to feel a weight settle onto his neck, as if in a curious way he sensed the more-than-chance coming together of their lives. It made him think of the day he had met Susan in the park, and how their light get-acquainted conversation had seemed queerly heavy and fraught with intimations of the future. (314)

The language of this first Ben / Mark meeting is also fraught with "intimations": the vague and shadowy ithyphallic innuendoes in "queer stretching" and "queerly heavy"; the overt comparison with the first meeting with Susan (that was suggestively sexual); and the subtle implications of the word "queer" (hardly accidental on the part of the narrator). Ben's initial reaction to Mark and his subsequent relationships fall somewhat short of raw sexual attraction, yet are clearly beyond friendship, paternal affection or mere remembrances of things past. Even King considers it "more than that." Everything in this passage carries the reader back to the nagging ambiguities of the opening sentence: that "almost everyone thought the man and boy were father and son"; and if they were not, what then? Perhaps— some would suggest—what Poe, in his satire "Lionizing," would have called "bi-part souls," or what "The Fall of the House of Usher" would philosophize away as "sympathies of a scarcely intelligible nature." Incidentally, it is more than passingly important that poker-faced young Mark appears innocent and virginal, by contrast with the rough-behaving and rough-talking teenage boys who play major roles in King's other stories: Todd Bowden, Gordie Lachance, Charlie Decker, etc.

Affectional male/male dispositions are not exactly unusual in King's stories, and from time to time suddenly surface in other characters. In *Christine*, teenagers Arnie Cunningham and Dennis Guilder do not engage in the kind of surrogate love-talk that passes for conversation between Ben and Mark. But there is an unexpected scene of embrace and intense affection that involves a measurable degree of sexual ambivalence, here and there tainted with embarrassing self-doubts. Arnie is the speaker in this candid car scene:

I knew what to do. Reluctantly, not wanting to, I slid across the seat and put my arms around him and held him. I could feel his face, hot and fevered, mashed against my chest. After that I went home myself. Neither of us talked about it later, me holding him like that. No one came along the sidewalk and saw us parked at the curb. I suppose if someone had, we would have looked like a couple of queers. I sat there and loved him the best I could. (56)

Sometimes, these mysterious male / male attractions are distinctly hostile, as in "Graveyard Shift," when Hall "went directly to the shower, still thinking about [his hated boss] Warwick, trying to place what it was about Mr. Foreman that drew him, that made him feel that somehow they had become tied together" (NS, 41). Or an odd mixture of hostility and affection on the very rim of the unconscious, as in "Apt Pupil," where the insidious relationships of the old Nazi Dussander (the pseudofather) and the young protégé Bowden (a pseudoson) border dangerously on the unnatural in more than merely sexual innuendo (cf. DS, 176, 191, 194). Similarly, in The Shining, a mentally disturbed former teacher (Jack Torrance) thinks about a former male student (George Hatfield), who seemed to him "almost insolently beautiful" in his tight faded jeans and Stovington sweat-shirt carelessly pushed up to the elbows to disclose his tanned fore-arms (111), and both of them talking about "knowing something" (113–14). In Pet Sematary, Louis Creed looks at his baby son Gage, "his heart abruptly filling with a love for the boy so strong that it seemed almost dangerous" (30–31).

The Ben-Mark affections do not exist in narrative isolation but belong to a set of parallels in 'Salem's Lot, specifically between fathers and sons (either literal or figurative) and, more generally, between parents and children. Mark's real father, the intellectual Henry Pe-trie,[12] is one who beats his son with a rolled-up newspaper (the "ritual whipping") from time to time (136) and is a kind of unacknowledged "king vampire," whose supposedly rational mind all too easily fills up with "thunder" against his son (293). A spiritual father, the alcoholic priest Callahan, who like Ben and Mark is also somewhat effeminate (specifically "womanish" on one occasion [331]), turns out to be a father without much faith in the very Catholicism that Mark has adopted (149–50, 300–306). Callahan eventually casts aside his crucifix (in whose power Mark believes even before his conversion) and yields to Barlow's blasphemous temptations (353–55). Sandy McDougall, the young mother of a ten-month-old baby

(Randy), is a vicious child-beater. Conversations between Susan and
her mother (Ann Norton) are openly spiteful and hostile, and culmi-
nate with Susan slapping her mother (191). Relationships between
the various members of the Glick family (Anthony, Margarie, Danny,
and Ralphie) are hardly ideal. King thus sets forth what, objectively
speaking, would appear to be the unnatural affectional orientations of
Ben and Mark over against more viciously unnatural, but socially
acceptable, familial hostilities. More than unconsciously, therefore,
King would have his readers rearrange, or at least reexamine, their
social/sexual priorities and perhaps clarify the too readily assumed
distinctions between natural and unnatural.

Several times in *'Salem's Lot* the refrain of Wallace Stevens' famous
poem on sensuality and death, "The Emperor of Ice Cream," is
quoted: "Let be be finale of seem" (181, 406). King's purpose in
"Jerusalem's Lot" and *'Salem's Lot,* as indeed in much of his writing,
is to tear at the "seeming" to get at the "being"—in a gothic sense,
to let rude realities take the place of clothed illusions. The often-
quoted first section of chapter 10 ("The town knew about darkness")
savagely tears away at the "false-fronted" homes of the Lot (i.e., the
"seeming") to reveal dismal secrets—wife-abandoned Albie Crane,
absent-minded Coretta Simons, self-abusing Hal Griffin, panty-
wearing George Middler, lecherous Reverend John Groggins, the
unnamed pyromaniac valedictorian of the 1953 class (i.e., the
"being")—secrets that the town keeps with its "ultimate poker face"
(212). What could be more morally disquieting than the contorted
business practices of reputable Lawrence Crockett, who describes his
sublegal real estate procedures as "going into the tunnel of love with
girl A, screwing girl B behind you, and ending up holding hands
with girl A on the other side" (80). How do these compare—*'Salem's
Lot* seems to be asking its readers—with Ben's secret signs of affection for Mark; an occasional handclasp and some words on impulse,
the amorous implications of which are never bodied forth: "I love
you," "I want you," "I need you"? (398, 405, 409).

Inevitably, therefore, the vampirizing that androgynous Barlow
inflicts upon so many—he whose face was "handsome in a sharp,
forbidding sort of way, yet as the light shifted, seemed almost
effeminate" (352)—is well deserved. In fact, many, if not most, of
the citizens of this normal American small town in rural Maine are
already (in King's opinion) social and psychological derelicts. Crockett's daughter Ruthie, for example, who ultimately "slept in enam-

eled darkness within an abandoned freezer close to [crude] Dud
Rogers" and "found [the hunchback's] advances among the heaped
mounds of garbage very acceptable" (310). Likable and sensible Mark
Petrie, indeed, is the only one who has the courage to finally realize
and say aloud of one of the outstanding pillars of the town: "My
father would have made a very successful vampire, maybe as good as
Barlow" (382). That the town's few innocents (Ralphie Glick, Jimmy
Cody, Matt Burke, Susan Norton, and the McDougall baby) should
also have to suffer is part of the terrifying vampire-martyrdom the
guiltless have to endure on behalf of the guilty.

King has deliberately positioned Ben Mears and Mark Petrie
among the innocent—two suspicious-looking males who, from the
point of view of gossipy Mabel Werts, insensitive Parkins Gillespie,
bullying Richie Boddin, hypocritical Ann Norton, and white-collar
criminal Lawrence Crockett, would be all too easily tossed into the
trash bin of sexual deviation. Against the historical malevolence of
the vampire's sexual behavior there is an air of innocence about the
relationship of vampire-resisters Ben and Mark that defies analysis,
and an involuted psychological complexity in the novel as a whole
that is impressive. Despite all the innuendoes about his delicate
nature, Mark Petrie, ironically, comes across as virile in will and
determination—a strong virginal male belonging to a little known
piece of folklore whereby a male virgin (almost always a boy) used to
be placed on a white stallion to be led around the grave of a
suspected vampire in order to destroy him.[13] In combatting the
vampire, even Ben Mears has a mystical moment of macho masculinity that occurs when the holy water accidentally splashes on his
hands and gives him a primeval "Force" and "Power"—defined as
"whatever moved the greatest wheels of the universe" (408). Feeling
this "hard sense of [luminous] sureness," Ben was, for the first time
in weeks, "no longer groping through fogs of belief and unbelief,
sparring with a partner whose body [in a literal sense Barlow's, but
in a psychological sense Mark's] was too unsubstantial to sustain
blows" (408).

Clearly, then, the psychological complexity in the relationship of
Ben and Mark should convince one that understanding Stephen
King's imaginary 'salem's Lot, Maine, is not so simple as merely
knowing that "Loretta Starcher wears falsies" (208). In one sense or
another—be it benign or malign—the whole damned town wears
"falsies." Living in 'salem's Lot, and reading a novel about that
demon-obsessed Jerusalem (the "namesake of the Holy Land's holiest

city" [xvii]) becomes a "daily act of utter intercourse, so complete
that it makes what you and your wife do in the squeaky bed look like
a handshake" (210). How appropriate that such a hate-encrusted
town should have been named after an eighteenth-century pig (mis-
called "Jerusalem") that "broke out of her pen one day at feeding
time, escaped into the nearby woods and went wild and mean" (17).

Taken either as a straight horror story or as an allegory of middlebrow America, *'Salem's Lot* is not only gracefully shaped in plot and
episode arrangements, but much more importantly in subtleties of
character penetration and intensity of moral indignation. Into this
psychological milieu, the rickety old clichés of Bram Stoker's *Dracula*
resuscitate and insidiously resurrect. The expose of mediocre bour-
geois values is such that *'Salem's Lot* may well enter the mainstream
of modern American fiction, taking its place not so much next to
other novels of horror (such as Fritz Leiber's *Our Lady of Darkness,*
Robert Block's *Psycho,* Isak Dinesen's *Seven Gothic Tales,* and Shirley
Jackson's *The Haunting of Hill House*), as beside similar social negative
portraits of middle-class society as Sinclair Lewis's *Babbitt,* Sherwood
Anderson's *Winesburg Ohio,* Philip Roth's *Goodbye, Columbus,* John
O'Hara's *Appointment in Samarra,* Saul Bellow's *Herzog,* and John
Updyke's *Rabbit, Run.* The middle-class citizens of the imaginary
town of 'salem's Lot that King is excoriating with such unrelenting
and absolute savagery are, of course, none other than his very own
middlebrow American readers, almost astronomical in number. Like
the already vampirized Eva Miller, many a mindless reader looks into
the mirror that is *'Salem's Lot* and sees nothing—not even a ghost-
reflection in the glass (371).

Chapter Three
Strange Powers of Dangerous Potential

A Lot of Splotches with No Meaning

Boys, generally twelve year olds, are among the most carefully developed and consistently explored of King's imaginary characters. What obsesses King about youth is by no means unique. Similar concerns appear in Western literature from Aeschylus and Euripides to Dante and Dostoevski: that is, the cause-and-effect relationships between (1) guilt and innocence on the one hand, and (2) suffering and survival on the other. That the interconnections can never be resolved to everyone's satisfaction does not keep King from perpetually rehashing the problem. To be sure, the cosmic guilt/innocence dilemma does manage to manifest itself in older characters as well—one thinks immediately of Johnny Smith in *Dead Zone*, Nick Andros in *The Stand*, Andy Dufresne in "Rita Hayworth and Shawshank Redemption," Alvin Sackheim in "Night Surf," and astronaut Arthur in "I Am the Doorway." But because preteen and prepuberty youngsters could hardly have done enough to deserve death, terror, or destruction, King rather insistently concentrates upon them, especially in the early novels.

If one includes the female protagonist of the first commercially successful novel, the vexed problem of the undeserved suffering of the innocent seems to have obsessed King from *Carrie*, through *'Salem's Lot* and "The Body" (composed almost simultaneously), to *The Shining* (1977)—and intermittently thereafter. The sixty-year-old black cook, Dick Hallorann, offers his version of the traditional cliché about injustice to the innocent at the end of *The Shining*: "There's some things no six-year-old boy [or girl] in the world should have to be told, but the way things should be and the way things are hardly ever get together. . . . Good people die in bad painful ways. . . . Sometimes it seems like it's only the bad people who stay healthy and prosper" (446). In this connection, it ought to be noted that *'Salem's Lot* divides its youngsters into three main types: (1) innocent boys who are spared (Mark Petrie), (2) innocent boys who are unaccountably destroyed (Ralphie Glick), and (3) obnoxious boys who deserve destruction and degradation (Danny Glick, but especially Richie Boddin). *The Shining's* six-year-old Danny Torrance belongs to the first type and seems to carry out King's theory that "children are better able to deal with fantasy and terror *on its own terms* than their elders are" (*DM*, 102).

Nicknamed "Doc"—to suggest perhaps a potential for self-healing—Danny is the son of playwright-alchoholic (and all-around failure) Jack Torrance and his wife Wendy. At the beginning of *The Shining*, an uncomfortable and resentful Jack is applying for a job as winter janitor of a luxury hotel in Boulder, Colorado, which his best friend and drinking companion, Al Shockley, has inherited and keeps as an investment (37). Awaiting Jack's return, anxious Wendy and six-year-old "Doc" are awkwardly and evasively talking about past events. Repeated instances of clumsy conversational evasions (especially in matters relating to Danny) dominate the introductory sections of the novel and prepare the reader for the six-year-old's unusual cardiokinetic abilities. One learns that Wendy is apprehensive about Jack's having lost a previous high school teaching position when, because of an ungovernable temper, he struck one of his students. Jack also broke his son's arm over a childish accident involving the ruined manuscript of a play (14, 27). Danny's easygoing forgiving-and-forgetting manner highlights his innocence and totally unspoiled goodness. As though nothing cruel had ever happened, even though he has just alluded to the arm-breaking incident, Danny innocently remarks, as only a child can: "I think I'll watch for Dad . . . Maybe he'll be early" (14). One also senses Danny's precociousness, for while his questions to his mother are typically childlike, his intuitions and perceptions are astonishingly acute.

How acute they are one does not fully grasp until chapter 4 (entitled "Shadowland"), in which King attempts an impossible intermixture of childish misunderstandings and unexpectedly mature insights. Even though only six years old, innocent little Danny already possesses almost supernatural mind-reading talents: "Mommy was lying on her bed in the apartment, just about crying she was so worried about Daddy. Some of the things she was worried about were too grown-up for Danny to understand—vague things that had to do with security, with Daddy's *selfimage*, feelings of guilt and anger and the fear of what was to become of them . . ." (26–27). From the beginning of *The Shining*, one senses that mind-reading Danny is already two people: a child and an adult. One of the consequences of Danny's astonishing cardiokinetic abilities, referred to as the "shine" (hence, the novel's title), is that he seems to merge into his own personality, at times, all the older people with whom he comes in contact (his mother, his real father, his surrogate father Dick Hallorann, etc.). At first, he is merely an image of his dramatist father. This father-mirroring is another version of the father-lost-and-regained obsession that has already been observed in *'Salem's Lot*, but here it takes a somewhat different psychopathic turn. On the simple level, Jack Torrance externalizes characters into his plays, but his son Danny appears to internalize the thoughts of "characters" into the "play" of his mind. This overlapping of characters, or absorption of one character into another, is an important aspect of King's work and shows up in various forms: from the blending of Barlow into the citizens of 'salem's Lot (vampirizing them and virtually vaporizing them into a single blood-sucking entity) to the blending of a black-and-white Hollywood image with the black-and-white personal life of the bored and jaded movie queen, Lily Cavanaugh, in *The Talisman*. Personality-mergings and the consequent personality-splittings, the fusions and fissions of the human psyche, are pursued with almost savage persistence in *The Shining*—though not always sucessfully. The roque mallet that goes smashing through the halls of the hotel, savagely swung by an irrational Jack Torrance, is an unconscious expression of this desperate need of Stephen King's to break, chop, splinter, and desperately reassemble the human psyche (cf. 396–98, 406–7).

Danny's mergings and splittings are managed in several ways. In "Shadowland," where the device of the interior monologue first develops in depth, the author employs several printing techniques to convey Danny's split-level thinking: long passages in regular print, italics (sometimes within parentheses), and capital letters (usually single words, but occasionally whole phrases). When used in the context of Danny's inner thoughts, capitals stand for words and phrases that Danny absorbs through his mind-reading capacities; but despite childish efforts, does not as yet fully comprehend DIVORCE, SUICIDE, BREAKDOWN, BUGHOUSE, DANGER, EMERGENCY, LIVE WIRE, THIRD RAIL, THE PLAY, LOST HIS MARBLES, MEN IN WHITE COATS, etc.—terms that usually involve his father in an uncompli-

mentary way. For Danny the most conspicuous of these incompre-
hensibles is oft-repeated REDRUM ("murder" spelled backward), a
"green fire" word that Danny first sees—or, perhaps one should more
accurately say, hallucinates—"flickering on and off in the medicine
cabinet mirror like a red eye" (32).

REDRUM flashes before Danny's eyes at about the same time and in
somewhat the same manner as "Tony," an invisible playmate—both
manifestations of the same psychiatric process. They appear in moments of anxiety and loneliness, when things get "woozy and
swimmy." A frightening and malevolent figure, Tony appears at the
"very limit of [Danny's] vision, calling distinctly and beckoning"
(29). Some of the more ominous "Tony-moments" occur when, all
conditions being ripe for a hallucination (uncomprehendingly per-
ceived by Danny as an "HA LOO SIN NATION"), Tony turns out to be
more of a presence than an appearance. King uses this chilling
technique in *'Salem's Lot*, when an unidentified child (the innocent
and appealing Ralphie) is offered up to the dark Lord of the Flies,
who remains silent and invisible amid the "sigh and whisper of leafy
branches and grasses" (73). A similar brief vignette in *The Shining* (a
chapter entitled "In Another Bedroom") is yet another instance in
which, for an innocent and appealing Danny lying alone in the
middle of the night, a mere Tony-presence is more unnerving than
an actual Tony-appearance:

[Danny] slipped out of bed and padded silently across to the window and
looked out on Arapahoe Street, now still and silent. It was two in the
morning. There was nothing out there but empty sidewalks drifted with
fallen leaves, parked cars, and the long-necked streetlight on the
corner. . . . With its hooded top and motionless stance, the streetlight
looked like a monster in a space show. He looked up the street both ways,
straining his eyes for Tony's slight, beckoning form, but there was no one
there. (56)

Like Randall Jarrell in his gothic poems of child-fears ("The Prince,"
"A Quilt Pattern," "A Sick Child," "Protocols," "Lady Bates," "The
Night Before the Night Before Christmas"), King, too, is capable of
raising hackles—as one reads, for example, of innocent Danny cran-
ing his neck out a window, one night, and hearing himself being
repeatedly called ("*Danny . . . Danneee*") by the fearful friend of his
imagination, his deadly other half, whose existence he cannot entirely shake off.

Although the origin of Tony's unusual name is never fully explained (though darkly hinted at), he continues to appear sporadi-
cally throughout the novel. Only gradually—if at all—does a reader
come to suspect an interrelationship between the middle names of
Danny's grandfather (Mark *Anthony* Torrance), Danny's father (John
Daniel Torrance), and Danny himself (Daniel *Anthony* Torrance); and
how the figure of Tony is a not-so-subtle outgrowth of these. On one
of the few occasions when Tony stands close, Danny realizes that he is
looking at a kind of older doppelganger, a "magic mirror" of himself
in ten years, an image that seems to pop out of the mirror maze of
Ray Bradbury's *Something Wicked This Way Comes*, where "things
collide, melt and vanish," and one sees "two, four, a dozen figures
where there should be only one" (chapter 15). More specifically, the
stamp on Tony's features was that of his playwright father, as if
"Tony . . . was a halfling caught between father and son, a ghost of
both, a fusion" (420). One recalls that, as a boy, Jack Torrance had
been "afraid that his father's shadow might fall over him while he
was at play" (223); and Tony seems a reembodiment of that older
paternal fear where "dream and reality had joined together without a
seam" (426).[1]
    The fission/fusion aspects of Danny's personality become extremely
complicated. Matters are not rendered less muddy by the fact that
the boy's nickname ("Doc") echoes the first name of the surrogate
father ("Dick"), a resemblance not without narrative, psychological,
and even phallic significance. "Tony" is the *invisible* dark half of a
divided psyche, a malign dark-half that recognizes its bleak kinship
with the biological father. A surrogate father, the black "Dick" Hallorann, is the *visible* but benign light-half. Because Danny is innocent and good-natured, one might be tempted to consider these
mysterious manifestations "mystical," though "schizophrenic" might
be a more appropriate term. Danny's father has similar divisive
experiences, only with desperate psychotic/phallic implications. As
indicated in a preceding chapter of this book, his "Tony" is a boy
called George.
    What happens in *The Shining* is that, having lost his New England
teaching position because of ill temper, Jack Torrance applies for, and
succeeds in obtaining, a job as winter caretaker in the Colorado
hotel, significantly called "The Overlook" (as if it were 'looking over'
all the activities of the Torrance family that will reside there isolated
throughout the winter). Though this luxury hotel closes down dur-

ing the winter months, it requires minimum maintenance. By managing to conquer his alcoholism and control his violent temper in such a quasi-contemplative environment, Jack Torrance should presumably be relaxed enough for his playwriting. Actually, Jack's mediocre efforts turn out not creative, but what one critic of the gothic novel, Judith Wilt, has called "decreative"—that is, destructive, in this case both to the hotel, and more tragically, to himself. [2] Jack fails as father, husband, caretaker, and most maddening of all, playwright.

The typical bad place of the gothic novel, the Overlook Hotel, has an evil history. It was once owned by a Howard Hughes-like millionaire, the "richest man in the world" (a certain Horace Derwent [155–58]),[3] and has apparently secretly retained the malevolent ghosts of its wealthy, indecent, and sometimes even criminal guests. Like the rented house in Oliver Onion's short story, "The Beckoning Fair One"—or even more, like the mansion in Poe's "House of Usher" that is believed to be almost sentient by its owner, the mad Roderick—the haunted Overlook, too, seems to resent intruders and trespassers. The three winter occupants, Jack, Wendy, and Danny, are thus inevitable targets of the hotel's unspeakable hostilities, a ghost-filled and ghost-merged hotel echoing with a "thousand stealthy sounds: creakings and groans and the sly sniff of the wind under the eaves where more wasps' nests might be hanging like deadly fruit" (136).

In pursuing this motif of the bad place with multiple identities, King manipulates portions of *Alice in Wonderland*, Poe's "Masque of the Red Death," and the famous legend of Bluebeard. Results are not completely satisfactory, often lacking the graceful nuances of the Dracula allusions of the earlier *'Salem's Lot*. The Wonderland story is needed, not merely to supply fantasy associations (as necessary as those might seem to be), but more subversively to turn a perceptive and sensitive six-year-old boy into a kind of male Alice. The philosophic concern of *The Shining* may be innocent suffering, but the psycho/psychotic concerns are clearly—though not clearly enough for some reviewers—the schizophrenic *person* (Jack), schizophrenic *place* (the hotel), and schizophrenic *thing* (a wasps' nest that will not die; an animal topiary that comes alive; and an empty barroom that fills with ghosts and an imaginary wonderland of evil people.

Though Alice/Wonderland allusions occur often enough, more important to the terror symbolism of *The Shining* are the closed door of

the Bluebeard legend and the reckless wild dance of Poe's "Masque."
Though few of the literary echoes are as carefully crafted as the
Cinderella and Oz legends of *Carrie* and *Pet Sematary*, nevertheless, in
the midst of all the schizophrenic complexities, King does work into
his novel some playful number symbolism — perhaps overplayful for
certain sophisticated readers. The hotel door number that Danny is
forbidden to open is 217. The number appears in three chapters
entitled respectively "Outside 217," "Inside 217" and "217 Revis-
ited." It was because of 217 that one of the maids was given "two-
weeks' worth of walking papers and told to get lost" as a consequence
of her accidental encounter with that peculiar "something," like a
noxious disease, that obsessed the Overlook (23, 87, 317). When
Danny is drawn to the forbidden 217 by a morbid kind of curiosity,
he remembers a story that Daddy had read to him, an all-too-real
story that seemed to equate Bluebeard's castle with the Overlook
Hotel, the corn-colored hair of Bluebeard's wife (Fatima) with his
mother's hair, and the mysterious closed door with 217, with the
passkey (as in the legend) hanging outside it. Blending the curious
boy into curious Fatima, as he had already blended him into curious
Alice, King makes the wife-analogy blatantly visceral—as when,
remembering his daddy's story, Danny is seized with a desire that
"itched at him as maddeningly as poison ivy in a place you aren't
supposed to scratch" (171).

Danny's curiosity about 217 becomes a "constant fishhook in his
brain, a kind of nagging siren song [Ulysses-like] that would not be
appeased." As one might expect, he finally does open the door. King
precedes the opening with a brief description of a "twisting jungle
carpet," and goes out of his way to point out that the carpet was
"blue," the obsessive color that King turns to at key points in his
stories to intensify the sense of terror. What Danny finds in the
bathroom of the apartment, after pulling back the shower curtain
(neatly described, though not strikingly original as terror traditions
go), is one of the novel's high points of horror. Significantly, the
skeletal apparition of room 217 appears on page 217, the point at
which the terrors of *The Shining* finally open up: "The woman in the
tub had been dead for a long time. She was bloated and purple, her
gas-filled belly rising out of the cold, ice-rimmed water like some
fleshy island. Her eyes were fixed on Danny's, glassy and huge, like
marbles. She was grinning, her purple lips pulled back in a grimace.

Her breasts lolled. Her pubic hair floated. Her hands were frozen on
the knurled porcelain sides of the tub like crab claws". Later identified as Mrs. Massey (318), this decaying female corpse was something that "had lain slain in that tub for perhaps years, embalmed
there in magic" (218).

A psychological terror point occurs about fifty pages later, incidentally, on a page with matching numerals, 271. Apparently in a
dream, Jack Torrance pulls back the same bathtub curtain only to
see—not the old woman the innocent Danny had seen—but instead
that "insolently beautiful boy" with the "Robert Redford" looks
(111) who had caused Jack's expulsion from his teaching position in
the New England academy: "Lying in the tub, naked, lolling almost
weightless in the water, was George Hatfield, a knife stuck in his
chest. The water around him was stained a bright pink. George's
eyes were closed. His penis floated limply, like kelp." These appari-
tions on pages 217 and 271 display superficial parallels in emphasizing (1) a floating body, (2) breast, (3) eyes, (4) genitals, and (5) the
general aura of death and decay. Like the Danny and Alice/Fatima
analogies, however, the male/female descriptions parallel each other
in more than mere literary style. Actually, they overlap and clash
violently, and psychological imbalances are chilling in what they
inexorably imply.

What the sexually immature six year old sees is a dead woman,
hideous indeed but matter-of-factly dead: ancient breasts lolling and
dark pubic hair floating—just about what one might expect a little
boy to notice (not female genitalia precisely, but mere "pubic hair").
But what the sexually experienced, alcoholic, and rather unstable
father dreams in the bathtub, on the other hand, is more disturbed
and perverted: a knife stuck in a boy's chest and a floating, almost
disembodied penis. One should hardly be surprised by the adjective
describing Jack's dream on the preceding page—"queer." Especially
queer is the fact that, before the end of the psychotic dream, Jack
Torrance realizes that the "supplicating face below him" is not
George's but Danny's" (273). Thus in his dream, like the revellers in
Poe's "Masque," Jack unmasks himself—indeed unmans himself. To
himself at least he is able to reveal his "secret sin," exposing the final
face of a "Red Death." Identifying himself with George's dead body,
Jack feels "weightless." Like George's limp penis, Jack, too, "floats."
This queer dream is his REDRUM (the precognitive "murder" pervert-

edly spelled backward in Danny's hallucination)—Jack's "red drum," his unconscious desire to annihilate attractive George Hatfield, affectionate son Danny, and apprehensive wife Wendy. REDRUM represents what Judith Wilt, in an astute comment on the gothic tradition, explains as the "secret sin that works itself poisonously out into the open, destroying at a distance of years or even generations."[4] What is destroyed in *The Shining* is the dramatist-drunkard's whole person, the washing away of body, soul, and consciousness, so that Wendy can say to her son, trying sentimentally to rationalize her husband's madness and murderous moods, "It's not your daddy talking, remember; it's the hotel" (375).[5]

Were *The Shining* more profound and catered less to popular passions for terroristic extravanganzas (what King himself sometimes calls the "gross-out"), one might compare the expansive, quasi-sentient Overlook Hotel to the ancient Egyptian god Atum, whose name means "the one who has been completely absorbing others" in the Heliopolitan cosmology of ancient Egypt.[6] One-armed Atum is a person, place, and thing (a god, a mound, and a phallus) that in his creative aspect breathes out of himself the primal dieties Shu (male) and Tefnut (female). The Overlook absorbs the spirits of its deadly guests, spews them forth when it pleases (like a demonic diety), and even blots up things. Unlike its Egyptian archetype, its nature, however, is decreative. Precocious Danny stammers out the opinion that "the people in the hotel" and "the *things* in the hotel. . . . The hotel is *stuffed* with them." Danny can hear them late at night, "like the wind, all sighing together" (323). King himself argues that a "man with a philosophic bent [like Dante Alighieri, one supposes] might have called it the sound of souls" (325). Wendy speculates that the quasi-sentient hotel is somehow "powered" by Danny's cardiokinetic skills, his so-called "shine"; and she fears that the hotel wants Danny in order to possess his life-force or life-spirit, and "absorb" it "into itself" (371). Happily, and with the assistance of Dick Hallorann (called back from a distance by "Doc's" psychic powers), the hotel that wants to be a god fails to blot up either the innocent one or his "shine." Ultimately, the Beckfordian Overlook is destroyed in a devastating explosion; and benevolent little Danny Torrance, surviving the implications of his last name, escapes the "torrents" of both his father and the hotel fire.

Setting the World on Fire

The villains in *Firestarter* (1980) belong to something called the "Shop," a government organization as insensitive and indifferent to human suffering as a hit man in an organized crime family. As part of the Central Intelligence Agency, their ostensible purpose is the protection of the interests of the United States; but in actual fact, for them murder and mayhem exist almost for their own sake alone. The behavior of shop members blurs the distinction between ordinary white-collar criminals and governmental investigative agencies presumably designed to protect the people and promote the general welfare. After murdering a victim, for example, they pull out fingernails just for kicks. According to an article that *Firestarter* attributes to *Rolling Stone* magazine, the Shop has been involved in such "colossal gaffes" and "crazy mistakes" as a "bloodbath" over an airplane highjacking by Red Army terrorists, in selling heroin to a criminal organization in return for information, and—most peculiar of all—in a communist takeover of a Caribbean island. They are pictured as so incompetent that if their "thousand or more employees had to go to work in the private sector, they would have been drawing unemployment benefits before their probationary periods were up" (144). To modify a phrase of King's, they are the "sublime architects" of criminality and incompetence (145).

The malicious and virtually conscienceless members of this Shop have an interesting assortment of WASP and ethnic names: Dr. Joseph Wanless, Albert Steinowitz, Orville Jamieson (known as "O. J."), John Mayo, and Herman Pynchot. That some of these names have heroic or distinguished resonances is not exactly unintentional—Orville, for example, suggesting Orville Wright; Mayo, the famous surgeons; "O. J.," football player O. J. Simpson; Dr. Albert Steinowitz, Dr. Albert Einstein; etc. When one adds other half-echoing names—Quincey, for example, that recalls perhaps President John Quincy Adams; a character called "Abe" (big, lean, and bearded, who like Lincoln hails from Kentucky [48]); and Bruce Rozelle (combining the names of rock star Bruce Springsteen and Commissioner Pete Roselle of the National Football League)—one begins to feel somewhat at home in the panoramic America of *Firestarter* against which King plays out his paranoid science fiction of terror, horror, and endless sexual innuendo. Frequent appearances of well-known bits of Americana also add to a reader's feeling of national familiarity: "Fire when ready, Gridley" (73)—"We'll think about it tomorrow, like Scarlett said," for tomorrow is "another day" (127)—making the world "safe for democracy" (56 ff.).

Prior to the beginning of the novel the Shop had decided to experiment with an hallucinogenic drug, "Lot Six," on twelve volunteers. Among these cheaply paid volunteers, most of whom died, were Vicky Tomlinson and college English instructor Andy McGee. The latter, whose name is a combination of two popular entertainment figures of the 1930s (the typical American boy, Andy Hardy, played by movie star Mickey Rooney, and the well-known radio comedian Fibber McGee), has the ability to influence people through a psychic something he calls a "push." Expectedly, Vicky and Andy marry and produce a child, Charlene Roberta, who unfortunately inherits and then goes well beyond her father's fatal talent for mental domination of others. As the experiment's director, Dr. Wanless, explains: "Andrew McGee became the X factor" (male to female, thereby reversing the chromosomal roles); "Victoria Tomlinson became the Y factor (female to male)"; and the little girl turned into "something we don't know," the "Z factor" (75). The unknown attribute, possessed by this girl whose name is an androgynous mix (Charlene/"Charlie"), turns out to be the ability to start fires at will—"able to light fires sometimes just by thinking about fires" (89). Little Charlie successively sets afire a Teddy bear, the shoes of a soldier, and a whole set of C.I.A. pursuers—not being able to help herself. This "bad thing" is bad enough; but the narrator expresses an apocalyptic fear that the lovable little seven-year-old "monster"— sometimes casually called "button," as if she ominously symbolized the atomic button that could bring on a nuclear confrontation—has lying, temporarily dormant within her, the "power to someday crack the very planet in two like a china plate in a shooting gallery" (80). Because of her ominous potential for universal earth-destruction, the Shop feels it must destroy the accidental child-fruit of its hallucinogenic experiment gone haywire, just as it has already eliminated the biological mother, the much less dangerous Vickie Tomlinson.

Whereas 'Salem's Lot begins with the interesting sentence, "Almost everybody thought the man and boy were father and son," Firestarter might well have as its theme (though not necessarily its opening line) that "Almost everyone thought that something sexually perverse was going on between the man and his seven-year-old female companion." After the mother has been eliminated by the Shop, Andy and Charlie race through the northeastern states in a vain attempt to escape their pursuers. In the course of the failed attempt (which occupies almost the entire first two hundred pages), they encounter the driver of a van, the owner of a farm, and some residents of a small New England town. Consistently—and oddly enough without outrage or moral indignation—these average American males assume the worst about Andy and Charlie: that Andy is either a kipnapper, or, more insidiously, a child-molester. The character resembling Lincoln hopes that Andy is "watching out" for the "little stranger." And when Andy acknowledges that he doing "as best I can," the unusually generous Abe sings out: "That's the name of the game"—deliberately hinting at the possibility of a sexual game (48–49). The owner of the farm, in his attempt to determine the relationship between the unknown man and girl, suggests sexuality rather broadly when he says, "Whatever else may be going on, it does not appear you've got her against her will" (109). Gossiping about Andy and his companion, some of the Vermonters slyly refer to "him" (i.e., Andy) and "whoever he's keeping over there" (180).

As if implications of incest and child-molestation were not enough, suggestions of androgyny—somehow always insinuated into a King novel—are subtly reinforced. It is somewhat jarring to find the name "Charlie," a name usually associated with boys, here constantly identifed as "she" and "her." King, of course, knows that many readers will make the necessary mental adjustments and perhaps be unaware of what the adjustment implies, and that those oriented toward female equality or unisexuality in names and behavior will silently approve of his apparent broad-mindedness. But all this is mere facade, a manipulation of the consciousness for what King is really after: putting and keeping the conscious mind in "neutral" and the "subconscious in high gear" (63). To reinforce the sense of androgyny, King employs whole sets of "small helping pushes" (157), drawing an analogy at one point between Charlie's pyromaniac abilities and boys' (not *girls'* notice, but boys') activities or sexual developments. Concerning his daughter's inevitable sexual maturing, Andy speculates: "What if [Charlie] began to light fires in her sleep as part of her own strange puberty, a fiery counterpoint to the nocturnal seminal emissions most teenage boys experienced?" (176). On an occasion when Charlie exerts her pyrotechnical powers, the "fingers of fire" she creates, "climb the ivy with the agility of a boy on midnight business" (120). Or, later, during one of Charlie's dreams, when she is galloping bareback on the horse called Necro-mancer, "she could hardly tell where her [female] thighs ended and Necromancer's [male] sides began" (301). Even such innocuous things as Charlene's emerging from a men's room with her male captors—and other such male/female conjoinings—cleverly manipu-late the unconscious and are instances of what, in another connec-tion, King calls "an invisible something that . . . seems to be feeding itself in a spiraling chain reaction of exponential force" (373). Such subtle androgynous "pushes" trigger an "almost hypnotic trace memory" in the person being pushed (in this case, the reader), setting up an "echo effect" that "could become a ricochet, and the ricochet could lead to . . . well, to *almost anything*" (273).

Innuendoes of incest, child molestation, and/or bisexuality inten-sify when Andy is finally captured by the Shop and is separated from Charlie for virtually the entire second half of *Firestarter*. There was little question of Andy's moral integrity with respect to his daughter. But once the Iago-like character with the unusual name of "Rain-bird" enters the picture, and in addition a curious mixture of perver-sion and normality ironically called "Pynchot," implications of psychological anomalies become more insistent and insidious. Like Polyphemus of Homer's *Odyssey*, Rainbird is one-eyed; and while not precisely a flesh-eater like his Greek counterpart (the chief of the one-eyed Cyclops), he is an indifferent and heartless flesh-destroyer. As part of his "main interest in life"—death itself—Rainbird once planted a bomb on a plane that ended up killing sixty-seven people (134). Out of morbid curiosity (with "lingering traces of Nazism" and "all the things Americans had fought World War II to put an end to" [191]), Rainbird liked to watch the faces of the dying and kills Dr. Joseph Wanless by holding closed the victim's nose and mouth. Thus this neo-Nazi—with idle indifference to human suffering—could watch that which interested him most: the "actual exhalation of the soul," the "exit from the body" (131). In killing Wanless (who is "wand-less," that is, without supernatural fairy power), Rainbird observes how the "eyes [of helpless victims] seem to lose their fear and fill instead with a great puzzlement—not wonder, not dawning comprehension, or realization or awe, just puzzlement" (134). Learning about "Charlie's fire-powers," he who was peculiarly "at peace with God, satan and the universe" (130), ponders (like a twentieth-century Herod or an innocence-destroying Antichrist) "what it would be like to kill a child" (134). Oddly, this Nazi-like thought makes him feel "very tender about her, very protective," for he knows that, eventually, "the girl would be his" (135)—"his" meaning "his" in death, but inevitably also "his" in sexual union. In the absence of incarcerated Andy, Rainbird hypocritically assumes the role of kindly friend and surrogate father, and by implication, incestuous lover, child-molester, and potential killer.

That affection develops between Charlie and Rainbird, but nothing beyond, is one of King's ways of dealing with what he calls the "finest emotion"—terror. Suspicions of improper behavior are, of course, entirely in the reader's mind, and nothing outright "nasty," though much hinted at, is actually articulated (*DM*, 21). This technique of evoking terror through evasion irritates some critics, as when, for example, nothing palpably awful ever emerges in the terror-closet in *Cujo*, or from the long phallic hose in the corridors of the Overlook Hotel in *The Shining*. But these are minor instances. One can imagine how repulsive an actual description of intimate Charlie/Rainbird relationships might turn out to be: that is, a physically deformed "John" with a sexually underdeveloped and possibly androgynous "Charlie," each out to destroy the other in incendiary copulation. Thus King can sometimes assume an air of pseudoinnocence about pursuing his "finest emotion" while, in actual fact, subtly disordering the psyche and "pushing" the gothic imagination in a variety of deviant directions.

Douglas E. Winter considers *Firestarter* King's "most sexual novel";[7] and considering the frequency of the Freudian extravaganzas—some of them quite bizarre—the view is not far off the mark. Among the unabashed erotica of King's uninhibited novels, surely the most mind-boggling is the behavior of the sexually self-indulgent and suicidal Dr. Herman Pynchot, a member of the Shop who is one of Andy's keepers, but one on whom Andy practices a certain number of "pushes" so as to facilitate an escape, which fails (Andy dies in the attempt). But in the process of exerting a series of mental "pushes" on Pynchot Andy chances upon his "disturbed personality . . . tightly corseted into an appearance of normality while God knew what forces might be delicately balanced underneath" (274). Though Andy notices something "slightly effeminate" about Pynchot (the same phrase used of Mears, Petrie, Callahan, and Barlow in *'Salem's Lot*), he does not know that Pynchot was a "closet transvestite" but "not gay" (277), who used to indulge himself sexually by dressing in his wife's delicate undies while listening to the grinding of the garbage disposal in the kitchen. In his twisted mind, the machine was a "vaginal" dark hole in the center of the sink guarded by a rubber diaphragm (276).

While practicing "pushes" on Pynchot, "a sudden cold and murderous voice spoke from deep inside [Andy], from some well sunk far into his subconscious. The cold voice said, *"Tell him to go home and commit suicide. Then push him. Push him hard"* (274). A similar satanic suggestion is made to the minister turned monster in *Cycle of the Werewolf*. But while the *Cycle*'s Reverend Lester Lowe does not take the suggested advice that comes to him quietly by way of a letter, Andy's "pushes" toward the Pynchot suicide are more irrational and insistent. The "somewhat effeminate" doctor does indeed go home, dress up in his wife's underclothes, abuse himself to the grinding sound of the disposer, and bizarrely commit suicide by plunging his arm into the machine, "vaporizing" his arm almost to the elbow, "sharpened like a living pencil, his blood splattered in the sink and on the Wood-Mode cabinets" (311). He commits this suicidal "pinching" as a result of Andy's push while alone in the house, his wife and children being away for the evening.

It is rather quaint to find Stephen King reported as believing in "most of the ideas expressed by Christianity"[8]. With suggestions of incest, suicide, child-molestation, bisexuality, transvestism, pyrokenisis, necrophilia, and mutilation, the American characters in *Firestarter* betray no such orientations or inclinations. The masturbatory suicide by arm crunching of Herman Pynchot harks back rather to the brutal blood-rites of the goddess Cybele of ancient Classical times, in whose name male devotees ritually castrated themselves and hurled their severed genitals at the bloody image of the *Magna Mater*.[9] In a headnote to *Our Lady of Darkness* (1977), Fritz Leiber quotes Thomas De Quincey's estimate of this savage deity: "the mother of lunacies, the suggestress of suicides" who "storms all doors at which she is permitted to enter."[10] King's Herman Pynchot, and perhaps King himself, seem perfect pagan adorers of such a *Mater Tenebrarum*.

Unlike the appealing gothics of *'Salem's Lot*, what often appalls in *Firestarter* is the pitiless ethics of a bleak and sexually grotesque America. It is naive indeed to suppose that, in describing the atrocities of the Shop, King is merely limiting himself to the excesses of the C.I.A.—as his Afterword seems to imply. By trace-echoing such attractive-sounding American names as Orville Wright, the Mayo brothers, O. J. Simpson, Albert Einstein, Samuel Morse, John Quincy Adams, Abraham Lincoln, Teddy Roosevelt, Booth Tarkington, and others, is he not rather speaking of the entire nation that the echoing names represent, an America "still full of odd dark corners and unsettling nooks and crannies" (403)? In one of those unsettling "nooks"—a sexual one—is nestled the yet to be fully developed fire-power of Charlie McGee. Still alive at the end of the novel and now alone, she has a story to tell and an unknown "something to show" (401). In other words, in King's lexicon of future horrors, the ultimate sexual revelation by fire is yet to come. The apocalyptic seventh veil has yet to be dropped. What has been thus far narrated in *Firestarter* was only the inchoate workings of an unexplained and uncontrollable incendiary/androgynous "Z Factor." What is ahead of the U.S.A. is future shock.

Chapter Four

One Touch of Horror Makes the Whole World Kin

The Stuff of Nightmares

Ever since World War I, and especially since the holocausts of such places as Auschwitz and Hiroshima, apocalyptic writings—that is, narratives of (1) universal malevolence, (2) world-wide destruction, (3) irrational symbols, and/or (4) eschatological visions—have become increasingly and almost neurotically frequent. Two of Stephen King's works are important contributions to this popular genre: his longest novel to that time (1978) *The Stand* (817 pages), and one of his shortest stories, "Night Surf" (eight pages). The former contains all four of the above-named characteristics, the latter (more bleak and futile) chiefly the first three.

The devastations in *Carrie*, *'Salem's Lot*, and *The Shining* may be limited to localities in Maine and Colorado, but there is clearly an apocalyptic atmosphere about the "recurrent power of evil" in all three novels (*SL*, 111).[1] The limited destructions in these three early novels are headed directly—almost prophetically—into the universal, end-of-the-world destructions of the fourth novel, *The Stand* (1978). The high school of *Carrie*, the Maine town of *'Salem's Lot*, and the Colorado hotel of *The Shining* broaden out to become the entire United States, which is what they really were originally intended to symbolize, if one is to trust King's claim that the Vietnam War, the Watergate disclosures, and America's assassinations and racial problems of the 1960s were the negative propellants of some early novels (*DM*, 398). The protagonist-speaker of "I Am the Doorway" says of his astronautic exploration of the hostile and inhospitable planet Venus (with "cloud cover . . . equals parts methane, ammonia, dust and flying shit") that "it was like circling a haunted house in the midst of deep space" (*NS*, 64)—King now apparently projecting the sodomitic Marsten House into the very solar system as the love-planet Venus. One might make up several possible formulas here to accommodate this expansion: haunted house equals city, haunted city equals nation, or haunted nation equals hostile universe, etc. But regardless of how a commentator might choose to formulate the gothic extension, the equation would be a modern version of the Roman and medieval *urbs-orbis* analogy, the "city" equated with "empire" and eventually the "earth"—if not the very "universe" itself.

Parallel to this classic city-world symbolism stands the New Testament image of the destruction of Jerusalem (cf. the original name of 'Salem's Lot), which symbolizes the destruction of the world that is to bring on the traditional Last Judgment as expressed in a well-known passage in Matthew (24:15 ff.). However, in the relationship between *'Salem's Lot* and *The Stand*, Last Judgment aspects of Christian escatology have been virtually eliminated. While some of the symbology of the Christian apocalypse has been exploited (especially plague, Antichrist, "lying wonders," and universal devastation), and while aspects of *The Stand* are, here and there, quite traditional and conservative (consider, for example, the arguments used by Frannie Goldsmith's father against abortion [54–55]), the Christian commitment is generally circumscribed, indeed is sometimes treated with sardonic humor. In *The Stand*, Christianity does not extend much beyond mere facade, the apocalyptic spirit more akin to the mythic imagery of Richard Wagner's *Götterdämmerung* ("Twilight of the Gods") in the nineteenth century, or the "Ragnarok" ("Judgment of the Gods") of the *Elder* and *Younger Eddas* of medieval Nordic literature.[2]

Apocalyptic dispositions always surface in Bible-influenced societies when human reason becomes incapable of resolving whatever distresses might happen to afflict a nation, or—as at the present time—consume the whole earth in irradiated madness. Although not all of King's narratives are apocalyptic, almost everything is touched by Scripture (usually negatively) and marked by what can only be called an "apocalyptic perspective." Without being consciously mystical or religious, the Argus-eyed hands and chest of astronaut Arthur in "I Am the Doorway" (*NS*, 73) hark back to the New Testament images of seven eyes in the forehead of the standing lamb, or the within-and-without eyes of the four living creatures (Revelation 4:6-8, 5:6). Clearly, a direct line connects the fire that comes from the mouths of the "two witnesses" to destroy their enemies (Revelation 11:5) and the incendiary powers that emanate from the mind of Charlie Magee to destroy her pursuers in *Firestarter* (a "child capable of eventually creating a nuclear explosion simply by the force of her

will" [80]). Though the cliché of the inexplicable manuscript derives
from Walpole, Poe, and Lovecraft, one can easily devise a connection
between the "yellowed foolscap," in "Jerusalem's Lot," mapped with
"spider-thin strokes of black ink" (NS, 8), and the apocalyptic scroll
"written within and without" and sealed with seven seals (Revelation
5:1).

Of course, the apocalyptic version of antirational mentality does
not flourish in an artistic and/or philosophic vacuum. Actually, artists' obsessions with the irrational extend at least to the beginnings
of the present century, and indeed well beyond, as the prophetical
writings and fantastical drawings of William Blake (1757–1827)
testify. What is exclusively twentieth century is the intensity of the
phenomenon. At the beginning of this century in northern Europe,
German expressionism initiated the irrational art movements with
attacks on objective reality—hence reason itself—through distortion, exaggeration, and symbolism. Later on, the surrealist movement, in the language of Andre Breton, Salvador Dali, and others,
added "convulsive beauty," "enchanted madness," "decalcomania of
desire," "psychic automaton," "delirious phenomenon"—artistic and
critical jargon that can be simply reduced to the "nightmare experience" and the "paranoid image." In his study of surrealism, Wallace
Fowlie pointedly observes that, in their aesthetic of the unconscious,
surrealists "could see a poetic unity joining such works as Nebuchad-
nezzar's dream in the book of *Daniel*, and the revelations made to St.
John on the island of Patmos, and [Lautreamont's] *Les Chants de
Maldoror*, and [Rimbaud's] *Une Saison en Enfer*."[3] Writing at the
present time, Fowlie might well include among the surrealist works
Stephen King's "I Am the Doorway," "Sometimes They Come Back,"
"Children of the Corn," and much of *The Stand*, especially the dream
episodes (81, 229–30, 365–68), and nearly every irrational appearance of Randall Flagg.

A half century or more separates the original expressionist aesthetic from the emergence of the mid-sixties horror novel in America, and a wide gulf separates the intellectuality of expressionism
(and later of surrealism) from the almost mindless popularity of the
apocalyptic horror novel of recent years. But the simple terms "distortion," "exaggeration," and "symbolism" apply perfectly well to
King stories in which one is likely to find such expressionist/
surrealist metaphors as—"like a skull that's been picked clean," "like
a blind conductor stretching out his hands over a lunatic orchestra,"

or "as if someone had scooped out his brains and put a hand grenade in his skull" (*NS*, 63–64, 71). As though a self-propelled prophecy, expressionism flourished in Germany prior to the distortions, exaggerations, and symbol-mongering of the Nazi hysteria. But once Nazism entrenched itself politically and initiated the holocaust and a second world war that climaxed in the atomic bombing of two Japanese cities, a seemingly permanent apocalyptic dimension was added to the surrealist philosophy.

The number 666 of Revelation 13:18, the number of the beast, is one of the most famous, and infamous, symbols in Scripture. Not accidentally, on page 666 of the paperback edition of *The Stand*, a character who has just unsuccessfully tried to commit suicide (Harold Lauder)—and is about to do so again, a second time successfully—inscribes a final entry in his journal: *"when the end comes, and when it is as horrible as good men always knew it would be, there is only one thing to say as all those good men approach the Throne of Judgment: I was misled."* One could hardly doubt that this journal entry is a statement of King's personal apocalypse; and it follows that faith in human progress, especially when that progress is dependent upon the triumph of human reason, is constantly circumscribed with doubt, insecurity, and ambivalence. The novels and short stories support the suggestion (in the words of *The Stand*'s Glen Bateman) that "we're here under the fiat of powers we don't understand" (473). In a conversation with Frannie Goldsmith—and this type of antirationalist reflection occurs at significant points in many King novels—Bateman comments on the stupidity of the human race and the limitations of human reason: "Who emptied the beaker loses importance beside the general truth: *At the end of all rationalism, the mass grave.* The laws of physics, the laws of biology, the axioms of mathematics, they're all part of the deathtrip, because we are what we are. . . . The fashion was to blame it on 'technology,' but 'technology' is the trunk of the tree, not the roots. The roots are rationalism, and I would define that word so: Rationalism is the idea we can ever understand anything about the state of being" (472–73). Many characters in King's stories—at least unconsciously—have this sort of philosophy. In *The Stand*, that perpetual adolescent, Harold Lauder, considers life, and most especially his own, as a futile attempt to "rationalize the unspeakable" (666).

Antirationalist outbursts are not confined to *The Stand*. Similar passages, in the form of either occasional brief observations or extended paragraphs, appear in other works as well. In *Rage* (initially published under the pseudonym Richard Bachman), the psychopathic teenage killer with the high I.Q., Charlie Decker, philosophizes like a Dionysian over what he considers a split-universe and the consequently Janus-faced distortions of human intellect and personality. His disdain for what others consider the Apollonian order of the cosmos is astonishing in one so young:

there's a Mr. Hyde for every happy Jekyll face, a dark face on the other side of the mirror. The brain behind that face never heard of razors, prayers, or the logic of the universe. You turn the mirror sideways and see your face reflected with a sinister left-hand twist, half mad and half sane. The other side says the universe has all the logic of a little kid in Halloween cowboy suit with his guts and his trick-or-treat candy spread all over a mile of Interstate 95. This is the logic of the napalm, paranoia, suitcase bombs carried by happy Arabs, random carcinoma. (33)

In Charlie Decker's version of Lauder's philosophy, the infernal dice are loaded in favor of the irrational, the inexplicable, and the imponderable—and ultimately the psychopathic. According to Charlie's point of view (considering who is articulating it and how much attention he accords it), this "mad mad world"—so-called by the Elizabethan dramatist Thomas Middleton—has shriveled up, meaninglessly and menacingly shaping itself into the "madman" with a "dead geranium" of T. S. Eliot's "Rhapsody on a Windy Night."

As omniscient narrator in *'Salem's Lot*, King speaks in his own name, commenting on that terrifying scene in which Hank Peters and Royal Snow descend, like the heavy souls of the damned, to the basement of the Marsten House to deliver what they think is a quaint piece of furniture, actually a vampire's coffin. This time, instead of debating the rationality or irrationality of the universe, King takes its idiocy for granted and, just as he often divides personalities, splits terror itself into two conflicting halves, in which the unreasonable half is the more overwhelming:

Hank felt a strain of fear enter his heart that he had not even felt in [Viet] Nam, although he had been scared most of his time there. *That was a rational fear.* Fear that you might step on a pongee stick and see your foot swell up like some noxious green balloon. . . . But this fear [upon entering the dark basement of the Marsten House] was childlike, dreamy. There was no reference point to it. A house was a house—boards and hinges and nails and sills. There was no reason, really no reason, to feel that each splintered crack was exhaling its own chalky aroma of evil. (86–87)

The various terror rooms of the Marsten House—the basement that is the night residence of Barlow, and the upper room in which Mears hallucinated the hanging figure—become microcosmic irrationals encased within a referenceless macrocosm, rather like Winston Churchill's "riddle wrapped in a mystery inside an enigma." What Mears imagines concerning his first meeting with Susan applies perfectly to a Marsten House that, metaphorically, seems "intent on grinding helpless mortals between the great millstones of the universe to make some unknown bread" (*SL*, 9). To obtain the right witch's dough for *The Stand*, all that was needed was some of the ominous symbology of the Book of Revelation: pale horse, wicked Babylon, great harlot, beast, seven seals, seven last plagues, Armageddon, etc. Under one guise or another, all of these appear—in spirit at least, if not as actual symbol. There can be no doubt, for example, that Las Vegas is Babylon, and the ironically named Nadine Cross the "great harlot," etc.

With only trifling exceptions, King's writings repeatedly betray a preoccupation with powerful evil forces, "all black winter and dark ice," possessing "nothing of God or Light" (*Cycle of the Werewolf*, 16), successfully battering human reason and biblical optimism in an arena of apocalyptic confrontation. As the ultimate ethical-irrational, this confrontation has three important aspects: (1) an innocence unjustly treated, like the beating of the McDougall baby in *'Salem's Lot* (38–39, 140–41); (2) a cruelty needlessly excessive, like the knifing of Jimmy Cody "stuck in half a dozen places" (397); and (3) a diabolical power seemingly irresistible, like the massive and everspreading malevolence of Barlow and his evil sidekick Straker. Little wonder, then, that 'salem's lot is filled with the unspeakable whisper that "Hubert Marsten kidnapped and sacrificed small children and sacrificed them to his infernal gods," a secret that even gossipy Mabel Werts "won't talk about" (200). A striking image—among many—of this tripartite sequence occurs toward the end of *The Stand* (760–61). A diabolical figure stretches out an index finger (representing the "irresistible power of evil"), and a "blue ball" no bigger than a pingpong ball leaps from the finger with a "faint ozone crackle." This searing ball of fire fuses shut the mouth of one of the protesting characters standing by (who obviously represents "innocence unjustly

treated"), making a charred trench in his cheek, and rolls toward the
back of his head, leaving a "grotesque bald strip behind it" ("cruelty
needlessly excessive"). Almost all the characters in *The Stand*, as also
in *Carrie* and *'Salem's Lot*, are entrapped in such diabolical apocalyp-
ses of terror and horror. Few escape, and even fewer triumph. When
they do conquer, it is not always *The Stand*'s fierce "finger of God"
that prevails, it is sometimes—as in *Cycle of the Werewolf*—nothing
more than a silly firecracker on a Fourth of July (70), or the "absurdly insignificant pop" of a Daisy air-rifle fired by a ten-year-old
crippled boy with a ridiculous name, Marty Coslaw (125).

Skeletal Fingers of the Accusing Dead

The main character in *The Stand* is not human, but rather a highly
contagious flulike disease, nicknamed "Captain Trips"—a superflu
that almost totally wipes out the population of the United States in
the year 1985, seven years after the publication of the novel. The
deadly epidemic results from a scientific experiment in which lethal
viruses are accidentally released into the atmosphere. One of the
characters describes it this way: "Your somebody in authority got a
bunch of bacteriologists, virologists, and epidemiologists together in
some government installation to see how many funny bugs they
could dream up. And they dreamed up a dilly" (158). Book 1 of this
tripartite, quasi-epic narrative—epic in its eight-hundred-page
length, if in nothing else—deals with the consequences of this scientific disaster, and is dated 16 June–4 July 1985. The 1985 date
follows chronologically that of George Orwell's *1984* (1948), when
the earth is in the total control of Big Brother and freedom of
thought and action, once inspired by the Declaration of Independence and the American Constitution, are completely annihilated.
While the Orwell novel plays no role in *The Stand*, King actually
extends the devastation from the cruel 1984 politics of Orwell's novel
to the crassly mismanaged 1985 biology of his own. Yet the elaborate
attempt to restore American democracy in the face of universal death
and devastation can be considered a response to Orwell, expressing an
unusual note of confidence in the lasting values of the American
political system (397 ff.).

The 4 July 1985 date that concludes book 1 is not without ironic
significance nor lacking grotesquely comical aspects when one of the
characters (sex-loose rock-star Larry Underwood) greets the morning

of a 1985 Independence Day with a buck-naked, "bump-and-grind" burlesque-rendition of "The Star-Spangled Banner" (246–47). What had been "proudly hailed" at the "twilight's last gleaming" by the woman with whom he was sharing a tight sleeping bag (Rita Blake-moor) was not the red-white-and-blue banner of the United States, but Underwood's "genital flag"—a piece of patriotic anatomy, though here flaunted and flagged about in an obviously undignified fashion that is not without importance to the flag symbolism (cf. the surname Flagg) of the novel. Interestingly, Karl Shapiro, in his novel *Edsel* (1971), also uses the flag and Independence Day symbolism in a sexual sense, when the quasi-impotent protagonist (college professor Edsel himself) finally achieves a successful orgasm to the tune of a star-spangled red, white and blue. In *The Stand*, however, the Fourth of July is also the day on which Larry Underwood, having slept with Rita Blakemoor, discovered she had overdosed and died in her sleep (370). In a sense, he has slept with a corpse.

The highly contagious flu of *The Stand*, with a 99.4 percent communicability, was nick-named "Captain Trips" when it reached California—a name deriving from rock star Jerry Garcia of the "Grateful Dead," one of the leaders of the drug cult in the sixties[4]—a nickname that appears glancingly in "Night Surf," where a similar devastating flu attack occurs (*NS*, 56). "Captain Trips" gives the novel, as well as the short story, important allegorical dimensions. For as drug trips go "tripping" across the United States (hypodermically from youth to youth), so the fatal disease goes "tripping" from person to person, both in novel and short story, with a death speed that turns out to be medically incredible. The devastating disease seems to express itself—sometimes actually personify itself—in the ominous figure of Randall Flagg, King's version of a pestilential Big Brother who is made to resemble both the superflu with its 99.4 percent communicability and the annihilating Antichrist of a two-thousand-year Christian tradition. Both Flagg and the imperious flu—to use the language of folklorists—were "shape-shifters." Usually on an *R-F* pattern, Randall Flagg randomly changed his name to Richard Fry, Robert Franq, Ramsey Forrest—though more often than not he is identified throughout *The Stand* as simply the "Walkin Dude." But even this *R-F* pattern is too localized and confining for the ubiquitous Flagg, and therefore the following more expansive suggestion is made: "Call him Beelzebub . . . Nyarlahotep, and Ahaz and Astaroth . . . R'yelah and Seti and Anubis" (743). The unusual disease itself is described by one of the characters (George Richardson) in language that parodies his shape- and name-shifting behavior: "With Captain Trips, the flu *itself* changed every time your body came to a defense posture. And it just went on shifting from form to form until the body was worn out. The result, inevitably, was death" (805). *The Stand* makes clear that there were those who believed that Randall Flagg, the "shape-changer" like A6, had "started the plague himself, that he was the Antichrist whose coming was foretold in Revelation" (637). In fact, the "dark man is as real as the superflu itself, as real as the atomic bombs that still sit somewhere in their leadlined closets" (665–66).

The deliberate interplay of the names "Trips" and "Walkin" (and later on "Trotts," as in Abigail Trotts) ought to be obvious enough, and the Dude's cross-country movements are emphasized, significantly, at opportune moments. The Dude's inexplicable peripatetics are first detailed in chapter 17 in rock song, refrainlike fashion: "the dark man strode south," "he walked rapidly," "he moved along, not pausing," "he strode on a steady, ground-eating pace" (118–22). These rapid-walking movements are underscored with effectively used clocking and knocking images, monotonously and metronomically keeping time (whenever the Dude comes hurrying along), like an ominous bass rhythm to an evil melodic line. Thus, "he hammered along" (120), "he rocked along, his feet easy in the boots which were comfortably sprung in all the right places" (121), and "his . . . dusty boots clocking on the pavement" (122). When he determines the destruction of one of his agents (Bobby Terry, for example), strange clock-rhythmic sounds are heard, "like rundown bootheels hammering swiftly along the secondary road macadam" (635). When he appears to Judge Ferris as a crow—a creature he not only commands (like wolves) but also transform himself into—he makes weird tap-tap-tap sounds upon the windowpane in the manner of Edgar Allan Poe's nevermore raven: "this *was* the dark man, his soul, his *ka*[5] somehow projected into this raindrenched, grinning crow that was looking in at him, checking up on him," and the "crow leaned forward and, very deliberately, tapped on the glass" (629). Clock images climax when one of the Dude's stooges finds "over a dozen five-and-dime plastic timers" to attach to his copper ignition system for the purpose of blowing up the enemies of Randall Flagg: "You set them for fifteen minutes or a half hour and when they got back to zero they went *ding* and you knew it was time to

take your pie out of the oven. Only instead of going *ding* this time
. . . they are going to go *bang*" (705). All the numerous foot-
clicking images appear to be setting up Randall Flagg as a doomsday
clock for a world whose final hour is about to strike.

Of the various traditional characteristics of the Antichrist (that he
would be born in Bethlehem, reign from Jerusalem for three and a
half years, rebuild the Temple of Solomon, and be received world-
wide as the messiah),[6] three interesting ones are emphasized in *The
Stand*: the supernatural powers, the ability to levitate, and the divine
pretensions. All are explored in unusual imaginative detail. Flagg is
presented, for example, with the ability to "suddenly appear in a
small, out-of-the-way burg" and "materialize like a ghost" (625).
When this ability to appear and disappear is combined with the
ability to levitate, Randall Flagg then seems to blend into himself
aspects of both human time and divine eternity.

With his ever-present sense of irony, however, King arranges an act
of private levitation at a moment when the otherwise-perceptive
Flagg suspects that he might have been making "stupid decisions" all
along and thus abruptly "decided to push it all aside and levitate."
This pseudodivine power always made him feel better: "looking out
at the desert sky, he proclaims himself God by insistently repeating,
"*I am, I am, I am, I AM*" (700). But Flagg is immediately confronted
with a succession of defeats, as when in an attempt to levitate, "it
was a long, long time before his bootheels would leave the sundeck,
and when they did they would only hover a quarter of an inch above
the concrete" (702).

Most unusual among the divine pretensions is Flagg's ability to
send forth his "eye." According to the cosmology of Heliopolis in
ancient Egypt (ca. 2780 B.C.), the primeval Atum, the single-armed
diety who had self-generated out of a primeval mound, had the
ability to send forth anywhere on the earth his single eye, known as
the "Wedjet"—representing the Egyptian Mother Goddess in her
destructive aspect. The technical, mythological name for the Egyptian eye, Wedjet, is never used in *The Stand*, but its search-and-seizure
behavior ought to be clear enough to anyone familiar with that five-
thousand-year-old mythology. Ancient Egyptian texts associate this
primeval eye with terror, fright, slaughter, howling, and cringing, as
in the spell that is #316 of the Egyptian Coffin texts.

With such gothic attributes, the ominous Wedjet is a perfect
companion for the pseudodivine Flagg, who (probably like the

reader) fails to understand the phenomenon (668): how, for example, he could have obtained such a detachable eye, or why he can use it. Its power is such that Flagg can throw a "sudden furious stare" at some wolves, and nearly a half a dozen would fall to fighting, "their gutteral sounds like ripping cloth in the stillness" (668). But the real purpose of this traveling eye (that sometimes falls "mysteriously blind" [668]) is to spy out potential dangers to Flagg and his associates. Most significant among its traveling extravaganzas are the ability to overcome an eagle, a traditional medieval symbol of apocalyptic triumph of Christ ("The eagle fell almost all the way to the ground, stunned, before recovering itself" [717]), and its corresponding inability to overcome a dog, the traditional gothic symbol of opposition to vampires. Despite its awesome power, the Wedjet too, like Randall Flagg himself, sometimes "flags"—a pun on his name that King himself occasionally uses, but a brief dialogue between Tom Collins and Stu Redman, toward the end of *The Stand*, seems to imply that the Walkin Dude, despite "flaggings," may come back (795).

Birthday Cake with Nitroglycerine Candles

Both the psychopathic killer Lloyd Henreid and the pyromaniac Trashcan Man (whose real name is Donald Merwin Elbert [762]) not only wander in the long-cast shadows of Randall Flagg, but are psychopathic embodiments of his Antichrist spirit. If any two characters should have been destined for flu destruction by Captain Trips, certainly Lloyd Henreid and Trashcan Man should have, but atomic detonation alone seems to have the power to clean up the earth by eliminating them. As moral cleansing agents, mere diseases are too weak.

Even though he is supposed to be the frightening "man with no face," Randall Flagg is a mere symbolic abstraction by contrast with the hideous specifics of Lloyd Henreid, a "pusbag" of criminality, a "scummy douchebag," who is unable to catch a cold, to say nothing of the superflu itself, even when someone sneezes into his face, "spraying him with thick spit" (171). His behavior in jail when all the "screws" around him are dying of superflu—that is, eating a cockroach, gnawing on the tail of a rat, negotiating the stiff body of his dead cellmate for future food ("Nothing personal, I ain't going to eat you, old buddy; not unless I have to" [234])—is so revolting as to be barely repeatable. Firebug Donald Merwin Elbert, known as the "Trashcan Man" (whose curious nickname echoes Lloyd's prison companion's, "Trask") is an "unknowing soul brother" (375). Drawn in a dream by the hypnotic powers of Flagg, "Trash" drags himself through Colorado's famous Eisenhower Tunnel, crying out repeatedly, "My life for you, my life for you" (364–81).

Trash is offering his life to the "light" at the end of the tunnel of death, the "light" being both Flagg himself and Flagg's imaginary capital, the seven-in-one city of the promised, the fabled Cibola of Hispanic and Indian folklore.[14] The legendary "Cibola" functions in Trash's imagination as a kind of infernal Jerusalem, a counterpart of the heavenly Jerusalem of Revelation 21:10-27, as Dante's infernal city of Dis is a counterpart of the earthy Jerusalem where Jesus was crucified. What the appropriately named Trash desires therein is not rest and peace, but rather shrieks, rapes, subjugations, and a "Great Burning"—"Cities going up like bombs. Cultivated fields drawn in lines of fire" (365).

While the figures of Lloyd and Trash might be the right and left sides of Flagg's demonic kingdom, more interesting are the pseudorational and often mutually contradictory manifestations of Flagg in American culture. Pockets in his "faded pegged jeans" were filled with "fifty different kinds" of "literature"—the "dangers of atomic power plants, the role played by the International Jewish Cartel in the overthrow of friendly governments, the CIA, the farm workers' union, the Jehovah's Witnesses . . . the Blacks for Militant Equality, the Kode of the Klan" (119). When Flagg, called by one of the characters (Glen Bateman) the "last magician of rational thought" (474), walked into a meeting, the backbiting, recriminations, and accusations would cease. Mysteriously, he brought to these meetings "some old and terrible engine of destruction," something a "thousand times worse than the plastic explosive made in the basement labs of renegade chemistry students or the black market arms obtained from some greedy army post supply sergeant"—a "device gone rusty with blood, but now ready again," carried to the meeting in which he intrudes like "some infernal gift." King observes that when the discussion that had been "hysterical babble" and "ideological rhetoric" began again, everything would surprisingly be "rational and disciplined—as rational and disciplined as madmen can make it, and things would be agreed upon" (120–21). In such a manner, the ubiquitous "Antichrist" infiltrated a "hundred different Committees of Responsibility." He participated in the civil rights marches of 1960 and 1961 and churches "exploded as if some miracle inside them had grown too big to be contained." Not unexpectedly, he encountered a certain Mr. Oswald [the assassin of President Kennedy], who was handing out tracts urging America to leave Cuba alone. Possessed of a "fiery grin," he terrified mothers who, seeing him, quickly used to "grab up their children and pull them into the house" (122).

Making Sense out of a Six-word Sentence

"Baby, Can You Dig Your Man?" is the repeated line in the rock song that makes singer-composer Larry Underwood wealthy and famous, a line that is repeated so often in the beginning of *The Stand* that it becomes a kind of motif, acquiring various layers of implication as the plot unfolds. The account of the creation and popularization of Larry's man-digging song in chapter 5 is preceded by the quarrel between Franny Goldsmith and her boy friend Jess Rider over Fran's unexpected pregnancy, and by the accidental escape of deadly flu viruses from the western California experimental laboratory. The question—"Can you dig your man?"— has one meaning (almost comical) in the context of the copulative carelessness that resulted in Fran's seemingly unfortunate pregnancy. In a mocking dialogue with her lover (Jess), the begetter of her unwanted child, she cleverly lists the possible errors that might account for her present condition: "Well, what I figure is *one*, somebody in the quality control department of the jolly old Orvil factory [manufacturer of birth control devices] was asleep at the switch when my batch of pills went by on the conveyor belt, or *two*, they are feeding you guys something in the UNH messhall that builds up sperm, or *three*, I forgot to take a pill and have since forgotten I forgot" (16).

The six-word man-digging question has yet another implication, quite bitter and sardonic, when scientist Billy Starkey conducts an imaginary conversation with his daughter (Cindy Hammer) to inform her of the sudden death of her young husband, whose ironical nickname is "Vic" (i.e., "Victory"). Starkey tries to explain the scientific mistake:

You see, there was a goof. Somebody made a mistake with a box. Somebody else forgot to pull a switch that would have sealed off the base. The lag was only twenty-three seconds, but it was enough. . . . The boxes were put together by female technicians, and they're put together circuit by circuit so none of them really know what they're doing. One of them was maybe thinking about what to make for supper, and whoever was supposed to check her work was maybe thinking about trading the family car. (31)

The accidental and fatal release of the experimental superflu virus (that produces death so universal as to turn the earth into a virtual crypt) is thus counterbalanced—and eventually counteracted—by the accidental impregnation of Franny Goldsmith (that will produce a child who will possess the biological power to "wear down" the virulence of the superflu and conquer it [805–6]). This child, like the child of the headless woman in "Breathing Method" (*DS*, 437–97), will be born within the twelve-day Christmas season (4 January 1986), drawing a somewhat imperfect yet obviously intentional analogy with the Christ child. The nickname of the child's father is "Jess," an abbreviated form of Jesse, the father of David in the Old Testament (1 Samuel 16). The child's ability to resist is the "stand" he makes against Captain Trips for several days after his birth (805–6)—hence the name of book 3, "The Stand" (dated 7 September 1985–10 January 1986), and the name of the novel itself.

Of the various sexual encounters throughout the novel, the most searing is the "infernal marriage" (678) between Randall Flagg and Nadine Cross, who has been saving herself for "something special." Nadine's inability to endure the cold phallic advances of Randall, although she has long been waiting for them, add layer upon layer of horror to the rock theme, "Baby, can you dig your man?" In bedding down Nadine and Randall in the context of repellant images, *The Stand* befouls sexuality by imagining its ultimate horror: a "caked and long-hidden lust," an "ageless pimple . . . about to spew forth some noisome fluid," "something terrible . . . beating with a life of its own beneath the notched coldness of his zipper." Copulation with Flagg is made as terrifying and forbidding as a descent into the ultimate ice-lake, the Cocytus, which forms the ninth and last circle of Dante's hell. One is reminded of what, earlier, Abigail Trotts said to Nadine Cross: "When you get there, you'll find out that hell is cold" (310):

And when the dead coldness of him slipped into her the shriek ripped up and out of her, bolted free, and she struggled, and the struggle was useless.

He battered into her, invader, destroyer, and the cold blood gushed down
her thighs . . . . and the moon was in her eyes, cold and silver fire, and
when he came it was like molten iron, molten *pig* iron, molten *brass*, and
she came herself, came in screaming, incredible pleasure, came in terror, in
horror, passing through the pig iron and brass gates into the desert land of
insanity. . . . (675–76)

It is not unusual for King to expand upon earlier myths, poems,
legends, and fairy tales. Here he zeroes into a missing aspect of
Yeats's "The Second Coming." He seems also to have in mind the
sexual encounter of the swan (actually Zeus) and the mother of Helen
in what Yeats considered an important companion piece, "Leda and
the Swan," especially the lines: "a shudder in the loins engenders
there / A broken wall, and Agamemnon dead." Unlike the Leda
poem, however, "The Second Coming" does not actualize the genital
contact between the parents of the Antichrist, observing only that
the "beast" "slouches to Bethlehem to be born." What Yeats lacks,
King here supplies: the sexual action. The Yeats poem (the name
mispronounced "Yeets") is actually dwelt upon at some length by
scientist Billy Starkey in one of the earlier sections of *The Stand*,
when he quotes a few significant lines, but especially emphasizes that
the "rough beast [i.e., "Captain Trips"] is on his way" (118).

Though much of *The Stand* is disjointed and needlessly
rambling—perhaps, carrying out the twentieth-century Yeats theme
of "The Second Coming" that "things fall apart" because "center
cannot hold"—there are genuine moments of imaginative power,
such as this bestial conjoining of those two abominations, Flagg and
Cross, whose names with their perverted patriotic and religious connotations have by no means been randomly selected. Caught in the
apocalypse of A6, the despairing scientist, Billy Starkey, is attempting to "dig" his man, that is, attempting to understand the prophetical Irish poet William Butler Yeats.

Ultimately, however, the true "baby" who can "dig" (i.e., "bury")
his man ("Captain Trips") is none other than Fran's illegitimate child,
baby Peter, the son of Jess, whose name has both religious and
Freudian connotations. Peter is the world's only hope. However, having made his "stand" as a baby against Captain Trips, Peter should,
when he grows up, try to make yet another "stand" by reminding his
own children that the *"toys are death," "flashburns," "radiation sickness
and black choking plague."* In his own strange way—and perhaps quite

unconsciously—Stephen King is developing his "baby" from an historical incident: a cryptic telegram, addressed to Secretary of War Henry Stimson at the Potsdam conference in July 1945, referring to the atomic bomb about to be dropped on Hiroshima as a husky "Little Boy" that has just been delivered.[7]

Developing an anti-Christian image from William Blake's famous poem "The Tiger," a grown-up Peter will eventually be able to warn future generations that some Lovecraftian *"devil in men's hands guided the hands of God when they were made"*—what Winston Churchill called, upon learning of the atomic bomb for the first time at Potsdam, the "Second Coming in wrath."[8] Peter's final admonition is that *"this empty world"* should be the future world's *"copybook"* (817), the copybook being, no doubt, King's eight-hundred-page *Stand*. Though this lengthy novel has brilliant subsections—little vignettes like the tender biography of deaf-and-dumb Nick Andros in chapter 13—the novel as a whole tends to be tedious. In attempting an American epic to rival Tolstoy's *War and Peace*, Dostoevski's *Brothers Karamazov*, Melville's *Moby-Dick*, and Mitchell's *Gone with the Wind*, King ended up producing in *The Stand* a pseudophilosophic speculation on Antichrist and the Apocalypse. Small wonder to find the author acknowledging that, during the composition of *The Stand*, he "actively hated the book" and considered it his "own little Viet-Nam" (*DM*, 399).

Like a miniature atom bomb, the eight-page short story "Night Surf" (analyzed in chapter 7 of this book) packs a far more powerful wallop than *The Stand* without bothering the reader with—desirable as they might be in the real world—tedious ramblings about democracy and the reestablishment of the Constitution. One of the ironies of the current taste in popular fiction is that whereas *The Stand* is extremely interesting to young readers (consistently described as their favorite among Stephen King's novels), the more brilliantly crafted "Night Surf" (based on precisely the same theme) does not seem to attract similar youthful enthusiasm.[9] Unlike the expansive *Stand*, an extravagant apocalyptic fantasy, "Night Surf" perhaps moves—in a context of rock music and the drug cult—too quickly and too close to the uncomfortable truth of universal selfishness and indifference to the sufferings of others.

Chapter Five
Two Terror Tales of a Town
Somewhere in a Gray Area

A romantically named town and a strangler-rapist bind together two diverse yet unusual narratives: the political *Dead Zone* (1979) and the psychological *Cujo* (1981), King's fifth and seventh novels. The town is the fictitious Castle Rock, Maine, and the strangler-rapist, a policeman, known throughout the town as a "fine officer and a fine man." Castle Rock had already appeared in "The Body," an insightful novella of parental abuses, youthful bashings, sexual self-questionings, and endlessly interlocked secrets. The town also appears in numerous short stories. Like 'salem's Lot, Anson Beach (in "Night Surf"), Tarker's Mills (in *Cycle of the Werewolf*), and many other Maine-localities that appear in King's stories, no such town exists at present. The pleasantly named town is intended as a pseudocover—a "mask" as it were—for the tragedies and horrors that reside therein. In the first part of *Dead Zone*, subtitled "Wheel of Fortune," the horror is a strangler-rapist who comes to be known as the "Castle Rock Strangler" (90); in the latter part, subtitled "Laughing Tiger," the tragedy is the Bible-thumping and nuclear-oriented prospective president, Gregory Ammas Stillson. As with the religious implications of Jerusalem's Lot in both novel and short story, the romantic-sounding name Castle Rock (which was the name of a popular Frank Sinatra song of the early 1950s) is yet another example of King's sensitivity to the superficiality of twentieth-century and/or American values and behavior. This point of view sometimes emerges in oddly clashing symbols, as when, for example, *Dead Zone* alludes to the nineteenth-century Polish cavalry fighting against the tanks and machine guns of the Nazi panzers and the *Wehrmacht* in World War II (113), or when a young wife rather carelessly loses her wedding ring in a toilet (177), or when some chipped angels, broken stars of Bethlehem, an "entire battalion of glass balls," and other "fragile Christmas tree ornaments" are counterposed with the madness and death of a mother (216–17).

Tragedies turned to traumas are common enough in King's stories: For example, Miranda's motorcycle-accident that causes Ben Mears anguished memories (*'Salem's Lot*), the murder of a brother that causes Jim Norman relentless nightmares ("Sometimes They Come Back"), the religious fanaticism of Mrs. White that causes her daughter Carrie much embarrassment and grief. In *Dead Zone*, the tragedy turned trauma is a near-fatal accident of a twenty-three-year-old man with the undistinguished name of Johnny Smith, a name that makes him a kind of American Everyman. As a consequence of a disastrous crash of two drag-racing cars, Johnny lies helplessly in a coma for four-and-a-half years (October 1970 to May 1975), awakening in an Eastern Maine Medical Center only to discover, now twenty-seven, that he has lost a good portion of his youthful twenties. Unexpectedly, and with a suddenness that matches the car accident itself, he has acquired, or perhaps merely intensified within himself, occult powers of precognition and telepathy. [1] The awakening is so thoroughly associated with his newly developed psychic powers that Johnny experiences a "sudden onrush of bad feelings, childlike in their intensity"; and "crude images of revulsion . . . assaulted him" (100). This telepathic clairvoyance gives Johnny the ability to foresee, among other things, Greg Stillson's presidential ambitions and ultimate inclination toward nuclear confrontation, and gives *Dead Zone* unexpected psychic, social, and political turns and twists.

While Johnny is comatose, an unidentified rapist kills several young women of Castle Rock, the rape-killings so arranged by King that, for the most part, they tend to occur while Johnny is comatose. Indeed, the rape-stranglings seem almost to emerge from the very blankness of the coma, as if sexual brutalities were merely the dark and evil side of an otherwise sunny and attractive personality, as if the rapist-strangler (who is eventually identified as the policeman Frank Dodd) was somehow Johnny's evil "other"—this Frankie and Johnny pair thus possessing something like Poe's "bi-part soul." In incessant dreams, Johnny's girl friend, Sarah Bracknell (later Sarah Hazlett), is aware of certain good-and-evil dimensions in her boy friend's personality: "Johnny in [his] Jekyll-and-Hyde mask . . . at the Wheel of Fortune concession" (62). Throughout the novel one is periodically reminded of Johnny's uncontrollable personality divisions. Rather playfully at first—as when Sarah reacts with a "strangled little shriek" on encountering a half-comical Halloween mask in the spooky corridor of Johnny's apartment house—

and then [his] face appeared before her, floating in the darkness, a horrible
face out of a nightmare. It glowed a spectral, rotting green. One eye was
wide open, seeming to stare at her in wounded fear. The other was squeezed
shut in a sinister leer. The left half of the face, the half with the open eye,
appeared to be normal. But the right half was the face of a monster, drawn
and inhuman, the thick lips drawn back to reveal snaggle teeth that were
also glowing. (14)

The little Halloween joke causes only momentary anger because
Sarah realizes that "you just couldn't stay mad at Johnny." Even after
being half-scared out of her wits, she "wondered if anyone had ever
succeeded in harboring a grudge against Johnny Smith, and the
thought was so ridiculous that she had to smile" (15). Yet from time
to time, when Sarah remembered Johnny, she visualized his face both
"half-light" and "half-dark" (134), with a smile always "charming,"
but somehow also "crooked" (138).

In chapters 4 and 5, an intriguing parallel develops between an
obviously guilty Frank and an apparently innocent Johnny. King
highlights the Jekyll-Hyde dimensions by juxtaposing two intriguing passages. In an attempt to understand Johnny's comatose condition, Sarah does a lot of library reading and comes across the tragic
story of a young English dockworker accidentally struck by a grap-
pling hook while working. His unconscious condition is similar to
Johnny's:

Little by little this brawny young dock-walloper had severed his connection
with the world, wasting away, losing his hair, optic nerves degenerating into
oatmeal behind his closed eyes, body gradually drawing up into a fetal
position as his ligaments shortened. He had reversed time, had become a
fetus again, swimming in the placental waters of coma as his brain degener-
ated. An autopsy following his death had shown that the folds and convolutions of his cerebrum had smoothed out, leaving the frontal and prefrontal
lobes almost utterly smooth and blank. (70)

While this passage concerns only the fate of the unfortunate English
dockworker, it anticipates with obvious and deadly precision, the
possible future deterioration of Johnny himself, who, if he had not
awakened within a reasonable time, might well have pulled into the
"prefetal position"—as the attending physician eventually points out
(112).

But intriguingly, a passage in the immediately preceding chapter
4 acts as a prelude to the description of the comatose Englishman

(who is a kind of symbolic Johnny Smith). It reports yet another kind of retrogression. Here the backward thrust is toward a psychological wound that never can be healed over. It results from the boyhood memories of this strangler-killer, whose mind suddenly harks back to the time when he was seven, and his mother, entering his room without knocking (as she always did), "caught him playing with his thing." By flinging back to this painful memory, at the moment when he is about to commit another of his rape-stranglings, Frank Dodd is, in a real sense, reversing time. Frank remembers how his mother, after her discovery, "began to shake him back and forth then, and he began to blubber with fear, even then she was a big woman, . . . and he was not the killer then, he was not slick then, he was a little boy blubbering with fear, and his thing had collapsed and was trying to shrivel back into his body. She had made him wear a clothespin on it for two hours, so he would know how those diseases felt. The pain was excruciating" (65).

While awaiting a young female victim (Alma Frechette) to walk into his trap, a trap that cruelly parodies the unwanted entrance of a mother into a seven-year-old life, the strangler-rapist's mind is momentarily obsessed with a childhood embarrassment (64–68). The potential here for imaginative interplay between interchanging Johnny and Frank is intriguing. While Frank's memory pulls him back to an excruciatingly painful incident—painful both physically and psychologically at the time when it occurred—Johnny's memory is perhaps disappearing altogether. Possibly, if the coma had lasted long enough, Johnny's whole psyche might have shrunk back to the very womb itself, like the "thing" in young Frank's maturing seven-year-old body that had "collapsed" and was trying to "shrivel back."

The parallel arrangement of these two painful passages is fraught with psychic, psychological, and physiological possibilities for dark fantasy and unspeakable horror. Both situations are indeed retrogressions. The psychological one is a backward stab of memory that destroys all moral restraints and rehurls the rape-murderer back into a present instance of antifemale violence. As *'Salem's Lot* has it, "childhood horror and adult horror had merged" (340). The physiological retrogression—only potential, since it never literally occurs in Johnny Smith—is a gradual and almost totally successful retrogression to a "prefetal stage," in other words, to a stage beyond the personal sexuality of Johnny Smith, almost to the very parental intimacy that had engendered him in his mother's body. It is no exaggeration to say that Johnny could become the "oatmeal swimming in the placental waters [his mother's womb] of coma." Because he survives the coma in Rip Van Winkle fashion, Johnny never turns into mere mental "oatmeal" (as seems to have happened to the English dockworker), but he does awaken childlike, for he seems to have "very little control over the functions adults are supposed to be able to control." "He could not walk," and on the way back from neurological tests, "he urinated on himself and had to be changed like a baby" (117).

Other interesting analogies abound. Frank's mother is a sexual neurotic who wants her detested son to experience genital pain that pathologically scars him for life. Johnny's mother, on the other hand, is a religious neurotic who believes that "heaven is somewhere out in the constellation of Orion" (63) and, expecting what is called the "rapture" by born-again fundamentalists,[2] is certain that God is going to send out a "fleet of flying saucers to pick up the faithful and buzz them off to Orion" (63–64). In her own way, Johnny's mother also marks her son with her religious frenzies. Vera Smith (whose first name means "truth") says more than once that "God has put his mark on my Johnny and I rejoice" (61). The Frankie and Johnny pair, as one begins to imagine, are "twins" emerging from a single neurotic womb; and each might readily interchange into the darker or lighter half of the other.

When Johnny comes out of his coma, his "eyes were the eyes of a man who has seen something terrible moving and shifting in the shadows, something too terrible to be described or even named" (100). Sometimes, even after Johnny's recovery, his eyes would turn "cruel and somehow inhuman." In spite of himself, Johnny becomes a "human blank," and "lurking behind the planes of his ordinary features, almost near enough to touch, was . . . the face of a killer" (238). Readers may recall Sarah Bracknell's "strangled little shriek" when she first saw the "horrible [mask] out of a nightmare," whose "right half was the face of a monster, drawn and inhuman" (14)—the word "strangled" describing her reaction (in view of what happened to Frank Dodd's female victims) now acquiring new implications.

The conclusion to "Wheel of Fortune" is melodramatic in the extreme and perhaps deliberately graceless: a naked Frank Dodd sitting on a toilet seat in the bathroom, with razor-slashed throat and black vinyl raincoat over his shoulders, and the words "I Confess" lipsticked on a sign tied to a string around his neck. King sardonically refers to this as "Frank Dodd riding a toilet seat into eternity, blood in his all-American blond hair" (258). The image reappears as a "ceramic parody of Rodin's *Thinker* perched on a toilet seat" in "Cain Rose Up," also concerned with a psychopathic killer (*SK*, 200). By contrast with *Dead Zone*'s overflamboyant ending of a rapist-strangler, the parallel figures of two mothers, Frank's and Johnny's, both "knowing" something about their sons, is perhaps more delicately drawn. Frank's mother (Henrietta Dodd) "knew" for years what crimes her son was committing (251), and Johnny's mother (Vera Smith), though dead at the end of "Wheel of Fortune," has her posthumous victory, for she always "knew" what talent God had given her son. The final lines of this first half of *Dead Zone* apply directly to Johnny and his mother: "he had fulfilled his mother's prophecy. If God had a mission for him, then he had done it. No matter now that it had been a kamikaze mission. He had done it. He was quits" (259).

But it requires no ghost come back from the grave to explain how this simple conclusion concerning Johnny Smith and his mother covertly and quite appropriately applies to Frank Dodd and *his* mother. After all, this Frankie and Johnny pair, according to the psychic symbology of the novel, are virtually bipartite malevolences. Frank indeed fulfilled his mother's prophecy in the sense that he carried out her pathological hatred of prostitutes and venereal diseases by killing young women. One recalls how Frank's psychopathic mother (like a similar purist-fanatic in the earlier *Carrie*) had cruelly scolded him as a little boy, frightening and brutally punishing him about his own elemental biology: "Do you want to have pus running out of it? Do you want it to turn black? Do you want it to rot off?" (65). Like the "hypnotic trace memory" or the "echo effect that could become a richochet" in the subsequent *Firestarter*, the parallel undercurrent (the "unconscious in high gear") that runs through these final lines of the first section of *Dead Zone* seems to be saying that, through the perverted will of Frank's mother, God had a mission for Frank even though it had been a "kamikaze mission" (i.e., rape-strangling of young girls). Whether *Dead Zone* as a whole is ultimately an effective novel is debatable and clearly a matter of personal gothic tastes; but King's skill in dealing with "character and nuance," as always, is superb, and the reader, as *Firestarter* recommends, must be as sensitive to character and nuance as a "blind man reading braille" (131).

Jumping into a Time Machine

The "Wheel of Fortune," the first subsection of *Dead Zone* (13–259), could stand alone as a self-contained novella and, with the exception of a few underdeveloped references to Greg Stillson, is virtually complete in itself. "The Laughing Tiger," the shorter second half of the novel, is sociopolitical and narratively less effective than the first. Conversations are often wooden, minor characters not especially interesting, and much of the plot labored or unnecessarily drawn out. The message of "Laughing Tiger," nevertheless, is an important ethical one—the moral obligation to destroy a potential atom-bomb-oriented president (Greg Stillson) before he gets a chance to irradiate the world.

Veiled with a certain vagueness, the symbolism is often more poetic and provocative than the plot. King's well-known train image always triggers deep feelings of loss and despair and is here used sparingly, but when trains do appear (albeit only metaphorically), they are things of stark and startling power. When Johnny looks at Frank's mother—in a sense, his own—for the first time at the end of "Wheel of Fortune," their staring is an "awful, perfect understanding," and "for that moment they seemed welded together" (251). But when Johnny looks into the eyes of the potentially dangerous Greg Stillson, their mutual looking—one might suspect a mutual attraction in "a perfect cameo of time as they stared into each other's eyes"—caused everything to come upon Johnny at once: "crammed together and screaming, like some terrible black freight train highballing through a narrow tunnel, a speeding engine with single glaring headlamp mounted up front. . . . There was nowhere to run, and perfect knowledge ran him down, plastered him as flat as a sheet of paper while that night-running train raced over him" (303–4).

As comes to be expected with King's train-obsession, rich images of terror and confusion follow such imaginative train-passages, what King here regards as the "soft roar of oblivion." Emphasis is upon something Johnny's mind perceives as a "blue filter," reappearing with deadly monotony for several pages ("blue filter began to creep in," "blue filter is deepening," "filter the blue filter," "flying through the blue"). In a kind of hallucination that results from the eye contact, two unidentified "motorcycle guys" (symbolizing, perhaps, the odd Frankie and Johnny fusions of *Dead Zone*) with sawed-off pool cues (like weapons, or more probably, disembodied phalluses) rush at

Johnny himself, who in this strained hallucination is riding a bicycle: "They were going to make believe Johnny Smith's head was the eight ball and they were going to blast it right into the side pocket, right back into the blackness of coma and he would never come out of it this time; he would never be able to tell anyone what he had seen or change anything. . . . He tried to backpedal . . . . Then the soft, swelling road of oblivion overwhelmed him and . . . he blacked out" (305).

King's peculiar obsession for blue—in *Dead Zone* growing directly out of sudden eye contact between Greg and Johnny in which they were "sharing everything"—can be found in just about every major narrative: the Bluebeard story reviewed prior to the opening of the fatal door in *The Shining*; or the lost blueberry bucket of the train-struck boy in "The Body"; or the blue chalk marks on the hands of Barlow in *'Salem's Lot* (363). Blue is a color King cannot seem to be long without at climactic terror points in his narratives.[3] In *Dead Zone*, the "blue filter" is used as a corridor, the "dull crome corridor" to the "dead zone." The "speeding engine," the "blackness," and the "oblivion" of the above-quoted passages are exactly what the blue filter is headed for: the "dead zone" of annihilation. In this novel, blue is consistently combined with yellow (though strangely never producing green), and further combined with the Oriental image of the "laughing tiger" to produce what is one of King's most unusual symbolic passages: "there was always that puzzling blue filter between, the blue filter that was sometimes cut by those yellow like tiger stripes . . . and a single tiger padding through miles of twisted metal, fused glass, and scorched earth. This tiger was always laughing, and seemed to be carrying something in its mouth—something blue and yellow and dripping blood" (317).

Two important realities—one projected into the future, one an actual medical fact—lie behind the shadowy symbology of trains, blue filters, and laughing tigers: (1) the political potential of having Greg Stillson become president of the United States and initiate an atomic war that will destroy the world, and (2) the medical fact that Johnny Smith has an "extremely well-developed brain tumor in the parietal lobe" (394). These two "realities" raise two corresponding questions of ethics, imponderables that have taunted and tormented humanity from the beginning of time.

The first moral difficulty involves the occult powers that develop as a consequence of the drag-racing accident. Johnny knows in advance, by mere touch, that Greg Stillson will eventually be elected president, only to become, either by accident or design, an atomic danger to both the nation and the world at large. Since this knowledge comes only by precognition and telepathy, is it his proper moral duty to save the nation and the world from universal destruction by destroying Stillson in advance of his becoming president? This is *Dead Zone's* new version of the age-old Hamlet question of whether or not, based on secret information from questionable psychic sources, it is morally defensible to eliminate dangerous persons like King Claudius (in *Hamlet*), Hitler, Jim Jones, the "Son of Sam," or Idi Amin. Of course, the dilemma can never be permanently resolved. A democratically oriented reader of the twentieth century might sympathize with noble Brutus's assassination of a dangerous Julius Caesar in order to save the Roman republic. Yet in the fourteenth century, an empire-oriented poet like Dante Alighieri can imagine the same so-called noble Brutus in the lower regions of his *Inferno* for treachery against his lord (canto 34). The situation can also easily be reversed, when a disgruntled and unstable John Wilkes Booth can see in "noble" Abraham Lincoln someone he personally thinks is a tyrant. King's twentieth-century horror tale complicates this eternal dilemma by raising doubts about the precise source of Johnny's precognitive abilities (just as Shakespeare himself toys and tinkers with the madness of Hamlet) and the biological, psychological, or psychic compulsions forcing the assassination of Greg Stillson.

Johnny's "almost flawlessly handsome" physiology (17) thus becomes a mask for the terrible things emerging from what gives the novel its title, Johnny's "dead zone"—known in medical language as spot amnesia (110), but in King's imaginative language is the seminal "oatmeal behind the eyes." This mental blank, out of which the earlier Frank Dodd almost seems to have emerged, is given a rational explanation by Johnny's attending physician (Dr. Samuel Weizak) to a gathering of reporters: "A part of John Smith's brain has been damaged beyond repair—a very small part, but all parts of the brain may be vital. He calls this his 'dead zone,' and there, apparently, a number of trace memories were stored. All of these wiped-out memories seem to be part of a 'set'—that of street, road, and highway designations. . . . This is a small but total aphasia which seems to include both language and visualization skills" (154). Johnny's newly found telepathic abilities are explained by the same physician in the following language: "another tiny part of John Smith's brain appears to have *awakened*. A section of the cerebrum within the parietal lobe. This is one of the deeply grooved sections of the "forward" or "thinking" brain. The electrical responses from this section of Smith's brain are way out of line from what they should be . . ." (154–55).

Throughout the first and longer part of the novel, "Wheel of Fortune" has been attributing Johnny's psychic abilities to an "enlightened zone," balancing off the "dead zone" that developed as a consequence of his four-and-a-half-year coma. But suddenly in the second half of the novel, there intrudes the symbolism of an oriental "laughing tiger" and the mysterious "blue filter"—the laughing tiger turning out to be the ominous Greg Stillson, and the blue filter, combined with the dead zone symbolism, comes to represent Johnny's fatal brain cancer (396). The end result of this curious mixture of symbology, psychology, and malign physiology is that Greg Stillson, through an almost successful assassination by Johnny, is destroyed because his cowardly use of a child as a shield is photographed (382–83). The accidental presence of a camera (capturing cowardice, and hence destroying a false macho-image before the voting public) turns out to be just as thorough as a bullet. Stillson has been "totaled."

In the strange world of imaginary Castle Rock, the assassination attempt is an impressionistic mixture of the actual and the symbolic. Blood-violence (as in "pistol-slug grooved his neck," "blood poured down and across his shoulder," "another bullet whizzed by his temple") is balanced off with smears of innocent, childlike images (as in "color washing out to the light robin's egg color of the vision," "warm fire flashed somewhere below and was gone," "sweet hum of the voices faded," "blurring into a high sweet humming sound" [382–85]). Most interesting of all is the ultimate ironic parallel between Stillson and Smith, important for a proper understanding of the novel. For when criminal Stillson shields himself with a child, he unwittingly parallels the earlier coma condition in which Johnny virtually disappeared into childhood. What Stillson does is a conscious crime; what had earlier happened to unconscious Johnny was, at least in part, a fateful return to innocence itself.

As noted in connection with passages in other novels, King is often quite powerful in blending the Dionysian (or passionate) forces with Apollonian (or restrained) impulses. It is this blend—or perhaps more accurately, blur—that gives the imprecise answer to the Hamlet-dilemma raised by "Laughing Tiger." The very language de-

scribing the aborted assassination, faces up to the realities of bloody
death, and at the same time, like the adolescent Ben Mears in the
Marsten House of 'Salem's Lot, runs away in uncertain fear and trembling. As common man Johnny Smith phrases it amid love-references
in a letter to his father: "I guess I was running away from Greg
Stillson and the thing I was supposed to do—like Elijah hiding in
his cave or Jonah, who ended up in the fish's belly" (390)—and later
on, "I won't play Hamlet any longer" (397). *Art of Darkness* suggests
that *Dead Zone* explores the nature of choice. But might it not be
more accurate to say that a plot deriving from a "dead zone" created
by a brain tumor—the tumor recalling a similar problem in Charles
Whitman, the "Texas Tower Murderer" in 1966 (the ostensible subject of "Cain Rose Up" [*SK*]) entraps its characters in a deterministic
universe of accidents, compulsions, and misfired intentions governing
inexplicable intuitions? Might it not be more consistent with King's
general philosophy to suppose that much, if not all, of this novel
explores the nature of nonchoice?

Idiot Mouth in the Dark of Night

Though plot and characters differ, *Cujo* picks up where *Dead Zone*
leaves off.[4] The Castle Rock cop turned killer-rapist, Frank Dodd, is
the conjoining factor. In the first line, Dodd is the "monster" who
came to the "small town of Castle Rock, Maine," and is identified as
having rape-murdered the same six women cataloged in *Dead Zone*.[5]
Though the novel is initially given a fairy-tale air through the use of
the phrase ONCE UPON A TIME, capitalized on an otherwise ominous
blank page, the "monster" Frank Dodd was not "werewolf, vampire,
ghoul, unnameable creature from the enchanted forest or the snowy
wastes." Rather, he was only a "cop with mental and sexual problems" whose name is now evoked by thoughtless Castle Rock parents
(parents who, in an enlightened twentieth century, should surely
know better) as a kind of boogeyman who would "get" children if
they "weren't good" and "didn't watch out": "*it may be his face you see
looking in your bedroom window after everyone in the house is asleep except
you; it may be his smiling face you see peeking at you from the closet in the
middle of the night, the* STOP *sign he held up when he crossed the little
children in one hand, the razor he used to kill himself in the other . . . so
shhh, children . . . shhh . . . shhhh.*"

Little five-year-old "Tad" (whose name half-echoes "Dodd") is introduced immediately upon the heels of the pro-and-con fairy tale introduction. Young Tad's problem is that he knows something unpleasant and unattractive resides at night in his dark and narrow bedroom closet, rather like Danny Torrance's Tony, except that Tad's terrifying Tony never really materializes. Initially, this unnameable thing seems to manifest its presence only when Tad is alone. Despite the attempts of the supposedly rational parents (Vic and Donna Trenton) to discourage Tad's inexplicable fears, King himself goes out of his way to persuade the reader to believe that "something" (invisible, though sometimes almost palpable) does indeed move and moan within that musty enclosure. Thus, later in the novel, when no one is in the house and the phone rings, and a potential tragedy is developing elsewhere, the "closet door stood open, and an unspeakable dry smell, lionlike and savage, hung in the air" (221). And still later, when an uneasy and overwrought Vic Trenton is alone in the bedroom of his son, who has been missing for days, he hears sounds emanating from the ghastly closet, and—as though in a dream—several times sees the closet door open. Earlier, in order to allay Tad's supposedly irrational fears, Vic had taken to writing a little verse containing such playful phrases as "Monsters, stay out of this room" and "You have no business here." But in a fine memory-haunted passage, King describes how these incantations soon come back to nag and annoy Vic, the boy's reasonable father, in a totally unexpected manner:

> Heart thumping heavily in his throat, Vic got up and went to the closet. He could smell something in there, something heavy and unpleasant. Perhaps it was only mothballs—that smell was certainly a part of it—but it smelled . . . savage.
>
> *Don't be ridiculous. It's just a closet. Not a cave. Not a monster's lair.*
>
> He looked at Tad's bear. Tad's bear looked back at him, unblinking. Behind the bear, behind the hanging clothes, all was darkness. Anything could be back in there. *Anything.* But, of course, nothing was.
>
> *You gave me a scare, bear,* he said. (282)

Like the sinister hallway hose of the Overlook Hotel that sometimes frightens little Danny in *The Shining*, nothing specific seems to materialize in, or out of, this bedroom closet: no werewolf, vampire, ghoul or unnameable creature. Having more implications that are at first apparent, the closet seems little more than a perpetually haunted enclosure harboring a shadowy and sometimes malodorous presence. But mysterious occupants of this symbolic closet do materialize in other ways. One of the most blatant is the exposure of the secret liaison between Tad's mother and a certain oversexed Steve Kemp. Of this affair, of course, Tad's father is totally ignorant until, by means of a cruel and crude note, Kemp chooses to reveal it in order to get revenge on Tad's mother for having rejected him as a lover. One can well understand, therefore, Tad's constant sensing that there is something obnoxious in the family closet. The pseudo-anonymous letter is a kind of "monster" that emerges from a clandestine affair that has been conducted in a kind of "closet."

But even more of a monster is Steve Kemp himself, one of the most bitter, vulgar, and revolting characters that King ever invented. In what could only be described as a mood of "half-mad jealous pique" for having been rejected as Donna's secret lover, Kemp smashes the furniture of the Trenton residence while the family is away and at the point of suffering a grievous wound over the death of young Tad. Kemp leaves as his "calling card," referred to as a "vengeful little *billet-doux*" (235), a wad of seed on the family bed (200). While he is not a rapist-killer like Frank Dodd, he is the kind of sex-obsessed drug-addict that Donna regrets she ever knew and certainly wishes she had never been intimate with. When one of the Castle Rock's officers goes into the Trenton house, he half expects to find the body of Donna mutilated and mangled in the same manner as Frank Dodd's six female victims. But as vulgar and revolting as Kemp turns out to be, he seems to reflect only portions of Frank Dodd's psychosexuality. An ill-tempered tennis player and mediocre town poet, Kemp convinces himself that his sex-trashing of the Trenton house is a "piece of revolutionary anarchy—offing a couple of fat middle-class pigs, the sort who made it easy for the fascist overlords to remain in power by blindly paying their taxes and telephone bills." Concerning Kemp's rationalization of his behavior in the Trenton house, the novel asks readers to reflect upon an obvious question: "Did that, maybe, say something unpleasant about where his head was at?" (202).

Of the novel's three main manifestations of the diabolical spirit of Frank Dodd—(1) the mysterious noncreature in Tad's closet, (2) the enraged lover of Tad's mother, and (3) the rabid Cujo—the first, albeit shadowy, is the most insistent; the second, the most ill-mannered and ill-tempered; and the third, the most immediately destructive. The St. Bernard dog belonging to the family of Joe, Charity, and Brett Camber has been mysteriously named for the pseudonym ("Cujo") of a member of the Symbionese Liberation Army (William Wolfe) that kidnapped heiress Patty Hearst in 1972 (131–32). Initially presented as lovable and friendly, the St. Bernard is bitten by some "brown insectivorous bats" that were "crawling with a particularly virulent strain of rabies" (19). The result is that, when the disease takes its full effect, Cujo attacks and kills Gary Pervier (whose name, incidentally, is sometimes mispronounced "pervert" [113]), and his owner, the garage attendant, lascivious Joe Camber.

Occupying most of the latter half of the novel, Cujo's most serious and vicious attack occurs when Donna Trenton and her son Tad are entrapped in their defective car for several days. Lying dead in a nearby house, neither Gary Pervier nor garageman and Cujo-owner Joe Camber can come to Donna's assistance. During these attacks, Cujo gives the impression that he is more than mere dog—almost for a brief moment, a rabid metamorphosis of Donna's insistent, sex-besot, and socially radical lover, Steve Kemp: "And a moment later Cujo's foam-covered, twisted face popped up outside her [car] window, only inches away, like a horror-movie monster that has decided to give the audience the ultimate thrill by coming right out of the screen. She could see his huge heavy teeth. And again there was that swooning, terrible feeling that the dog was looking at *her*, not at a woman who happened to be trapped in her car with her little boy, but at *Donna Trenton*, as if he has just been hanging around, waiting for her to show up" (149–50). Here the Kemp analogy is more implied than directly stated. In another passage, however, an association of Cujo with Frank Dodd is more explicit. When the county sheriff of Castle County, George Bannerman, attempts to neutralize the rabid Cujo, the following thoughts run through Bannerman's mind just prior to his sanguinary demise: "The dog bored in again. Bannerman tried to dodge away but the dog anticipated him, it was *grinning* at him, and suddenly there was more pain than he had ever felt in his life. . . . Screaming, he got both hands under the dog's muzzle again and yanked it up. For a moment staring into those dark, crazed eyes, a swoony kind of horror came over him and he thought: *Hello Frank. It's you, isn't it? Was hell too hot for you?*" (272). In *Dead Zone*, Sheriff Bannerman was the chief instrument in the pursuit and final "capture" of rapist-killer Frank Dodd. By here having the Dodd-like Cujo kill Bannerman (274), even though the

Dodd associations are, for the moment, entirely in the mind of the victim, King telescopes two novels of horror. To use the image King himself employs, "it was like two half pictures coming together to make a three dimentional whole" (286). Considering what follows, however, it is more like several partial pictures (Kemp, Dodd, Cujo, etc.) coming together to make a massive multifaceted horror.

Toward the end of *Cujo*, King introduces an attorney general called Andy Masen (whose last name deliberately resembles Erle Stanley Gardner's famous detective Perry Mason), an attorney general whose God is "logic" (265). Despite the fact that this attorney general's elaborate ratiocinations do little to solve the mystery of the disappearance of Donna and Tad Trenton, Masen has a philosophy that can be used, by extension, to explain the relationship between the two Castle Rock novels: "he saw each event as a point from which a finite number of possibilities radiated" (266). If one were to consider the rape-murders of Frank Dodd as the main events or points of *Dead Zone* and *Cujo*, then a "number of possibilities" or "implications" do indeed "radiate." The quasi-visible /quasi-palpable monster that haunts Tad's closet, the irrational behavior of Steve Kemp, and the unluckily rabid and savage man-killing St. Bernard dog, Cujo—all three, in varying degrees, could be considered deliberate manifestations of Frank Dodd's psychopathic spirit. Considering, too, that the Frank Dodd of *Dead Zone* is the sinister half-mask of Johnny Smith—and further, that this handsome and presumably benign Johnny Smith is, symbolically, "everyman" or the Common Man—one can begin to understand the involuted labyrinth of Jekyll-Hyde interconnections that King is designing. That even the name of the obnoxious Steven *Kemp* sounds suspiciously like Stephen *King* adds to psychological and philosophical complexities that, by contrast with Andy Masen's finite number of possibilities, are (both in *Dead Zone* and *Cujo*) more accurately considered "infinite" in their implications. Each page of these two novels is an endlessly revolving door of gothic inventions and involutions with the grinning face of King himself endlessly reappearing.

Infinity multiplies into infinity—or "steam spills into steam" as Hart Crane phrases it in his poem "Harbour Dawn"—when one considers that the novel *Cujo* also stands in important relationship with the "Cujo" of the once notorious Symbionese Liberation Army that kidnapped Patty Hearst. The name of that lovable and amiable St. Bernard echoes that of a "radical robber of banks and kidnapper of rich young heiresses" (132)—creating yet another Jekyll-Hyde paradox and turning the novel into a kind of allegory of social evils; and, strange as it may sound, despite some brutally explicit sex-passages, perhaps even a kind of morality novel.

Conspicuous among the SLA allusions of the novel is Tad's closet of mysterious smells and groans and equally inexplicable openings and closings. When Patty Hearst was captured in 1974, she was hidden in a closet for the first month and transferred to another and slightly larger closet in another building. At the trial, she reported that she was raped by two different men ("Cujo" and "Cinque") in the first closet and, after being tied in a garbage can, was roughly loaded into the trunk of a car and deposited in yet another closet for a few weeks. The court account of the Patty's closet rapings has been reported as follows:

"Did there come a time when one of the women came to you [Patty Hearst] and talked to you about getting it on with someone?" . . . Yes, Angela Atwood. Where? In the closet. "She said that in the cell everybody had to take care of the needs of other people. She said I was gonna sleep with Willie Wolfe [*Cujo*]." The corners of Patty's thin mouth turn down, and she begins breathing heavily. "So I did." Wolfe [*Cujo*] came into the closet that same night. . . .

And one week later, did someone else come to the closet for the same purpose? Yes. Who was it? It was *Cinque* [Donald DeFreeze]. Did he do the same thing? Yes.[6]

King's interest in Patty Hearst is well documented. Prior to the composition of *The Stand*, King had worked on a roman à clef based on Patty's experiences with the SLA. It was to be expected, therefore, that names, symbols, and incidents would inevitably intermix in his mind and crop up, from time to time, in a variety of forms. Donald DeFreeze, the so-called "Cinque," is one of the manifestations of the Antichrist figure in *The Stand* (122); and his last name, *DeFreeze*, is unconsciously echoed by a Cujo-terrified Donna when she assumes—in a typical Stephen King pun—that her husband will perhaps "assume we went out to catch . . . a couple of ice creams at the *Tastee Freeze*" (205).

As in classical musical compositions, King is working out formulaic parallels that are variations on a universal theme. Frank Dodd's raping killings of young girls, the Cinque/Cujo violations of Patty Hearst, Kemp's sex-trashing of Donna Trenton's body and house, and the St. Bernard's blood-rape of Gary Pervier, Joe Camber, George Bannerman (and indirectly of little Tad Trenton)—these, and others, are interacting parallels in which we are all involved.

Though a crafty student of psychology, King is sometimes reluctant to assign ultimate causes. The behavior of the SLA cannot be considered as the cause of anything that occurs in *Cujo*. Rather, the SLA was a manifestation of a universal Lovecraftian malevolence that "shambles" in the universe in the manner of the dark forces in "Jerusalem's Lot" and is, in the dynamics of such a universe, more or less inescapable. Consequently, no matter how much Vic and Donna try to convince young son Tad that "there are no monsters here" or that "monsters are entirely in the imagination," the "old monster [Cujo] kept his watch still, and [Tad] was slipping, slipping, slipping away" (285). As a "rational woman," Donna did not believe that the rabid Cujo was "four-footed fate," the "Reverend Dimmesdale," "Moby Dog," the "Ghost of Sins Remembered," or the "reincarnation of Elvis Presley." Yet, in an "instant," she *knew* that the dog was something more than just a dog" (204–7). The "unhinged idiot mouth" (59) is King's metaphor for the closet door with its mysterious openings and shuttings that somehow never give birth into an actual "monster"—"idiot" because it has no ordered explanation, and "unhinged" because the closet-mouth can never be permanently locked or sealed shut. Even the medieval epic *Beowulf* (724a) uses the image of "mouth" to describe the door of haunted Danish hall, Heorot (the gentle "hart"), that is occupied by a man-eating monster, Grendel (the cruel "grinder"), for twelve years.

In the context of the psychological and multilayered horrors of *Cujo*, the elegant quotation that King selects from W. H. Auden's "Musée des Beaux Arts" as a poetic foreword concerning the classic sky-fall of Icarus, while no one is watching or shows concern, seems tepid indeed:

> About suffering, they were never wrong,
> The Old Masters: how well they understood
> Its human position; how it takes place
> While someone else is eating or opening a window
> or just walking along. . . .

A passage from the Roman poet Ovid concerning the annual destruction of Athenian youths by some Cujo-headed Minotaur in a psychological Cretan labyrinth might have been more appropriate to the main thrust of the novel. *Cujo* is not about classic "suffering" in the manner of a Renaissance painting; it is rather about the meaningless mangling of youthful innocence.

Chapter Six

Impossible Cars and Improbable Cats

Crudely Drawn Human Faces

H. P. Lovecraft characterized the typical protagonist of an Edgar Allan Poe story as being a "dark, handsome, proud, melancholy, intellectual, highly sensitive, capricious, introspective, isolated, and sometimes slightly mad gentleman of ancient family and opulent circumstances; usually deeply learned in strange lore, and darkly ambitious of penetrating to forbidden secrets of the universe."[1] While the strangely behaving protagonist of *Christine*, Arnie Cunningham, is not attractive (at least not initially), nor of ancient family or opulent circumstances, nevertheless much of Lovecraft's delineation is surprisingly appropriate. Arnie is indeed stubborn, melancholic, intelligent, sensitive, capricious, egocentric, and strangely behaving. As for his isolation, teenage Arnie was a natural "out"—"out with the jocks because he was scrawny"—"out with the high school intellectuals . . . because he had no specialty"—"out with the druggies because he didn't do dope"—"out with the macho pegged-jeans-and-Lucky-Strikes group because he didn't do booze." While he is not handsome in the Poe mold, his physical appearance, especially his ugly face—"his glandular machinery had gone totally bananas"—simply reinforces his isolation (1–2). He was therefore "out" with the girls also. Concerning Arnie's melancholy, his only friend, Dennis Guilder, the sympathetic narrator of the first and third sections of King's eighth major novel, *Christine*, pathetically observes that "If you hit him hard enough, he'd cry" (2). Arnie's Poe-like eyes were a "fine and intelligent gray, the color of clouds on an overcast autumn day" (14); yet with Poe-like capriciousness, Arnie's eyes sometimes reflected "black water and glee," and "far down within them," one could see—"dancing"—the "twisting, decomposing body of a drowned man" (235).

Capriciousness is what gets the story going. Having never had a date in his life (14), Arnie falls in love with, and is stubbornly determined to purchase, a bashed-up old 1958 Plymouth Fury nicknamed "Christine." He falls for the feminine Fury, a real "beauty," long before he falls for the more beautifully real Leigh Cabot (136); and considering his awkwardness in relationships with women (his mother Regina included), the "she" and "her" in the description of the pathetic Plymouth to which he is so fatally attracted are not without psychological import (cf. 194). The attraction to Christine is that of a talented teenage auto mechanic who has been forbidden by academic-oriented parents to pursue his mechanical skills: "his hands were sensitive and quick with machinery; it was only when he was around other people, particularly girls, that they got clumsy and restless" (17). What are mere feminine pronouns in the narrator's description are much later recognized as the "terrible female force [i.e., the pagan fury] that animated her" (427):

She was a bad joke. . . . The left side of her windshield was a snarled spiderweb of cracks. The right rear deck was bashed in, and an ugly nest of rust had grown in the paint-scraped valley. The back bumper was askew, the trunk-lid was ajar, the upholstery was bleeding out through several long tears in the seat covers, both front and back. It looked as if someone had worked on the upholstery with a knife. One tire was flat. The others were bald enough to show the canvas cording. Worst of all, there was a dark puddle of oil under the engine block (7).

The phrase "Arnie had fallen in love" is used immediately before and after this catalog of rusting and decaying disasters. Arnie purchases the Plymouth, prophetically considered a "damned thing" by friend Dennis (16), from a crafty old oddball, Roland D. LeBay, who resembled a "cold November wind" that "could think" (12). While this "cold November wind" turns out to be a ghastly undesirable—a crude version of the Nazi Dussander in "Apt Pupil"—he is yet another manifestation of King's penchant for surrogate fathers who, for good or ill, supply the missing paternal link in a young male's parental requirements. Arnie considers his inadequate father, Michael Cunningham, little more than a henpecked fool: "[My mother] talks to him like a donkey, she rides him like a donkey, and he brays like a donkey" (355).

In lieu of the "ancient family" and "opulent circumstances" that Lovecraft claimed for Poe's heroes, Arnie is given aristocractic parents

who were "university people to the core" (17)—academic pseudoli-
berals, the kind that Stephen King seems to despise. With protests
and teach-ins, they believed in and supported integration, antiwar
movements, racial balances in schools, restraints on police brutality,
hotlines for runaway kids, ERA, vegetarianism, alternatives to fossil
fuels, and protection of abused wives and unwed mothers. Yet,
ironically, like that "cold November wind," Roland LeBay, they,
too—especially the mother—had refrigerated personalities: "Regina
. . . forty-five and handsome in a rather cold semi-aristocratic way—
that is, she managed to look aristocratic even when she was wearing
bluejeans, which was most of the time. Her field was English, but of
course, when you teach at the college level, that's never enough; it's
like saying 'America' when someone asks you where you're from. She
had it refined and calibrated like a blip on a radar screen. She
specialized in the earlier English poets, and had done her thesis on
Robert Herrick" (18). The free-thinking Cunninghams live in a
fictitious Pennsylvania college town called Libertyville and are associated with an obscenely named Horlicks College. The father is a
history professor.

As the novel progresses, Arnie develops involuted psychosexual
relationships with his female-named car, Christine. One of the consequences of this love affair with a crazy car is that his domineering
mother (whose first name, Regina, means "queen") loses control over
her son. Thoroughly acquainted with her minor seventeenth-century
poet (Robert Herrick), the "refined and calibrated" Regina is unable
to communicate with Arnie and totally incapable of getting her son
to comprehend the depth of his disastrous infatuation with a twenty-
year-old, beat-up old Plymouth Fury. It is not without significance
that a social-minded mother educated in a parochial school, where
she presumably would have learned to appreciate the supernatural,
should have a son who becomes enamored of a diabolical car with the
pseudoreligious name of "Christine." Though a more sympathetic
character than Regina, Father Callahan in 'Salem's Lot is also imbued
with a sense of social commitment and follows similar patterns of
liberal behavior. Like Regina, the seminary-trained priest has more
interest in secular progress ("better prisons," "better cops," "better
birth control," "better sterilization techniques" [SL, 149]) than he
has in the spiritual power of the cross of Christ. Hence in a melodramatic moment, when strong faith in the crucifix—in objective reality, nothing more than a symbol—is needed to ward off the

overpowering malevolence of the vampire Barlow, the drink-dependent Catholic priest is a dismal failure (355). In a major crisis with her son, Regina also fails. Unlike Callahan, Regina's problem is not alcohol, but a desperate need for sex to calm her nerves. King reports that every night, the "refined and calibrated" Regina Cunningham used her husband's "dutiful and joyless" penis as a "sleeping pill" (248).

The Hollywood-like flawlessness of Arnie's girl friend, Leigh Cabot, belongs in a nineteenth-century Arthurian idyll. Arnie's attraction, beginning about a third of the way through the novel—he being a somewhat late bloomer—is intended to prove him a sexually normal all-American boy, superficially not unlike Todd Bowden in "Apt Pupil." Once Arnie's facial appearance improves, "his acne and pimples gone," he "looked okay." In fact, best-friend Dennis carefully observes, "he looked more than okay" (140)—was "almost handsome" (118). The novel thus sets the stage for what should turn out to be a sentimental romance between an attractive teenage couple, like that of the fatally victorious Cinderella pair (Tommy and Carrie) at the high school prom in King's first published novel. Leigh Cabot is described as "just beautiful, with no qualifications. Her skin was fair and perfect, usually with a touch of perfectly natural color . . . and her figure was lovely—firm, high breasts, a small waist that looked as if you could almost put your hands around it . . ." (137). The loveliness of Leigh contrasts markedly with both the crabbed personality of Regina and the ridiculously bashed-up condition of the *Christine* in its first appearance. These three are like the ancient fates (Clotho, Lachesis, and Atropos) that dominated gods and men in Greek mythology, for they direct and control every aspect of Arnie's life, each female weaving him her own fateful web.

Yet despite the physical attractions, as well as attractiveness, of Arnie and Leigh, the affair goes badly; the jealous and malevolent Plymouth Fury intervenes. This "Fury" is a modern adaptation of the Erinyes, the furies of ancient Hesiodic mythology sprung of the gushing blood of the castrated Ouranos, and like the three fates also tripartite (Megaera, Alecto, and Tisiphone).[2] According to the mythology of Hesiod, believed to be a contemporary of Homer, the furies came into existence during the lovemaking of Ouranos (meaning "heavens") and Gaia ("earth") as a consequence of a brutal castration episode by son Chronos ("time").[3]

Though one must be careful not to press the analogy too far, a rough but important parallel can be drawn between these Hesiodic Furies sprung from the phallic blood of the mutilated "heavens" and the 1958 Plymouth Fury sprung from the loined malevolence of Roland D. LeBay—that "cold November wind," who seems to have invested his offspring car with "supernatural power" (434). This 1958 Plymouth Fury possesses all the qualities of the Erinyes: the persevering anger of Alecto, the blood vengeance of Tisiphone, and the furious jealousy of Megaera. Like Christine (who, in Christian symbology, represents a kind of demon-Christ overflowing with a will-to-evil such as could only derive from an cold Calvinist divinity), the ancient Furies were the embodiment of unfeeling or abstract justice. Theirs was an ethic without concern for the motivation behind a crime, a justiceless obsession for crime itself. Like these ancient avenging Furies, the Plymouth Fury (and also the cold Regina Cunningham) pursues in blind anger, vengeance, and jealousy those who come within the compass of her attention. Arnie seems an Orestes-like teenager caught between a Clytemnestra-like mother (whom he annihilates through contradiction [348]), and Erinyes-like Christine-Fury (who almost annihilates him [491]).

In subtle symbols, the Christianity-negating qualities of both the irrational Regina and the unspeakable Christine are skillfully exploited in a well-drawn winter scene at Christmas. One should bear in mind when reading this that Roland D. LeBay had been earlier compared to a "cold November wind" that "could think," a cold-wind image that is never far from the surface of the novel (cf. 135, 207, 237, 355).

Mother Nature didn't seem at all that motherly that evening as early dusk gave way to full dark and then to blizzardly night. She [like Regina and Christine] was a pagan fearsome old witch that night, a harridan on the wind [like Roland D. LeBay], and Christmas meant nothing to her . . . she blew the large nativity scene [the figures of Joseph, Mary, and baby Jesus] in front of the police station into a snowbank where the sheep, and goats, the Holy Mother and Child were not found until a late January thaw uncovered them. (359)

It is impossible to say which of the two female forces (both fearsome old pagan witches, like blizzardy Mother Nature) is the more cruel: the psychological antagonisms of Regina or the psycho-supernatural horrors of Christine.

Obviously the beautiful Leigh Cabot as the object of Arnie's erotic interest turns out to be the object of Christine's eccentric malevolence. Leigh complains that making love to Arnie in that particular Plymouth Fury "seemed a perversion worse than voyeurism or exhibitionism—it was like making love inside the body of [your] rival" (196). Leigh develops a "vague dislike of walking in front of [Christine's] new grill, or closely behind the trunk." She fears that the emergency brake might accidentally release, or that the gearshift might slip out of park and into neutral "for some reason." She never entertained such thoughts about her family car. Nevertheless, when she was seated inside Christine, she felt engulfed—"swallowed" is how she prophetically phrases it (196).

Both Leigh and her next lover, Arnie's best friend Dennis, have premonitions about Christine that prove prophetic. In Leigh's case, a casual McDonald's hamburger (while she is sitting in Christine) causes a near-fatal choking incident, rendered in excruciating anatomical detail for two pages (270–71). Leigh is saved by the skill and presence-of-mind of a hitchhiker who happens to know the Heimlich maneuver for saving choking victims. While Leigh's salvation is sheer luck, the choking incident is made to seem the result of an asphyxiating stench that permeates the interior of Christine from time to time. It is interesting that, when she is gagging and at the point of death, Leigh resorts to fragments of an old repentence-prayer: "*O my God, I am heartily sorry for having offended thee.*" Yet while her salvation by Heimlich occurs upon the utterance of this aspiration, her confusion is such that at one point she reverses the intention of the prayers by desperately mumbling: "*I am . . . for offending . . . this is my act*" (271).[4]

In Dennis's case, a seriously debilitating football accident occurs immediately after a nightmare (the "slit trench" of the "unconscious"), in which Dennis sees the "decomposing corpse of Roland D. LeBay lolling obscenely in the shotgun seat as the car roared out of the garage at me, pinning me with the savage circles of its headlights" (167–68). The dream-power of Christine extends outward into the waking world to cause a crippling accident on a football field; and the reader has no difficulty making the connection between Christine's power and the end of Dennis's football career. Dennis comes "within about a centimeter of being paralyzed from the waist down for the rest of [his] life" (169)—a form of castration and / or impotence that mind-reading Christine seems able to impose at will on any male she pleases. An important parallel exists between the psychologically emasculating powers of Regina over her husband Michael, and the near total destruction of Dennis's lower parts by Christine.

While this novel is generally effective, and well deserving of its popularity, some of the gothic horrors tend to be conventional and could be easily interchanged with those of other King narratives. There is little difference between a car that destroys in *Christine*, a house that destroys in *'Salem's Lot*, a dog that destroys in *Cujo*, or a place that destroys in *Pet Sematary*, seeing-eye hands that destroy in "I Am the Doorway," malevolent boy-ghosts that destroy in "Sometimes They Come Back," or a contaminated fog that destroys in the novella, "The Mist" (*SK*, 21–133). But one of the more interesting science-fiction attributes of the Fury is her penchant for time-reversal, a quality she shares with the famous mechanism in H. G. Wells's *Time Machine* (1895) and the carnival in Bradbury's *Something Wicked This Way Comes*. It is a penchant she also shares with Michael (a past-obsessed historian) and Regina (a backward-looking literary scholar). In addition to appearing to drive herself (though the driver is actually the decaying Roland D. LeBay), and her self-healing and self-repairing talents (paralleling and probably causing Arnie's facial, physical, and social improvements), Christine has an odometer that runs backward. Her one radio station, *WDIL*, plays only golden oldies from the year of her manufacture, 1958.

Why 1958? The date harks back to one of the few periods in twentieth-century American history that could be regarded as an "Era of Good Feeling"—the years of the Eisenhower presidency (1952–60), that deceptive calm before the Cuban missile crisis; the Kennedy assassination; the Vietnam War; student violence and protests; Watergate; black, gay, and women's liberation; the rock music of the Beatles; the Iran hostage crisis; and Reagan's conservatism. Christine, therefore, harks back to her birth in an American pseudo-Eden. But like the ominous oasis in the midst of the violent corn fields in "Children of the Corn," the paradise is illusory, haunted with false dreams and future disasters. As an omen of what the future holds, the car radio plays rock 'n' roll music of the fifties, leading into an intriguing little death-dialogue, as Arnie, Leigh, and the knowledgeable stranger listen to the car radio.

On the radio, the Big Bopper finished and Richie Valens came on, doing "La Bamba."

The hitchhiker shook his head and laughed. "First the Big Bopper, then Richie Valens. Must be death night on the radio. Good old *WDIL*."
"What do you mean?" Leigh asked. . . .
"They [all] died in a plane crash. With Buddy Holly." (266)[5]

This conversation occurs just before the choking incident. Later, after Leigh's close call with death, the car radio again evokes the false Eden of the Eisenhower era, this time not by playing music but by giving news reports that appear to confirm the stranger's interpretation. The good news is only one sentence long, followed by a succession of reports on crimes, accidents, and atomic weapons (278–79). Especially notable is the announcement of the sudden death of rock star Eddie Cochran,[6] the same rock star with whose lyric about the "car made just for me" the novel begins. King thus carries out the ultimate death-orientation of the three subtitles of *Christine*: "Teenage Car-Songs," "Teenage Love-Songs," and "Teenage Death-Songs."

This backward movement in time is a movement toward birth and beyond, and, as stated elsewhere by King, is a "pulling apart the links between past and present" (*Dead Zone*, 135). Christine's self-repairings and music/news/echoes of an unrecoverable past have their parallels in the coma of the young English dock-walloper, who "had reversed time and become a fetus again, swimming in the placental waters of coma" (*Dead Zone*, 70). On the symbolic level, the Plymouth Fury represents Arnie's unconscious hostilities toward Dennis, Leigh, and others; and at least in one respect, Christine's back-in-time compulsions express Arnie's penchant for self-annihilation or even total nonexistence. In the time-frame of the novel (1978), Christine is reaching back twenty years. But twenty years earlier, Arnie Cunningham would not yet have been in existence. His parents would not yet have married, possessing that youthfulness that free-thinking Regina and Michael would like to have possessed forever, and, possessing it, would have pushed Arnie past their sexuality back into their very bodies, rendering him, in a sense, part seedling and part egg (158).

To return to Lovecraft's delineation of the Poe protagonist: intelligent as he might be, Arnie is not "deeply learned in strange lore" in the romantic manner of the nineteenth-century gothic hero, nor "darkly ambitious to penetrate the mysteries of the universe." Nevertheless, in tampering with Christine, Arnie has tampered with the impossible and the improbable. Along with Roderick Usher in Poe's famous short story, Arnie too is capable of proclaiming: "I must abandon life and reason together in some struggle with the grim phantasm, *Fear*." That Arnie should only appear to be "saved" ("I think things are going to be okay now" [491]), and that Christine, even though crushed down into a mere metal cube, should still "reach out its hands toward the present" and "bite" (496), is Stephen King's inevitable drift toward the concluding despair of "The Fall of the House of Usher," whose "storm" is always "abroad in all its wrath." In *Christine*—generally successful in blending ancient mythology, pretentious academe, teenage immaturities, and gothic symbology—the "storm" is a multileveled "November wind" that "could think." The narrator Dennis Guilder, who eventually becomes a conventional junior high school teacher after the death of his friend Arnie Cunningham, worries that this "cold November wind"—none other than the infamous Roland D. LeBay himself—might be "working its way east," perhaps into another King novel, and "saving me for last" (503)—"me" being you the reader.

In a Misspelled Cemetery

While it is not unusual, as in all fifty-one chapters of *Christine*, for the sections of a King novel to be introduced with phrases from rock music and/or poetry, which thereafter run through the narrative like a haunted refrain, *Pet Sematary* is unusual in that each of its three sections begins with a biblical paraphrase that continues from section to section. Unexpected indeed are both the religious tone of the headnotes and their continuation. What is quoted (or rather simplified) is the raising of Lazarus from the dead (John 11:11–44). In the first of the three paraphrases, Jesus is compelled to explain to his unsophisticated disciples that when he said that Lazarus was "sleeping," he was speaking metaphorically. "Sleep" meant "death." The first Lazarus paraphrase, therefore, prepares the reader for what is to follow; and to be sure, before 211 pages of the first section are completed, six death-sleeps will strike down characters in breathless succession—one nightmare hardly absorbed before another occurs or is narrated in flashback. These deaths all crop up under extremely unpleasant circumstances. Three major deaths of part 1 are those of the auto victim Victor Pascow, the house cat "Churchill," and the elderly Norma Crandall. The three minor ones are all presented in retrospective flashback: the dog "Spot," Stanny B., and the ten-year-old Zelda, whose death coincides with the Jewish Passover. Both Pascow and Churchill, who seem to be interchangeable symbols of one another, are killed on a mysterious road, a disaster about which there are numerous hushed and haunted warnings.

The death of Victor Pascow sets up a death-and-resurrection pattern for which the Lazarus reference was merely a pale prelude. First referred to as "dying boy" (70), Pascow plays a comparatively small introductory role, but his tragic death by accident weaves a dark background to the seemingly light and playful scenes of the two-year-old Gage Creed learning how to walk and talk, whose death and resurrection in parts 2 and 3 will ultimately develop into the major mystery of *Pet Sematary*. Ultimately, this Victor Pascow—a kind of ghost-Christ, whose Jewish-sounding name is a pun on "Paschal" (pertaining to Resurrection and / or Passover), becomes a core around which the hauntings of the resurrection-novel spiral. He is repeatedly alluded to and remembered, even in dreams (83–87, 314–19). Pascow's first appearance is as a motorcycle victim in a hospital, with head half-crushed, neck broken, and collarbone jutting from a "swelled and twisted right shoulder" (72). Though obviously dead, he nevertheless seems alive enough to groan out "syllables . . . slurred and unclear"—syllables that unexpectedly turn into oracular pronouncements, few of which are understood by the attending physician (or by the reader): "It's not the real cemetery," "The soil of a man's heart is stonier," "Injun bring my fish," etc. These meaningless mumblings are uttered by a corpselike Pascow, whose eyes are "vacant, not-seeing, rimmed with blood"—whose "mirthless" mouth is "grinning the large grin of a dead carp" (74).

The attending physician is Louis Creed, protagonist of *Pet Sematary*, who has just moved into the university town of Ludlow, along with wife Rachel, daughter Ellie, son Gage, and the house cat Churchill, not insignificantly nicknamed "Church." Louis does not understand the dying Pascow's dismal utterances. But on the night after Pascow's death, the deceased (his body still cold in an autopsy drawer in Bangor) pays a dream-call on his attending physician, the rationalist and hard-headed realist, Dr. Creed, and, like an ancient Greek "psychopomp," conducts the alarmed physician through the "pet sematary" about which he had made his first oracular remark. A true specter, Pascow retains his final grisly appearance: head bashed in, dried blood "in maroon stripes like Indian warpaint" on his face, and collarbone jutting "whitely" (83). The ghostly meandering of Pascow and Creed through the cemetery is a visual and auditory hallucination that seems headed nowhere—except that a pile of dead branches (the much-repeated "deadfall") turns into a moving "heap of bones" that "writhed and clicked together, mandibles and femurs and ulnas and molars and incisors; [Louis] saw the grinning skulls of humans and animals. Fingerbones clittered. Here the remains of a foot flexed its pallid joints" (86). In this graveyard setting, Louis hears Pascow's third and last prophetic utterance, less cryptic than the preceding two, but obviously more ominous: "Your destruction and the destruction of all you love is very near, Doctor" (87). All this occurs to the dream-smell of death and the "maddening" dream-click of bones, and produces a "hopeless crawl of horror in [Louis's] belly." Yet, playing the hard-headed rationalist even in his dream, Dr. Louis Creed believes that his "waking mind will discover [the dream's] inconsistencies" (85).

The second important death is Church's. Though the Church-cat is only three years old, nevertheless its eventual death (someday from natural causes at a ripe old age) has already been the subject of an uncomfortable discussion between Louis and his daughter Ellie. Louis has tried to convince Ellie that her beloved Church cat "might still be alive when you're fifteen," and "that's a long time away." But Ellie has reacted angrily, saying that "it doesn't seem long to me" (50–51). The sharp, little theological dialogue between father and daughter that follows these comments on Church's "long life" significantly anticipates subsequent disasters:

"Honey," he said, "if it was up to me, I'd let Church live to be a hundred. But I don't make the rules."
"Who does?" she asked, and then, with infinite scorn: "God, I suppose."
"God or Somebody," he said. "Clocks run down—that's all I know. There are no guarantees, babe."
"I don't want Church to be like all those dead pets!" she burst out, suddenly tearful and furious. "I don't want Church to ever be dead! He's my cat! He's not God's cat! Let God have His own cat! Let God have all the damn old cats He wants, and kill them all! Church is *mine*!"

This far from comforting father/daughter exchange on the "intractability of death," "its cruel unpredictability," and "its imperviousness to argument or to a little girl's tears" (51) has an icy irony about it that chills and chills as events unfold. Within seventy pages of the cat-death dialogue, and forty pages after the Pascow dream sequence—and indeed on a very cold November evening when old Norma Crandall is at "Thanksgiving church service"—the housecat "Church" does indeed die. He is unexpectedly killed on that fatal "road" (sometimes spelled like the Down East pronunciation, "rud"). This is a sudden misfortune that not even the hard-headed and realistic Creed can get himself to believe. Hearing from his strange and legend-filled old friend, Jud Crandall, the news of a dead animal lying truck-struck on the road, he fervently wishes to himself: *"Don't let it be Church"* (123). "But, of course," Stephen King coldly and matter-of-factly observes as events yield themselves to fate, *"it was Church."* As with Victor Pascow, the cat is killed on the road—in this case, an ominous "rud" about which there had been many warnings from the beginning of the narrrative.

This is not all. On a deadly cold evening, the cat is buried in the old pet cemetery (consistently misspelled "Sematary" just as the road is consistently mispronounced "rud") "in a grave two feet wide and three feet long," mockingly thought of as a "Cadillac of a grave for a damn cat." As for the graveyard itself, it was a mysterious old gravesite of Maine Indians: "The Micmacs believed this hill was a magic place. . . . Believed this whole forest, from the swamp on north and east was magic. They made this place and they buried their dead here, away from everything else. Other tribes steered clear of it—the Penobscots said these woods were full of ghosts" (137). For Church the old Micmac magic works, for, shortly after the cat burial, the cat returns from the grave, behaving almost as if he had never died. While Pascow's haunting was largely dream—or at least, the "return" could not easily be distinguished from a dream—Church's return is clearly a Lazaruslike cat resurrection; and "cool as a cucumber Dr. Creed" (146), hard-headed realist and nonbeliever, is the first witness to this old Indian mirage.

It is at this point that Church's return from the dead and the Lazarus quotation from the Gospel of John begin to conjoin, and also that, if he has not already done so, the perceptive reader begins to suspect an impious connection between the cat's nickname ("Church"), the Hebraic name Pascow (suggesting Passover), the raising of Lazarus from the dead, and the theme of the Easter resurrection. The more one keeps these bizarre parallels in mind, the more they direct *Pet Sematary* toward a parable of unbelief—even indeed a "revolt" against Christian resignation—all the more sardonic because the hard-headed physician/protagonist's last name is an impossible "Creed." Sometimes subtly, sometimes bluntly, King keeps enforcing a cat-equals-Christianity analogy; and one would have to be obtuse indeed not to notice how sharply double-edged are even the most offhand references to the church cat, of which the following comment is typical: "*Church* had died at the best possible time" (291).

In his unexpected returns, perhaps Church, more than anything else in *Pet Sematary*, turns the rational Dr. Creed into a helpless believer—not in the Christian revelation as preached by St. Paul (that faith is vain if one does not believe that Christ rose from the dead [1 Corinthians 15:14]), but rather in the "skeletal remains of some long dead monster . . . slain by [Geoffrey Chaucer's] *parfait good and gentil knight* (46), or in the fierce Wendigo, the "creature that moves through the north country [whose touch can] turn you into a cannibal" (364).[7] In poisoning off Church (397), Creed in a sense is killing one form of belief (black magic) only to encourage another (even blacker and more hellish), for "from somewhere in the shadows above there came a giggling—a cold and sunless laughter that made the skin on Louis's back prickle" (400). As in a medieval morality play (like the fourteenth-century *Everyman* or the fifteenth-century *Castle of Perseverance*, where all characters are abstractions), *Pet Sematary* slowly but inexorably turns into a fearsome morality novel of an "invisible vulture [that rides] the air currents above" (396)— medieval and broodingly gothic only in the most unflattering senses of those much-misabused terms.

The third major death in part 1 is that of the eighty-year-old Norma Crandall, the wife of Jud Crandall, Louis's surrogate father (212–15). She dies of old age and cancer. The inclusion of her death demonstrates that "except for childbirth, [death is] the most natural thing in the world." In a sense, her death overstates the obvious— necessary not only to intensify gothic glooms and prepare the reader for the triumphant horrors of parts 2 and 3, but more immediately as a response to Rachel's irrational—or should we call it "rational"?— outburst that "there's nothing natural about death—*nothing*" (56). Left alone after a sharp exchange with Rachel over whether five-year-old Ellie should be told about death, hard-headed Dr. Creed says to himself while tilting a dustpan filled with spilled flour (symbolically, human remains) into a wastebasket (symbolically, the grave): "In the end there [are] only the clock, and the markers, which [become] eroded and nameless in the passage of time. Even sea turtles and the

giant sequoias have to buy out someday" (57). Thus Norma Crandall's death at eighty-plus gives this horror novel of inexplicables and
imponderables, a focal point of normality (hence the name "Norma").

But far more important in one's pursuit of the sheer pleasure of
terror is the flashback to the death of ten-year-old Zelda Goldman by
her sister Rachel, Louis's wife. While the implications of her name
are not as blatant as those of Creed, Norma, and Church, Zelda's
name does begin with the same rare final letter of the alphabet as
zombie and, her final illness and death, according to the lengthy
account by Rachel, does indeed evoke the figure of the "living dead,"
not unlike the comatose young Englishman in *Dead Zone,* who had
shriveled up to an almost prenatal position:

Louis, we watched her degenerate day by day, and there was nothing anyone
could do. She was in constant pain. Her body seemed to shrivel, pull in on
itself, her shoulders hunched up and her face pulled down until it was like a
mask. . . . we *wanted* her to die, Louis, we *wished* for her to die, and it
wasn't just so *she* wouldn't feel any more pain, it was so *we* wouldn't feel any
more pain, it was because she was starting to look like a monster, and she
was starting to *be* a monster. . . . And sometimes she'd touch me with her,
her hands, her birdy hands, and sometimes I'd almost scream and ask her
not to. (203–5)

Rachel was only eight years old when Zelda's tragic death occurred
(206); but because Rachel carries this sorrow inside herself, like one
who inly mourns, she comes more and more to resemble the Rachel
of Jeremiah 31:15 and Matthew 2:18: "In Rama was there a voice
heard, lamentation, and weeping, and great mourning, Rachel weeping for her children, and would not be comforted, because they were
not." This biblical analogy is tragically vivid after the shocking death
of Rachel's two-year-old son Gage: "That day's penny-dreadful events
were only complete when [Rachel] was pulled, screaming, from the
East Room of the Brookings-Smith Mortuary, where Gage lay in his
closed coffin . . ."(229).

One of Zelda's inadvertent contributions to the plot of *Pet Sematary*
is the nickname she has for a picture, hanging upon the wall, from
one of the Oz books that she liked before she got sick with
meningitis. It was a picture of Oz the Great and Terrible,[8] "only
Zelda always called him *Oz the Gweat and Tewwible* because she
couldn't make that sound," that is, the letter *r* (207). Her conspicuous mispronunciation correlates with Jud Crandall's inability to pro-

nounce English words properly, but especially with the misspellings
that appeared in the cemetery tombstones. These misspellings and
mispronunciations seem to imply a philosophy powerfully expressed
by the contemporary American poet Howard Nemerov, who describes
a mess of thick-weaving vines that entangle a half-fallen tree as a
"wandering calligraphy . . . enthralled to a magic constantly misspelled."[9] Not especially significant in its first appearance, the mispronounced phrase from *The Wizard of Oz*, like so many repeated
elements in *Pet Sematary* (and in King's stories generally) modifies
and intensifies in meaning upon each repetition:

Sure—she just wants to make sure I don't go up in a puff of smoke, Louis
thought and almost smiled. But then that thought called up another one: *Oz
the Gweat and Tewwible*. And the smile died. (213)

Oz the Gweat and Tewwible has just fallen on top of my son's coffin, Louis
thought dazedly (247).

Louis stopped at the Orrington Corner Store, bought two six-packs of
cold beer, and called ahead to Napoli's for a pepperoni-and-mushroom pizza.
"Want to give me a name on that, sir?"
Oz the Gweat and Tewwible, Louis thought (284).

King cleverly arranges these references to the "Gweat" and
"Tewwible" so that most of them occur in Louis's mind. The most
telling is clearly the following that equates this ominous Oz with a
dying-and-decaying power more primal than the Divinity defined by
the New Testament: "*No, not Christ. These leavings* [masses of rotting
flowers in a cemetery] *were made in propitiation of a much older God than
the Christian one. People have called Him different things at different times,
but Rachel's sister gave Him a perfectly good name, I think: Oz the Gweat
and Tewwible. God of dead things left in the ground. God of rotting flowers
in drainage ditches. God of the Mystery* (344).
This view clearly tears away at the veil of simple piety that the
Lazarus headnotes of parts 1–3 might weave. The belief in a power
beyond recognizable human-shaped dieties goes back in Western European tradition to the Greek dramatist Aeschylus (sixth century
B.C.), who proclaims in his *Agamemnon* a belief in an ultimate being,
"Necessity," an abstract entity similar to Aristotle's "Unmoved
Mover," to which were subjected the Olympian gods (Zeus, Poisedon,
Athena, Aphrodite, etc.) and even the three fates themselves (the

Clotho, Lachesis, and Atropos who were previously mentioned in connection with *Christine*). The irreconcilable difference is that whereas Aeschylean "Necessity" was a mathematical entity beyond good and evil, the "Gweat and Tewwible" Lovecraftian Oz is unmistakably sinister. The Jupiter of Percy Bysshe Shelley's massive poetic play *Prometheus Unbound* (1820) is a similar malevolent diety (2.4:19–23).

In Shelley's *Prometheus*, however, malign Jove is overthrown by a goodness within the interior of the earth, the Chthonian Demogorgon. But from the graves of the animal cemetery with its frequently misspelled epitaphs (cf. SMUCKY THE CAT, HE WAS OBEDIANT; TRIXIE KILT ON THE HIGHWAY; MARTA OUR PET RABIT, etc.), and from the mispronounced names of illiterate divinities of reconceived fairy tales (like *Oz, The Gweat and Tewwible*), no such benevolent resurrection will ever occur. No matter how innocent or inadvertent are the misspellings and mispronunciations throughout *Pet Sematary* (especially the endearing verbalisms of two-year-old Gage: "dweems," "kite flyne up to the kye," "Chuggy-Chuggy-Choo-Choo"), everything is endued with the futility of death. [10] In the imagination of Dr. Creed (the nonbeliever), the earth itself seems one vast Egyptian gravestone-pyramid on which is inscribed: HERE LIES RAMSES II, HE WAS OBEDIANT (136). As one critic phrases it, in discussing the psychological convolutions of the horror story: "Irrational fear [initially, in this instance, the mere death of a pet cat] can split open the known world to reveal the underlying nightmares, both of the individual and the age, in all their ambiguity and self-contradiction."[11] Stephen King's *Pet Sematary*, therefore, must ultimately revert to the cry of the unjustly punished title character of Shelley's *Prometheus*, chained by a cruel Jupiter to a mountain in the Caucasus: "Ah me! alas, pain! pain ever, forever" (1.1.29). In Shelley's nineteenth-century symbology the cry proves temporary; in King's twentieth-century *Pet Sematary* the cry is eternal.

Chapter Seven
Night Shift:
Harbinger of Bad News
Comprehension of the Final Ending

Most of the short stories in *Night Shift* (1978), a representative anthology of Stephen King's short fiction, begin with dramatic situations so interestingly rendered that curiosity is immediately aroused: the payoff blackmail negotiations, for example, of betrayed husband Cressner and wife-lover Norris in "The Ledge"—the crafty reflections of the anonymous killer-narrator (alias "Springheel Jack") in "Strawberry Spring"—the almost offhand descriptions of the sinister Chapelwaite of half-mad Charles Boone in "Jerusalem's Lot." More often than not, opening scenes have an intensity and directness that impact upon the reader immediately, and are occasionally—as in much of "The Boogeyman" and "The Mangler"—even highly comical. In tales of pure terror, something unnatural (oversized rats, mysterious killings, death-dealing diseases, magical mechanicals, and unexplained wall-noises) is rather quickly insinuated into the narrative. Consequently, a strangeness or peculiarity recurs with an insistence that ultimately screams for resolution, what King abstractly calls the "comprehension of the final ending." Not unusually, the repetition (often in varied form) is a phrase, quotation, theme, or question repeated with dramatic effect not unlike the well-known incremental techniques of traditional ballads on tragic themes. Sometimes the refrainlike phrases are simple, as in the title repetitions occurring in "I Know What You Need" or "I Am the Doorway." In others the repetitions are more involuted. In "Sometimes They Come Back," the line and scene repetitions are dramatically interlocked. The recurrence of Jim Norman's terrifying "old dream" (143, 146, 148, 152) interconnects with the similarly patterned appearances in Jim Norman's classroom of three dead teenagers, those vicious ghost-killers who seem to emerge mysteriously from the teacher's recurring nightmare (150, 153, 157).

In these short stories the narrative moves swiftly toward a terrifying resolution. The movement is menacing and cunningly designed.
(1) Some*one* or some*thing* surfaces to present supernatural information
essential to the plot, as with Donald Nell, who, without realizing
what he is doing, informs English teacher Jim Norman that the three
teenage killers have been dead for some time and are now residing in
"Millford High School" (actually a cemetery), from which, as Donald
Nell jokingly points out, "no one ever graduated" (158–61). Or, (2)
a character may be "in" on something supernatural that subtly helps
to deepen the mystery while, at the same time, partly resolving it.
The traditional information source is the classic book of demonic
lore, such as the infernal *Mysteries of the Worm*, dealing with "whatever faceless powers exist beyond the rim of the universe" (25),
discovered in the desecrated chapel of Jerusalem's Lot by Charles
Boone. Or, somewhat less anciently, the book entitled *Raising Demons*
that Jim Norman consults to rid himself of diabolical torments and
persecutions of his teenage ghost-killers (166). Another classic
"knower" is the person who has kept himself demon-informed. In
King novels and short stories, such knowers are not unusually school-
teachers like Matt Burke in *'Salem's Lot*, who has been "researching
vampires," and reviews the entire tradition of vampire behavior and
extermination (318–22). From reading "Frazier's [*sic*] *Golden Bough*,"
English professor Mark Jackson, in "The Mangler," knows that "there
are almost as many spells for casting demons in as for casting them
out" (81). Though only a preteenager, *'Salem's Lot's* Mark Petrie
knows how to deal with vampires from reading comic books of terror
and the supernatural (280).

But the one who "knows" is not always the same as the one who
"learns." This process of discovery is little different from the *anagno-
risis* ("discovery") of Aristotle's *Poetics*, wherein the philosopher ana-
lyzes the various aspects of Greek tragedies—tragedies which,
though mythic in source, were clear precursors to the modern gothic
tale. King sometimes telescopes the two into what might be called
"knower-learners." In the short story, "The Monkey," Hal Shelburn
starts out knowing a good deal about the behavior of wind-up toys,
yet he learns much more as an ominous toy monkey appears and
reappears despite burials, destructions, and carefully contrived disap-
pearances (*SK*). In "I Am the Doorway," narrator Arthur is a good
example of the horror tale's ill-fated knower-learner who, having
"gone further than any human being had gone . . . and came down

hard" (64), would desperately desire to move backward in time so as to "unknow" and "unlearn."

Through the use of human reason, common folklore, or pseudoreligious symbology, this knowing tends to involve either an invocation of, or resistance to, an evil entity that often has shape or form only by virtue of metaphor. What *Danse Macabre* sometimes refers to as the "thing without a name" might (57, 77, 150), in some instances, be more accurately called the "thing without a shape." While the tangible terror in "Jerusalem's Lot" is the "face . . . that yawned in a toothless, agonized grin" (20), the ultimate horror—the ultimate Lovecraftian horror—is the thing that "shambles beyond the stars" (31), residing in "pathless wastes beyond the edges of the Universe" (33). Some thing-without-a-shape occupies the massive ironer in "The Mangler" and, when actually seen, turns out to be "huge and black . . . bulked to a tremendous height," metaphorically sensed in images that are absurd, if not downright comical: "gaping hungry mouth filled with steam" or "glaring electric eyes the size of footballs" (91). In "Children of the Corn," the infernal thing without a shape is "something green," with "terrible red eyes" the "size of footballs" (276). In "Sometimes They Come Back," the evil entity is merely a voice in a dark nighttime classroom asking for offerings and sacrifices (mumbling "What do you offer?" / "Give me what is mine!"), but ultimately is no more than a "deep silence" swelling with "something unseen," a "thickness . . . that seemed to fill the belly and throat with gray steel," an "electric potential" (167)—and, at the very end of the story, dissolves into a "something," a "shadow," or "perhaps only an intuition" (170). As is constantly suggested in Lovecraft's "Dunwich Horror," "Rats in the Wall," and "Colour Out of Space," *Danse Macabre* offers the opinion that what are merely "shadowy forces"—things without shapes—are so powerful that they could destroy all humanity "if they so much as grunted in their sleep" (63).

King's short stories sometimes conclude with O. Henry–like endings, which, though momentarily pleasurable to millions of unsophisticated readers (who are only concerned with what horror "finally happens"), have been justly censured by perceptive reviewers. "The Boogeyman," much of which is masterful comedy wherein a simpleminded father confesses to the murder of his children, unfortunately turns preposterous in the last eight lines when the masked and gloved psychiatrist, to whom the father has been confessing his crimes, turns out to be the boogeyman-in-the-closet, with a voice that sounded like a "mouthful of seaweed" and a "spade-like claw" for a hand (104). Similarly, though somewhat less adolescent, "Strawberry Spring"—initially effective as the narrator describes murder-rapes on a college campus—weakens considerably in the final lines when the narrator suddenly turns out to be "Springheel Jack" himself, the secret murderer.

By contrast with such pop-magazine conclusions, "The Last Rung on the Ladder," one of the few nongothic stories in *Night Shift*, moves relentlessly toward its resolution with a delicate dynamism, the iron fist of a cruel fate gripping the reader in the velvet glove of a casual narrative style. Unlike the absurdly clichéd endings of "Strawberry Spring" and "The Boogeyman," and unlike the cliff-hanging, nail-biting melodrama of "The Ledge" or "Quitters," the pathos of a tender brother-sister relationship that unaccountably drifts into distance, indifference, and ultimately despair, is one of the subtlest psychological studies that King ever devised, the kind of "soft" story that Gordie Lachance (the sensitive male narrator of "The Body") would be terribly afraid to admit that he ever wrote. Instead of mysteries shambling beyond the edge of the universe, or nameless—shapeless things with football eyes, the terror is little more than a subtle whisper, thereby stirring up feelings all the more deeply disquieting: "funny little drafts in the house that had never been there before," "strange currents in the air that had not existed down below," "mysterious updrafts . . . in the third loft" (281–84). The ending surprises without exasperating the reader or insulting his intelligence—a sister's expectation of salvation by a brother as she "swan-dives" to her death from a skyscraper ("I always knew the hay would be there" [290]). Oddly enough, "Last Rung" is less popular among horror-readers addicted to what is sometimes called "shudder gothic"[1] as some of the more formulaic tales of elemental terrors, such as "Gray Matter," "Battleground," and "Trucks."

The three short stories analyzed in this chapter ("Night Surf," "Children of the Corn," and "I Am the Doorway") have been selected because of the grace and finesse with which they are narrated and their ultimate terrors skillfully unveiled. Three interesting literary techniques emerge. The conclusion may be (1) subtly muted, as in "Night Surf," where the dying narrator quietly remembers past pleasures of sunburned flesh. Or, (2) cunningly developed from earlier hints, as in "Children of the Corn," where the mysterious unknown who "walks behind the rows" is revealed as possessing precognitive abilities that flow inevitably from all his other diabolical powers. Or, (3) revealed with a savage suddenness, as in "I Am the Doorway," where the reader himself comes to "know" and "learn" of the severed hands and the eye-encrusted chest—in a total anticipation of an apocalyptic contact between steel claws and diabolic eyes, as inevitable as it was unexpected.

It's Earlier than You Think

The title of the short story "Night Surf" echoes and seems to pun upon the title of the entire anthology in which it appears, *Night Shift*. Futility prevails, hopelessness dominates, and a sense of early death insinuates itself into every character. Desolation and despair are poignantly expressed by the ebb and flow of the night-tides that were like "foamed black glass" (54)—or the self-feel of the narrator's face, "its grain and texture . . . narrowing so swiftly . . . no dignity in it" (59)—or the memory of carrying bodies of college students in dump trucks and "burying them in mass graves with payloaders" (56). To paraphrase the title of Pirandello's famous play, Stephen King's "Night Surf" might well bear the subtitle "Six Characters in Search of Annihilation," a meaningless annihilation that encompasses them in every futile thing they see or do: the "restless, moving humps of the [black] waves, topped by delicate curls of [white] foam" (57), an empty beer can that "landed with a hollow clank on the cement walk that went around the building" (59), and the sand that was "white and duned, marked only by the high-tide line—twisted skein of seaweed, kelp, hunks of driftwood" (53).

This tightly structured and progressively constricting short story details the final flickering hours of some young people, neatly arranged in three sets of two: the sex-partners Bernie and Susie, the self-centered lovers Kelly and Joan, and the weird tag-alongs Needles and Corey. They live in a world where virtually everyone has succumbed to the deadly flu A6, sometimes unexplainably called "Captain Trips"—the same disease with the same nickname that "scrubs the whole human race" in *The Stand*. The six have gravitated to a quasi-imaginary Anson Beach, Maine, and some of them expect to be "dead by Christmas," lying perhaps in somebody's front room, while a "weak winter sun" casts "meaningless windowpane patterns" on a dusty rug (56). In addition to the six, a few straggling survivors are heard only as voices on Corey's expensive and ever-present radio: some "backwoods deejay" on station WKDM in Portsmouth, Maine, who had gone "nutty religious," and a "bunch of kids" who had taken over the transmitting facilities of WRKO and WBZ, two Boston-based radio stations.[2] Each character deals with A6 according to personal needs and whims. The nutty-religious would "play a Perry Como record, say a prayer, bawl, play a Johnny Ray record, read from Psalms . . . then bawl some more," etc. The teenagers gave out only "gag call letters, like WDOPE or KUNT or WA6 or stuff like that." Simply identified as the "guy on the radio," someone was reading dirty limericks while a girl in the background asked him where he put the beer. Before they are even mentioned, the superficiality of these voices is symbolically anticipated by Corey's big radio / tape player that was hardly more than a "nice-looking hunk of junk" (52).

In Giovanni Boccaccio's description of the attitudes and conditions attending the Black Death in the city of Florence, Italy, in the fourteenth-century, he observes that the bubonic plague "had instilled such horror into the hearts of men and women that brother abandoned brother . . . wives left their dear ones to perish and, what is more serious and almost incredible, parents avoided visiting and nursing their own children, as though these were not their own flesh."[3] King's twentieth-century Americans might well be engrafted into the social conditions of medieval Florence. Only, if possible, the behavior of the six is even more cruel—their brutality unspeakable. They come across a semiconscious and raving victim of A6, whose "head was bloated to the size of a football and his neck looked like a sausage" (54). Though he was mumbling about his grandmother, he was in sufficient control of his senses to identify himself as Alvin Sackheim,[4] come all the way from New York. Without pity or conscience, they tie him to the observation gadget, go rooting around for dry brush and hunks of driftwood, and pile the dead branches and twigs up to the victim's waist. Needles ignites the pyre with his Zippo lighter—and in the only moment acknowledging physical pain throughout the entire incident, Bernie reports that "at the end, just before his hair caught on fire, the guy began to scream" (55).

With carefully managed understatement, King gives his readers bits and pieces of dialogue to underscore the callousness of his six characters. While the pyre is burning, for instance, Needles asks

Bernie for a cigarette. Bernie points out that there are about fifty cartons directly behind him. But while Needles is slapping away a mosquito that is "ominously probing his arm," he says, "Don't want to move"—indirectly indicating his pleasure at the sight and smell of burning human flesh, and his reluctance to miss a single delicious moment of Sackheim's fiery holocaust. Even the use of Bernie's name in the context of this incident—a not too subtle pun—seems to suggest that "Bernie's" time for "burning" may come earlier than even he supposes. To reinforce this implication, King reveals Bernie's inner thoughts when, later on, he sat and "smoked" and thought about Needles "flipping back the top of his Zippo, spinning the wheel [as though playing Russian roulette], making fire with flint and steel like a caveman." The surprise comes when Needles acknowledges that he himself is already ill with A6, and then "lit a match and held it under the angle of his jaw" where one could see the "first triangular smudges, the first swelling" of the fatal disease (56).

Superficially, the two lovers Kelly and Joan seem benign enough: Bernie could see them by the edge of the water, walking with their arms around each other, looking like "an ad in a travel agent's window" (56). But their love is like the "delicate curls of foam" that mask the "restless moving humps of the waves" (57). Hot for each other, they are icily indifferent to the sufferings of others. Hand-holdings, sudden laughters, and mutual self-absorptions, rather than diminishing their negative dispositions, tend to accentuate them. Two comments give the reader an interesting insight into their hardened hearts. As though he had been watching a collegiate pre-game bonfire instead of the Sackheim holocaust, lover-boy Kelly exclaims: "Some fire!" As if she were making an inquiry of a travel agency (following neatly from King's travel-agency analogy of the Kelly-Joan beach wanderings), Joan indifferently wonders whether the enflamed and screaming Sackheim "came all the way from New York, like he said" (54).

Kelly and Joan, however, are mere backdrops to the more visible and outspoken sex partners, Bernie and Susie. It is difficult to say which of the two is the more repulsive: Susie laughing and being "turned on" by Sackheim's mumblings about his grandmother as he is being readied for the fire, or Bernie revolted by Susie's appearance and behavior while at the same time assenting to intimate relations. Thinking about Susie, Bernie notes that "she is getting fat, and if she lived long enough . . . she would get really flabby . . . was already mouthy" (52). Responding to her advances with an inexplicable kiss, he sees "she was wearing too much lipstick and it was like kissing a greasy plate" (55). Finding her clothed in one of his shirts, he realizes that he "hate[d] that," especially because she "sweats like a pig." When Susie wants to sit down beside him, he blurts out: "I doubt that it would be wide enough for both of us" (59). Commenting in general on her obnoxious temperament, he thinks to himself: "She wasn't like a jukebox; you never had to put in a dime and she never came unplugged" (57).

Yet despite this nastiness, Bernie alone of the cruel six seems to have something like a conscience. Corey's decision to burn Sackheim, in which everyone enthusiastically or indifferently joins, seems to bother Bernie. Sensitive to this, Needles says, "You're thinking about that," and attempts to ease his own conscience: "I don't think he even knew it was happening." To which Bernie responds, "*He knew*" (56), and later has sweaty dreams about the incident: "a bloated blackened head and a charred skeleton . . . smelled *burnt* . . . talked on and on, and after a while I couldn't make out a single word" (58). It is a nuance worth noting that whereas Bernie wakes up from his frightful dream "breathing hard," the tying and binding of the mother-moaning Sackheim was "turning on" Susie, who was really "breathing fast" (55).

The seventh malevolence is the sea itself and its natural associates: the moon that attracts it and the beach that attends it. Broodingly, malevolently, and menacingly, "Night Surf" keeps returning—again and again—to the sea, as if it were curtain raiser, protagonist, denouement, and indeed the dark final curtain in a tragedy called A6. It does more than symbolize A6; it "is" and goes beyond—is "bigger than the world," "eater of all the dirt and all the crap" of the typical American vacation beach: "candy wrappers and popsicle sticks in the sand, all the beautiful people necking on their beach blankets, intermingled stench of exhaust from the parking lot, seaweed, and Coppertone Oil." For the T. S. Eliot of "Dry Salvages," the "river / Is a strong brown god—sullen, untamed and intractable." But for apocalyptic King, the sea is more infernal, one of the chthonian "dark gods" that must be propitiated (54) in the manner, perhaps, of Odysseus propitiating the goddess Artemis with the sacrifice of his virgin daughter Iphigenia—only more ominously. The equation dark sea equals dark god is never directly stated, but is hinted at in undulating patterns of repetitions. Sea images—such as the "foamed black glass," the "moving humps of the waves," the "running boil of the water," the demanding "thunder of the breakers"—draw the reader toward the inevitable subject of Corey's books about witchcraft and black magic, and especially toward his "telling us that if we made a sacrifice to the dark gods, maybe the spirits would keep protecting us against A6" (54). The sea in the elegiac poetry of fellow New Englander, Robert Lowell, is similarly unrelenting, devouring, and Plutonian when he addresses the drowned body of a sailor-cousin, Warren Winslow: "The winds' wings beat upon the stones / . . . and scream for you and the claws rush / At the sea's throat and wring it in the slush."[5]

With respect to A6, "Night Surf" (like "Children of the Corn" and "I Am the Doorway") possesses what Lovecraft required of all weird tales, "certain atmosphere of breathless and unexplained dread of outer, unknown forces."[6] The deadly flu, unlike its appearance in *The Stand* (chapter 4), is never explained but is a Lovecraftian "deadly force" that simply expands and destroys. However, with respect to the sea and its associates (sand and moon), "Night Surf" would appear to move contrary to Lovecraft's further claim that the "true weird tale" possesses the "suspension or defeat of those fixed laws of nature which are our only safeguard against the assaults of chaos and the demons of unplumbed space." King goes out of his way to stress the importance of one "fixed law," that is, the gravitational power of the moon itself, for the restlessness of the sea, the thundering of the breakers, and the cold dampness of packed sand "would go on as long as there was a moon to pull the water" (57).

Associating the moon with delicate finger-images and employing his technique of incremental repetition and variation, "Night Surf" evokes an uneasy lunar madness in some strikingly haunting lines: "In the faint moonlight," for example, "Needles already looked half dead, with circles under his eyes and pallid *unmoving fingers like pencils*" (53)—or Susie's "*laquered fingernails twinkled* dimly 'with the half moon that had risen about a half hour ago" (53)—or the "moonlight stitched inky crescent-shapes and shadows . . . across everything" darkly illuminating the "deserted lifeguard tower" that pointed toward the sky "like a *finger bone*" (53). Thus everything in "Night Surf" is dark, dismal, and dull-illumined, what Edmund Spenser in his *Faerie Queene*, describing the interior of a dragon's lair, called a "little glooming light, much like a shade" (1.1.122). This muted atmosphere makes the brightness of a summer sun in the final lines all the more blinding. It is as if the pupils of one's imagination had widened to accommodate the pages of preceding gloom, only to have the glare of a hurtling mid-summer sun sear itself directly into the eye of one's consciousness. Meandering back mentally to an earlier girl friend (now probably dead of A6), Bernie remembers a beach date with her and how "I had put oil on her back, and she had put oil on mine, the air had been hot, the sand bright, the sun like a burning glass" (60). Not only do the adjectives "hot," "bright," and "burning" contrast with the sand that is elsewhere cold, dark, and damp (and at one point even a death-suggesting sand-clot on Susie's blouse and skin [57]) but by a clever indirection, the oiled body, the bright sand, and the burning sun—in their own subversive way— echo back to the useless fire-sacrifice of a hapless Alvin Sackheim, about which an indifferent Kelly could find nothing more compassionate to say than: "Some fire!"

Corn Children with Corn Names

The "diabolical young" is an important motif in such novels as William Golding's *Lord of the Flies* (1954) and Charles Robinson's *The Children* (1982) and such similarly themed films as Wolf Rillas's *Village of the Damned* (1960) and Anton Leader's *Children of the Damned* (1963). This malevolent-child motif is an aspect of the apocalyptic narrative—one of its less noted aspects—and is used intermittently in *'Salem's Lot*. In one scene, the vampirized Danny Glick, a "hideous entity" (only twelve years old, with "skin grave-pale" and "eyes reddish and feral"), appears at young Mark Petrie's window in order to "play with you," and when invited into Mark's bedroom, shows a face "suffused with an expression of vulpine triumph" (239–40). In another scene, all the vampirized children of 'salem's Lot (Richie Boddin, for example, with "black chips of coal" for eyes, and lips "ruby red" [370]) occupy and control the school bus of child-hater Charlie Rhodes to destroy him, the malevolent child—to alter William Wordsworth's famous dictum—becoming the "father of the thoroughly malevolent man."[7] But diabolical youth are not entirely unexpected in *'Salem's Lot*, since both young and old in that novel, with the sole exceptions of Ben Mears and Mark Petrie, have been transformed into "evil entities" by Barlow and his henchmen. The situation that obtains in the short story "Children of the Corn" differs in that the young that occupy the mysterious corn fields of Gatlin, Nebraska, are already "pagan devil children" (*NS*, 276). They are lying in wait for someone to sacrifice.

Names are important in this story of blood rites offered to a heartless corn-god who, in one of King's typical reiterations, is the ominous "he who walks behind the rows"—the sacrifice here being the crucifixion-mutilation of a husband and wife, entrapped travelers, in the midst of a children-haunted, Eden-resembling cornfield. The suddenly doomed couple, innocently driving through three hundred miles of cornfield in Nebraska, are called "Vickie" (an "ex-Prom Queen") and "Burt." But their complete names most likely would have been Victoria and Albert! Unlike their nineteenth-century namesakes, this unroyal Vickie and Burt hate one another, are on the verge of divorce, but end up unwillingly "united" as a crucified couple, victims who just happened to be in the wrong place at the wrong time, viciously sacrificed victims of devil-children to devil-gods—as sheerly accidental as Sackheim's in "Night Surf."

Of considerable symbolic importance are the name changes that have been occurring among the malevolent young, all of whom have undergone an infernal rebaptism and are given new names with Old Testament associations: Amos, Isaac, Zepeniah, Rachel, Moses, Job, Japheth, and David. Names of New Testament personages with their Sermon-on-the-Mount implications of kindness, gentleness, and forgiveness are scrupulously avoided, hostilities against the New Testament evidenced by the discovery of a mutilated bible, with sections of the New Testament "chopped out" by "someone who had decided to take on the job of amending good King James with a pair of scissors" (267).

Of the Old Testament names given to these young people—all of them younger than nineteen—five stand out in a special way: Adam and Eve, Ruth and Malachi, and David. According to the records accidentally found by Burt, who becomes both "knower" and "learner" in this story, no births were recorded for a nine-month period between 5 September 1964 and 16 June 1965. Theorizing that most of the parents had been killed during that period of time, Burt discovers that the first recorded birth after an unexpected nine-month hiatus is that of an "Eve" Tobin, followed ironically—as though in deliberate reverse of the sex pattern of Genesis—by an "Adam" Greenlaw. The Eve/Adam associations are sustained by the discovery of an Eden-like patch of cornland without crows, bugs, weeds, yellow blight, etc. (275). Just as the new Victoria and Albert are destined to be the sacrificial victims to the corn-god in order to sustain an imperial paradise, so the new Adam and Eve are doomed to be the death-progenitors of a new devil-oriented society that exists in deliberate, diabolical parody of Scripture. But while the purpose of the original Adam and Eve was the origin of the human race, it appears to be the purpose of the new Adam and Eve, albeit only symbolically, to lead the malevolent young to extinction. They are in a sense the death-mother and death-father of the new human race, and the fact that they accomplish nothing in the story, and virtually disappear after their names are mentioned, only reinforces their use-lessness.

Two other names, Ruth and Malachi, play roles more important than Adam and Eve in the conclusion of the story. Malachi is the name of the last prophet and last book of the Old Testament in the King James version. The male teenager who has this name is respon-sible for the impregnation of a young girl named Ruth, whose name, deriving from the Book of Ruth, is traditionally associated with corn, kindness, and Christ. The gentleness of Old Testament Ruth is one of the most memorable in Hebrew scriptures, ironic because Ruth, herself a Moabite, is not Hebrew, yet in the Matthew gospel her name is included among the ancestors of Christ (Matthew 1:5). Hence her pregnancy in King's story is significant since it suggests the possiblity that a future redeemer might be able to break the back of the diabolical dispositions of the pseudo-Hebrew corn-children. Not only has this corn-girl Ruth conceived a child by Malachi, she has also "conceived a secret hatred for the corn and sometimes dreamed of walking into it with a torch in each hand when dry September came" (278).

However, because the malice that "walks behind the rows" sees everything, "even the secrets kept in human hearts," it is not likely that Ruth will live long enough to carry out her secret design to burn the fields. Also, because the life span alloted to the devil-children, graciously called their "Age of Favor" (277), is reduced from nineteen years to eighteen in punishment for a transgression (as if in mockery of Genesis 6:3, where the life span of humanity has been reduced from Methusalah's incredible nine hundred and sixty-nine years to one hundred and twenty), is it not likely that Ruth's offspring, nor Ruth herself, will survive long enough to ancestor a new messiah. By contrast with the "good news" of the New Testa-ment, the "bad news" that King is suggesting through the use of biblical name-parodies is that the situation in the gothic cornfields of Nebraska is hopeless. Evil forces ultimately conquer! It is no accident that the young man whose place Malachi had taken was a "David," and that David—the name of most famous ancestor of Christ—had walked into the cornfield at the age of nineteen years and been destroyed. Thus, as in Roger Zelazny's science fiction story, "Game of Blood and Dust,"[8] King's "Children of the Corn" seems to suggest that every avenue of future control over the destiny of the corn-children has been successfully blocked by an omnipotent, omniscient, and omnipresent power of evil, a "corn-power," over which no human being has control or even minimal influence. The repeated blood-and-dust death image in Zelazny's unusual story might be taken as an appropriate theme for King's:

> ". . . I am blood. I go first."
> "And I am dust. I follow you."

As the Cumaean sybil says to Aeneas in Virgil's epic when she and he, in the lower world, are discussing the ironclad will of the fates, "Abandon hope by prayer to make the gods / Change their decrees"—so here in the cornfields of Nebraska all appeal to pity through prayer is useless. Even closer in futility to the intrusions of doomed Victoria and Albert into those Nebraska hell-fields are the dark words that the traveler in Dante's *Inferno* notices over the gates of a lower world that he is about to enter with no certitude of ever finding a safe outlet—words that, in the case of the devil-land of King's devil-children, ought to read: "Abandon all hope, you who [accidentally] enter here."

Outer-Evil from Venus / Inner-Evil on Earth

"I Am the Doorway" is a perfect example of the "surrealist gothic" discussed in connection with *The Stand*. Like the mythical king of an imaginary Camelot, the protagonist is an astronaut called Arthur who, along with fellow astronaut Cory (the "core" or "heart" of the matter), carry out a space mission to the planet Venus, armed with "five souped-up TV cameras and a nifty little telescope with a zillion lenses and filters." This is their twentieth-century Arthurian romance. Half-jokingly, half-seriously, Arthur and Cory are asked by the NASA people to "find some nice, dumb little blue men for us to study and exploit and feel superior to," or "even the ghost of Howdy

Doody" (62). Superficially, the astronauts find "nothing but nothing"—"no vegetation and no sign of life." Nevertheless, despite negative results, the love/sex planet presents a frightening image of death and unspeakable horror. In Arthur's grim words: "It was like a skull that's been picked clean" (64). It turned to be the twentieth-century equivalent of the waste land in Chrétien de Troyes's twelfth-century *Perceval*.

What happens is that the ocean landing of the return trip is so rough that Arthur is hospitalized for two years, can no longer walk, and, like the vampires in *'Salem's Lot*, is "dead from the waist down" (*NS*, 69). Thus he comes to resemble the impotent Fisher King in the medieval *Perceval*, except that here the waste land comes before—and perhaps causes—the impotence. What happens additionally is that Arthur's fingers become itchy, redden into "tiny perfect circlets . . . of infection," the flesh, disgustingly, becoming "soft and gelid, like the flesh of an apple gone rotten" (66–67). Were it not for the illustration on the front cover of the 1979 Signet edition, a novice reader is not likely to guess what follows. Eyes appear on Arthur's hands, eyes that have the power to explode whatever they focus upon, yet have the power to enliven the crippled Arthur in the process so as to give him "life" below the waist. At such times of destruction, Arthur can "stand" (69)—his standing covertly symbolizing the restoration of phallic power that climaxes, or only appears to climax, in the destruction by explosion of whatever the finger-eyes decide to dislike—which seems to be anything earthly (animal, vegetable, or mineral) that they look at.

It is no accident that "whatever had gotten hold of [Arthur] had done it in deep space or in that weird orbit around Venus" (70), Venus being the traditional planet of love or sexuality. In this piece of science fiction, the earth-victims are exclusively male (an incredulous Richard, to whom the whole impossible story is being recounted [72] and the unnamed innocent boy in frayed denim cutoffs who walks along the beach at sunset)—although, to be sure, there is nothing to indicate that orgasmic destructions would always have been so sexually limited. Unlike the androgynous vampires of *'Salem's Lot*, however, they destroy with their eyes, not their mouths. According to *Danse Macabre*, such inexplicable horror is of the "predestinate" kind, "coming from outside [from the planet Venus] like a stroke of lightning" (62). It is thus that King demeans and denigrates into an abyss of horror the sentimental old medieval cliché, part of the well-known Petrarchan love tradition, that human eyes were like lovely stars.

Arthur tries to explain to the incredulous Richard that he has become the "doorway" or "window" through which alien beings can peer upon hated earthlings to annihilate them. This door image is the story's primary metaphor and title. "I am the doorway" is a stark parody of a line from the sermon on the Good Shepherd ("I am the door" [John 10:9]) that is repeated incrementally with greater and more maddening power each time Arthur utters it (61, 66, 69–70). Apparently, the phrase had already been part of the conversation between Arthur and Richard prior to the beginning of the story itself, for Richard "repeated thoughtfully" what he has just heard: "You are the doorway," as if trying to understand what Arthur has been trying to say. King adroitly draws the title of the short story (which a reader would already have seen) into the beginning of the story itself. Thus the first appearance of the biblical parody is already an echo and a repetition. As though devil-possessed, Arthur tries to explain what it is like to share a body with an alien creature: "It was a feeling like no other in the world—as if I were a portal just slightly ajar through which they were peeking at a world which they hated and feared" (66). These eye-aliens are what *Danse Macabre* characterizes as things-without-a-name (50), their anonymity dovetailing perfectly with that wretched unnamed boy (71) whose head exploded "as if someone had put a hand grenade in his skull" (63) when Arthur held out his hands toward him (in greetings, perhaps—or in warning).

Through this "hand-doorway" the outside evil—or whatever it is—is able to enter into Arthur and become an inside evil, manifesting itself in the unwanted eyes. A brutal parody of outside-inside motif occurs when, in a fit of resentment, Arthur attempts to destroy one of the eyes (now an "inside" evil) by poking at it with the tip of a pencil (an "outside" evil) and "felt excruciating agony slam up [his] arm" (70). It was this unwise "self-blinding" that stirred up latent eye-angers and led directly to the destruction of the beach boy in the frayed denim cutoffs. The death and mysterious burial of this boy, and later of Richard [72], occur merely because they are "looked at" by astronaut Arthur. Their deaths-by-explosion are preceded by countless images of looking: looking at the planet Venus, looking out over the dunes, looking at one's own face and seeing a monster, seeing over the rim of the universe a distorted, living monolith—the suspicious looks and lookings of the investigator from the Navy department.

"I Am the Doorway" concludes with a succession of science fiction nightmares. After the death of the unnamed boy, Arthur notices the "first signs of structural change" in his hands as the fingers slowly begin to shorten [72]. Although it is not so specifically described, the hands are slowly turning into other "heads," metamorphosing poor Arthur into a kind of three-headed monster, a Cerberus perhaps, the fierce three-headed dog who guards the River Styx in the lower world of Virgil's *Aeneid*. To avoid the monsterizing of his person, Arthur soaks both hands in kerosene, and before the alien eyes realize what he is about to do, plunges both hands into fire. Thus, with unexpected suddenness and an ultimate suicidal momentum, King has insidiously arranged for his protagonist—his Arthurian victim, as it were—to fulfill a famous, but highly controversial, injunction concerning both "eyes" and "hands" in the Sermon on the Mount: "If thy right eye is an occasion of sin to thee, pluck it out . . . and if thy right hand scandalize thee, cut it off" (Matthew 5:29–30).

But the attempt to eliminate the eye-aliens through self-mutilation proves futile. King not only devastates the Hebraic images of moral restraint implied in the famous gospel passage, but (almost without warning) hurls his helpless reader "over the [Lovecraftian] rim of the universe and into the fires of hell itself" (71)—suicide ("shotgun into my mouth") being the only alternative for this tormented, twentieth-century Arthur. Muted images of oppressive air, bright sand, and burning glass in the conclusion of the eight-page "Night Surf"—images that subtly suggest more than they actually say—pale by comparison with what surrealist Salvador Dali used to call the "paranoid image," the simple line with which "I am the Doorway" concludes: "There is a perfect circle of twelve golden eyes on my chest."

The image is nuclear and apocalyptic, and virtually explodes in the face of the reader with the force of an obsessive and almost hallucinatory irrational—the "seamed and fissured face as enigmatic as . . . driftwood sculptures" (62). One point of power in the final line (among several) is the "naturalness" of the perfect circle of twelve that—in its own way, deadly and golden—echoes the "unnaturalness" of the inhuman eyes themselves, earlier conceived as perfect circlets (66–67). Astronomically discredited medieval symbols of divine perfection[9] since Johannes Kepler's discovery of the three laws of planetary motion,[10] these perfect circles from outer space are designed to contrast with the "eccentric orbit . . . radical and deteriorating" of Arthur's rocket exploration of the planet Venus (63–64). The NASA people had been "praying" that the astronauts would find something "to study and exploit and feel superior to" (62). But the answer from outer space only confirmed an old "error" of the Dark Ages about perfect circles, and in this story science experiences the fate of the beachboy who had the misfortune to be looked at by the aliens: "as if someone had scooped out his brains and put a hand grenade in his skull."

Chapter Eight
Fantasies of Summer and Fall
Full of Sound and Fury

With brief seasonal subtitles, *Different Seasons* (1982) attempts to bind together four unusual novellas of varying lengths and moods. Taken from the optimistic "Essay on Man" of the eighteenth-century English poet Alexander Pope, "Hope Springs Eternal" is the subtitle of the vernal season, "Rita Hayworth and Shawshank Redemption"— a subtitle that is, at the tag-end of the violence-ridden twentieth century, little more than a pleasant, but not quite believable, cliché. The second and longest of the novellas, the sinister "Apt Pupil," is a "Summer of Corruption"—an apparent variation on the "winter of our discontent" from the oft-quoted opening line of Shakespeare's *Richard III*. The third and autumnal season, "The Body" (widely acknowledged as the most nearly autobiographical of King's works), flirts with the attractive deceptions of an American Eden and is, consequently, a "Fall from Innocence." The fourth, "The Breathing Method," easily the most fantastic of the group, is appropriately subtitled with Shakespeare's late fantasy-romance, *The Winter's Tale*. While this brilliant quartet of tales does not deal with the unabashed horrors and terrors of the more famous novels, nevertheless, according to King's personal observations, "elements of horror can be found in all of the tales, not just in 'The Breathing Method'—that business with the slugs in 'The Body' is pretty gruesome, as is much of the dream imagery in 'Apt Pupil' " (*DS*, 502). Although (as noted in chapter 1 of this book) King raised sharp objection to psychiatrist-author Janet Jeppson, when she suggested that he has been "writing about it ever since"—"it" being the train accident that killed a young playmate—he admits in his afterword to *Different Seasons* that, with respect to horror in general, only "God knows why," sooner or later, "my mind always seems to turn back in that [gothic] direction (502).

"Rita Hayworth and Shawshank Redemption," the first "season," is the most strangely titled of all King's stories, the kind of story

("with a homosexual rape scene") that Susan Norton's mother com-
plained that "sissy-boy" novelist Ben Mears had written. Taking
place in an imaginary Maine prison called Shawshank, the story is
supposedly narrated by one of the inmates (nicknamed "Red"), a
clever entrepreneur who can "get it for you" for a price, that is,
obtain whatever a prisoner might like, or need, from the outside
world: pictures, comic books, posters, panties from a wife or girl
friend, etc. Red's hundred-page story concerns a banker-prisoner,
Andy Dufresne, sentenced to life imprisonment because of incriminating circumstantial evidence in the murder of his wife and her
lover. Though consistently denied parole, and tragically unfortunate
in attempting to prove his innocence, Andy becomes the financial
wizard of the prison ("quiet, well-spoken, respectful, non-violent"
[95]), with an unusual smile and a cool far-away look. Red is in-
trigued by Andy's strange requests, two in particular: a rock-hammer
and a Rita Hayworth poster. What Andy is doing with these
objects—the Hayworth poster changing to other shapely females as
the years go by—is revealed only at the end of the novella, when the
reader learns that for years and years (1949–75) Andy had been
digging himself a tunnel, and successfully concealing the cellblock
escape route (the "hole") behind sexy, and inevitably distracting, pin-
up posters.

Both the prolonged tunneling and the subsequent escape are as
improbable as the incriminating evidence that incarcerated Andy in
Shawshank State Prison in the first place (18–25). But King makes
the narrative plausible by having whole sections of Red's account
reported as gossip, rumor, and prison talk, slowly turning Andy
Dufresne into a legendary folk hero about whom (like Robert Frost's
Paul Bunyon, Washington Irving's Icabod Crane, or some medieval
Arthurian knight) one tends to expect the unexpected. Unlike the
final section of *Carrie*, which attempts to verify everything through
newspaper reports, eyewitness accounts, and court transcripts, here
King exercises his ingenuity by having everything sustained through
sheer guesswork and speculation.

Of all the plot improbabilities in "Rita Hayworth and Shawshank
Redemption," however, the most hilarious is the author's success in
hiding in his rectum a one-hundred-page (or more) manuscript about
Andy Dufresne's life, prison escape, and detailed plans for secret life
in Mexico (30, 101). On the occasion of the author-prisoner's parole,
this rectal secreting is done so as to escape detection from guards

during a strip-down physical examination prior to final release. Thus what the average King enthusiast has been devouring with such interest derives from the same part of the human anatomy that is naturally used to eliminate foul-smelling body wastes, but was "unnaturally" violated (and presumably also much enlarged) by the prison "sisters" during one of their many sodomitic escapades.[1] Both this rectal literary joke, and the impossibles and improbables of the quasi-legendary prison career of Andy Dufresne, give the Popean subtitle, "Hope Springs Eternal," a rather hopeless resonance indeed—implying, one supposes, that if you believe this "story," you will believe just about anything.[2] The "redemption" part of the title has various implications, not the least of which is the elimination of the Bible-quoting Warden Norton, who never so much as cracked a smile and "would have felt right at home" with those infernal New England preachers, the "Mathers, Cotton and Increase" (56).

"The Breathing Method," the fourth and last "season," and a gothic/fantasy successor to such traditional Christmas stories as the medieval romance *Sir Gawain and the Green Knight* and Charles Dickens's *Christmas Carol*, is an out-and-out tall tale best suited to winter in which, as one editor points out in connection with Shakespeare's *Winter's Tale*, "no one expects any probability."[3] In folklore and legend (the Roman *Saturnalia*, ancient rituals surrounding the birth of Mithra, the tradition of the *modrenacht* among the Angles, etc.), the season of the winter solstice (21 December) is often filled with fantasy. The main incident in the fourth season is the birth of a child from an accidentally decapitated woman (Sandra Stansfield) occurring "on the eve of that birth we have celebrated for two thousand years" (462). The young woman is unmarried and wearing a false wedding ring, and this mysterious and/or magical birth thus parallels, or even parodies, the traditional Christian belief in the virgin birth recounted in the gospel of Luke. Despite the potential for blasphemous satire (which King does not elsewhere resist), the parallel is not overstressed, and at several points only gently reinforced: (1) by a quotation from a Roman Stoic that might well have come from the Pauline epistles, to the effect that *There is no comfort without pain; thus we define salvation through suffering* (461, 482–83); and (2) by having the tall tale of an impossible Christmas Eve birth told by an eighty-year-old physician, who thereby parallels the author of the gospel of Luke, traditionally believed to have been a physician, from whom the story of the virgin birth is almost exclusively derived.

Without demeaning the power of these spring and winter narratives, "Rita Hayworth" and "Breathing Method" appear as prologue and epilogue to the central tales of summer and fall that are among King's finest creations: "Apt Pupil" and "The Body." The former concerns a thirteen year old's not-quite-accidental discovery of a Nazi war criminal living secretly in California, while the latter recounts the adventures of several twelve year olds who set out to find the dead body of a boy struck by a train, and in the process one of them (the teller of the tale) makes significant discoveries about his personal sensitivity and poetic proclivities. Taken together, "Apt Pupil" and "The Body" are youth-oriented companion pieces, offering in-depth analyses of young boys who can easily take their place among King's other preteens: Mark Petrie, Richie Boddin, Danny and Ralphie Glick, Danny Torrance, and Marty Coslaw. Interestingly, in both "Apt Pupil" and "The Body," King again explores depth after desperate depth of feelings about father-son relationships that are central to a sympathetic understanding of much of his work—a psychological dimension too often glossed over by reviewers, who seem to harp exclusively on elements of terror, horror, and the supernatural. [4]

Corpses that Refuse to Stay Buried

The protagonist of "Apt Pupil" is a thirteen-year-old "innocent" in the pleasant-enough beginnings of this California revelation, but a seventeen-year-old criminal in its tragic conclusion. A stereotypical American boy of WASP background—the family was Methodist (164)—Todd Bowden has the kind of "summer" face that might easily be found advertising Kellogg's Corn Flakes: hair the color of ripe corn, white even teeth, lightly tanned skin marred by not even the first shadow of adolescent acne" (109). Despite the gradual deterioration of Todd's personality throughout this 175-page "Summer of Corruption," his face matures but never loses its boyish attractiveness: "young, blond, and white" (281). Even toward the end of "Apt Pupil," when Todd is one of four victorious boys named to Southern Cal's All Stars, the newspaper photograph is "grinning openly out at the world from beneath the bill of his baseball cap" (254). When identified as the probable killer of local derelicts, he is remembered as having an "ain't-life-grand" air about his improbable face (282).

In addition to a happy-time television reaction to nearly everything (good or bad), several other aspects of Todd's personality—

always superficially favorable—receive considerable attention: his "aptness" as a school student, his high degree of intelligence and foresight, his full-blooded teenage slang, and his outstanding athletic abilities. These apparent positives in Todd's All-American makeup, however, inevitably deteriorate. So boyishly appealing and attractive at first, showing "perfect teeth that had been flouridated since the beginning of his life and bathed thrice a day in Crest toothpaste" (113), his smiles sour into the sardonic expression of a psychopath beaming out "rich and radiant" (131) as he eagerly absorbs Nazi stories about gas chambers, conspirators hung by piano wires, or lampshades designed of human skin. On one occasion, when the old concentration camp commander (Kurt Dussander, whom Todd all-too-willingly befriends) is forced to tell Todd about the experimental nerve gas (poetically nicknamed *Pegasus*) that caused its victims to scream, laugh, vomit, and helplessly defecate, the All-American Boy is happily consuming two delicious chocolate Ring Dings. Even old reprobate Dussander reacts negatively, not only in being forced to remember horrors he himself eagerly perpetrated in German concentration camps, but especially because of Todd's enthusiastic "That was a good story, Mr. Dussander" (136). Ironically, King puts in the mouth of the old Nazi, wanted by the Israelis for being "one of the greatest butchers of human beings ever to live" (262), reactions that are likely to pass through readers themselves when he says aloud to the boy, "You are a monster." Innocent-looking Todd reminds Dussander that "according to the books I read, *you're* the monster, Mr. Dussander," who sent thirty-five hundred a day into the ovens "before the Russians came and made you stop" (127). The next time Dussander (in something resembling teenage slang) is tempted to damn Todd as "putrid little monster," he only *thinks* it (135), keeping to himself his disgust with Todd's behavior, even though that behavior is viciously patterned after his own (giving an inkling of King's attitude toward the relationship of postwar American behavior to the Nazis.)

The name Todd suggests "toddy," a pleasant drink of brandy or whiskey mixed with hot water, sugar, and spices. Like the boy's blue-eyed All-American appearance, therefore, his name has sweet connotations. Winter suggests a sinister undercurrent—quite apt, one might add—to this attractive first name, since "Todd" is similar to the German word for death, *Tod.*[5] Kurt Dussander's name derives from *Peter Kurtin, Monster of Düsseldorf*, a novel about an actual

criminal included in Father Callahan's recollections of gothic junk
in *'Salem's Lot* (296). But Dussander's American pseudonym is the
kinder-sounding "Arthur Denker," the first name deriving from the
mythic medieval king,[6] and the patronym from yet another German
word, "thinker" (*Denker*). The fake last name covertly suggests the
octogenarian's cleverness in concealing his true identity by skillfully
avoiding detection and capture by sharp Israeli authorities for so
many years. Dussander's ability to "think" things through is so
masterful that inexperienced Todd, who at one point had the potential of being an absolute blackmailer, comes to feel that "his skull
had turned to window-glass and all things were flashing inside in
large letters" (201). The living room of Dussander's house contains a
neat symbol of all the false facades in "Apt Pupil" (Americans and ex-
Nazis included): "the fake fireplace" that was "faced with fake bricks"
(115).

The Jekyll/Hyde qualities of the Todd/Denker names seem—and
indeed *are*—the exact opposite of what they pleasantly suggest, and
have parallels in some unusual literary techniques. The most important of these is the series of empty-headed clichés, banalities, prov-
erbs, and (on Todd's part) slang simplicities that are placed in plot
situations in such a way as to point up their utter shallowness. As
names reverse (e.g., from sweet "toddy" to grim "death"), so do the
cliché-drenched conversations among the doomed older characters.

Important among these typically American pseudoprofundities are
the following. Todd's parents "don't believe in spanking" because
"corporal punishment causes more problems than it cures" (115).
Todd's father (Dick Bowden) thinks that "kids should find out about
life as soon as they can—the bad as well as the good." His silly
rationale is that "life is a tiger you have to grab by the tail, and if
you don't know the nature of the beast it will eat you up" (120).
Dick Bowden balances off his wife's cliché, "Waste not, want not,"
with his own innocuous "Not by a long chalk" (138). Todd's teacher
(the well-intentioned Mrs. Anderson) lectures the students of the
California school (of which sweet-looking Todd is one) about finding
"YOUR GREAT INTEREST," hers being "collecting nineteenth-century
post cards" (117). The guidance counselor (satirically nicknamed
"Rubber Ed," "Sneaker Pete," and the "Ked Man" by mocking high
school students) idiotically supposes that his rubber-covered Keds
gives him "real rapport" with the students. He too has an assortment
of dismal colloquialisms on which he thinks he can structure educa-

tional success: that he could "get right down to it" with the kids, "get into their hangups," knew what a "bummer" was, and understood and sympathized when "someone was doing a number on your head" (166).

The upshot of all this "right-thinking," superficial claptrap that passes for wisdom—a parody of certain educational practices that dominated American society during the period of the 1976 bicentennial, the time-frame of the story (206)—is that Todd Bowden, one of the young people these insights were supposed to direct into proper channels of patriotic behavior, becomes a Nazi admirer and hobo murderer. King is not saying that benign and "liberating" clichés are inherently wrong or that they cause Todd's inclination toward social misbehavior. Rather, his gothic perspective is that benevolent philosophies, reduced to thoughtless aphorisms and innocuous clichés, are utterly powerless against the boy's adamantine malevolence. Todd, too, is entrapped in his own kind of verbal superficiality, mostly teenage American slang that might have been considered "cute" in something other than a California neo-Nazi context: "Gotcha," "Right on," "You'll go ape," "School's cool," "Crazy, baby," "It blows my wheels," "Blasts from the past," etc. Only infrequently does Todd trot out some really humorous wit, as on the occasion when his mother brings up a matter that Todd does not want to deal with, and he leaves her with the wise crack: "I've gotta put an egg in my shoe and beat it" (134). All too frequently, unfortunately, his mind reverts to mindless banalities, as when, entrapped by Dussander, he thinks of a "cartoon character with an anvil suspended over its head" (202).

Possibly offensive to some readers—and this may explain the negative criticism of "Apt Pupil" by some reviewers—is the fact that the Nazi proves the more elegant and perceptive in language skills than the sentimental, cliché-ridden Americans, who—as Dussander scornfully points out—"put photographs of firemen rescuing kittens from trees on the front pages of city newspapers" (202). Thus at the dinner table with Todd's parents, when offered another glass of cognac by Todd's mother, Dussander gracefully declines with the proverb, "One must never overdo the sublime" (149). When in the office of the guidance counselor, Dussander convinces his listener by pretending he "was raised to believe that a man's family came before everything" (169)—a cliché, to be sure, but just about the only one in the entire novella known to be false at the time it is uttered. When Todd is

completely entrapped by the old Nazi's psychological counterthrusts,
Dussander comforts the boy by suggesting that "no situation is
static" (202). When confronted with murderous hatred in Todd's eyes
("that dark, burning, speculative glance"), Dussander realizes that he
had to protect himself, because "one underestimates at one's own
risk" (175). At the complex business of what might be called "verbal
survival," Dussander is extremely crafty: careful to manipulate false
words, while never falling victim to them, always rising above his
own (and others') deceptive language to remain—desperately necessary for a former Nazi—free to survive! Adolf Hitler once asserted
that "something of even the most shameless prevarication will find
lodging and stick,"[7] but Dussander is several notches beyond mere
Nazi lies and prevarications. Whatever he does, he pulls off with
considerable finesse and with an enviable command of language that
makes him all the more dangerous because his basic malevolence is so
difficult to detect by naive Americans—like the Bowdens and the
Frenches in this novella—who are too easily satisfied with facades
and superficialities. As Dussander says on the occasion of his deceptive visit to the office of the guidance counselor in the guise of Todd's
grandfather: "In my time I have stayed ahead of Wiesenthal and
pulled the wool over the eyes of Himmler himself," and "if I cannot
fool one American public school teacher, I will pull my winding-
shroud around me and crawl down into my grave" (165).

One of the perhaps less obvious purposes of "Apt Pupil" is to
dramatize the confrontation between an intelligent but inexperienced
teenager (whose German name means "death") and an intelligent but
far more sinister, yet "extremely urbane," ex-Nazi (whose German
pseudonym means "thinker"). King engages in a skillfull balancing
act, seesawing the blackmail potential of the boy over against the
psychological counterthrusts of the Nazi, highlighting differences in
language they both use. What to the boy is "grooving on it," "getting off on it" (i.e., the Nazi atrocities), to language-sensitive old
Dussander is the behavior of an aficionado (121). At first the boy and
his American slang seem to win out. For example, every time Dussander "tried to slip into generalities" concerning the atrocities, the
"gooshy stuff" that the boy liked to hear about, "Todd would frown
severely and ask him specific questions to get him back on the track"
(131). With "absurd American self-confidence," and pummeled by
his own knee-jerk slang, Todd never studies the "possible consequences" of the memories he has stirred up and set aswirling (198–

99). He acts like the "sorcerer's apprentice, who had brought the brooms to life but who had not possessed enough wit to stop them once they got started" (141). This insensitive, damn-the-torpedoes behavior on the part of an All-American boy, who had been raised by well-meaning parents "without all those needless guilts" (181), and got an A + on a Nazi research paper from a teacher who never gave such grades, proves fatal. Once the sleeping specters of a pitiless past have been awakened, literate Herr Dussander reverts to Nazism again. "Nostalgia" for a history of gas chambers and hideous ovens takes over his whole personality (135), and like an articulate Red Death that might please even Edgar Allan Poe himself, holds "illimitable [verbal] dominion over all."

What distinguishes Stephen King from a mere hack writer grinding out novels for popularity and a fast buck is that, in "Apt Pupil," he himself never gets self-deceived by the clichés of his own conceptions. Though the subsidiary characters of "Apt Pupil" (Dick and Monica Bowden, Ed French, etc.) are entrapped by clichés, they are still multidimensional, much deeper than the bromides in which they so ardently believe. Dussander himself may be "one of the greatest butchers of human beings ever to live," but he is no pasteboard Hollywood Nazi. He may scorn American slang and wince every time young Bowden utters one of his teenage "witticisms," but every once in a while even Dussander "marvel[s] at the American love of jargon" (159).

Especially interesting is a final exposure to American slang that occurs at the end of the novella when Dussander takes the poison pills he has always kept in clever reserve. Beginning to grow dim with death, Dussander overhears the "quavering" but "triumphant" voices of some cribbage players using typical card-game talk: "How do you like *those* apples" and "I'll peg out"; and for the first time in his snobbish old life, the conceited concentration camp commander acknowledges to himself that Americans do indeed have a "turn for idiom," what he is finally and sentimentally capable of realizing is "wonderful." In his last moments, the childless octogenerian finds himself wishing he could tell his "apt pupil"—a kind of surrogate Nazi son—that "talking to him had been better than listening to the run of his own thoughts" (266). In reading these final meanderings, one must remember that the "apt pupil's" questions and answers had been mostly slangish, and that Dussander's conversation, though conniving and degenerate, was *always* literate, elegant, and graceful.

On his deathbed, the old Nazi inclines toward the Americanisms he had been scorning for more than a hundred pages of narrative. He enters his eternity with the idea that he is somehow—in the American slang—"pegging out." Of course, Stephen King does not resist a final twist of the ironic knife. Criminal Dussander cannot possibly "peg out." For hands with "hungry fingers" were "reaching eagerly up" from his deathbed to "grab him" (like the wrathful souls of the River Styx in the seventh canto of Dante's *Inferno*); and Dussander's death thoughts "broke up in a steepening spiral of darkness, and he rode down that spiral as if down a greased slide, down and down, to whatever dreams there are" (267). As he dies, it is as if the tongues of the "unquiet dead" (the former victims of his gas chamber atrocities) were crying out to him their own colloquialism: How do you like *these* apples, Dussander?—his eternity being suddenly recognized as a nightmarish place where there is absolutely no possibility of ever "pegging out."

Dussander's desire for "rest," while dying from a deliberate overdose of pills, is disrupted by a fear of hideous dreams that the dead and damned might have to endure. His thoughts, of course, echo Hamlet's famous soliloquy, "To be or not to be"); and this technique of literary echo is typical of King, who sometimes—though not here—goes out of his way to specifically justify a literary allusion. The glancing reference to Hamlet's famous fear ("for in that sleep of death what dreams may come"—hardly an original thought at this late date) interweaves ominously into the wise sayings, banalities, and bromides that hammer away at "Apt Pupil" for more than a hundred pages. Dussander may be a former Nazi, but he is the kind of sophisticated old degenerate who would have read and in part probably memorized *Hamlet*, a Nordic play on a revengeful Nordic subject. It is consistent with his temper and flair for the histrionic to pass away into the "dreams" of death with a graceful Shakespearean flourish.

The Target Was a Dead Boy

Nothing in the novels of Stephen King, not even the autobiographical parts of *Danse Macabre*, is so intensely personal as the two-hundred-word introduction to "The Body," the third novella of *Different Seasons*, composed immediately after the first draft of *'Salem's*

Lot and exploiting nonvampire aspects of masculine identity—this time in teenage boys. "The Body" is supposed to be narrated by protagonist-novelist Gordie Lachance, who is the presumed author of the introduction. But the mask is papery thin, and more than once—by including adaptations of previously published short stories[8] and by concluding the novella with blatantly autobiographical snatches (432)—the problematic psyche of Stephen King breaks through. From time to time, there are glancing autobiographical parallels even among other characters. In *'Salem's Lot*, Ben Mears, when under suspicion of combined murder and perversion, quotes Mark Twain (who significantly has the same first name as Ben's young mirror-image, Mark Petrie) as having said that a "novel was a confession to everything by a man who had never done anything" (97). While such popular stories as "Graveyard Shift" may recount the terror of an actual descent into the basement of a rat-filled factory, "The Body" makes deeper psychological cuts into the "everything," the "dreadful possibilities," the "awful . . . unknown"—and attempts "to look the [subconscious] Gorgon in the face" (*SL*, 374). As the poet Hart Crane once phrased it, the "scimitar" of self-appraisal found "more than flesh to fathom in its fall."[9]

Punning on his own name, Gordon, the protagonist-novelist of "The Body" realizes what a "thin film there is between your rational man costume—the writer with leather elbow-patches on his corduroy jacket—and the capering, Gorgon myths of childhood" (418). Lachance (though actually King) works out his word-problems more matter-of-factly than some twentieth-century poets, but no less poignantly. In "Burnt Norton," T. S. Eliot believes that "Words strain / Crack sometimes break, under the burden, / Under the tension, slip, slide, perish, / Decay with imprecision." Lachance-King's repeatedly stated anguish is simply that the "most important things are the hardest things to say" because they "lie too close to wherever your secret heart is buried"—interesting sensitivity on the part of one who, under his own name, elsewhere explains that the "business of creating horror is much the same as the business of paralyzing an opponent with the martial arts . . . finding vunerable points and then applying pressure there" (*DM*, 68). The tripartite appearance of the secret-heart motif (289, 390, 395) obviously indicates its sensitive importance, but one cannot help remembering the "life of careful academicism" (i.e., Matt Burke's in *'Salem's Lot*) that "refuse[d] to plant an intellectual foot on any ground until it had been footnoted in triplicate" (299). The vulnerable point for Gordie Lachance, as also for novelist Ben Mears in 'Salem's Lot, is the secret self, the creative and sensitive nature that can all too easily be cruelly misunderstood. The secret self of alcoholic Father Callahan of 'Salem's Lot, for instance, was the effeminate face of "Mr. Flip," his imaginary boyhood companion with "thin white face and burning eyes," the "thing that hid in the closet during the days and came out [at nights] after his mother closed the bedroom door" (352).

Assuming a poetic and almost mystical posture, Gordie recognizes that "words shrink things that seemed limitless when they were in your head to no more than living size when they're brought out." Tellingly, this popular twentieth-century author of horror tales—for one must remember that King more than Lachance is speaking here—reveals his personal horror: that the "most important things . . . are landmarks to a treasure" that "your enemies would love to steal away." Later in the novella, a half-retarded boy (Vern Tessio) tries to retrieve a "quart jar of pennies" hidden under the front porch of his house. Unfortunately, like Lachance-King's landmarks to a treasure that one's enemies would love to steal away, Vern's treasure map was accidentally burned by his mother (an "enemy") along with old homework papers, candy wrappers, comic magazines, and joke-books, in order to start the cook fire one morning, and Vern's map for locating his copper treasures went "right up the kitchen chimney." Vern is half-afraid that his crafty brother (yet another "enemy") might have found the secret penny jar, an explanation that was clear enough to all his twelve-year-old buddies (whose corpse-searching activities form the basis of the novella), but "Vern refused to believe it" (297). Toward the end of the novella, Lachance-King will wrap up his secret in a symbol, a missing blueberry bucket, perhaps imaginary, belonging to a dead boy (Ray Brower), whose train-struck body is what the morbidly curious boys are seeking.

The momentary formula in the penny-jar incident, however, is King equals Lachance equals Vern, and this ought to be apparent to perceptive readers. But as Henry James points out in his "Art of Fiction," too often such subtle symbolic parallels are likely to be overlooked. Therefore, the protagonist-author of "The Body" who has—in James's phrase—"reasons of his own" for considering these sensitive parallels important, continues more explicitly in his introduction so that the reader can "see it": "*And you may make revelations that cost you dearly only to have people look at you in a funny way, not understanding what you have said at all, or why you thought it was so important that you almost cried while you were saying it. That's the worst, I think. When the secret stays locked within not for want of a teller but for want of an understanding ear."* The entire novella is balanced and counterbalanced with this need-to-reveal versus fear-to-reveal paradox, and thus the ultimate revelation turns out to be nothing more than a blue symbol (the "blue bucket" that Gordie goes groping after in the incessant pursuits of his imagination [419–20]), timeless yearnings for meaning and understanding, perhaps not entirely understood even by the author himself—imponderables that the death-haunted poet Percy Shelley, in his *Prometheus Unbound*, sought for in the "unascended heaven / Pinnacled deep in the intense inane" (3:203–4).

Several portions of these fearful needs are repeated on the occasion when Gordie prepares to keep nightwatch for his sleeping buddies against improbable ghosts. What Gordie Lachance sees is not a "grotesquely ambulatory bedsheet" stealing spectrelike through the trees (38), but something so delicately ambiguous that one cannot tell, for an instant or two, whether it is girl or female deer: "her eyes weren't brown but a dark, dusty black"—"she looked serenely at me"—"my stomach and genitals filled with a hot dry excitement" (389). Deliberately paraphrasing Robert Frost's poem, "Two Look at Two" (except that in this case it becomes a boy looking at a doe—as it were, "one-looking-at-one"), the four-paragraph passage sounds Gordie-depths of Frost-like feelings of delicacy and sensitivity. King even exploits the implications of Frost's name when Gordie is "frozen solid" with fear and awe and perhaps even loving expectation. For a brief and ecstatic moment, Gordie has chanced upon his American Eden.

A similar echo (this time from Frost's "After Apple-Picking") occurs in *'Salem's Lot* when novelist Ben Mears compares looking at one of the avenues of the soon-to-be-haunted town to "looking through a thin pane of ice—like the one you can pick off the top of the town cistern in November," and everything is "wavy and misty and in some places it trails off into nothing" (*SL*, 13).[10] The Frost allusion in *'Salem's Lot* is perhaps not so subtle as that of "The Body," although in both instances the quasi-quotation is intended to emphasize delicate aspects of the male psyche, a matter of considerable significance in both novel and novella. Interestingly, both Ben and Gordie, novelist-protagonists in successive and presumably entirely different stories, are delicately drawn together through an allusion to momentary Edens in Robert Frost's poetry.

It is on the tip of Gordie's tongue to tell his companions about the sudden appearance of the doe and the wonder and astonishment it caused, but he ends up keeping it to himself. In fact, "I've never spoken or written of it until just now, today." Gordie privately acknowledges in his novella what he never would have openly acknowledged to his adventuring twelve-year-old pals: that the delicate, or should one say feminine, feelings about a beautiful doe, rather than the machismo of actually looking at the mangled and decaying body of a boy struck by a train (obviously the main thrust of the story), were the "best part of that trip, the cleanest part" (390). All this by contrast with the diminished pleasure that literary success produces in a maturer Gordie of later years, writing being once associated with "guilty masturbatory pleasure," but later—at the time of the composition of "The Body"—associated with "cold clinical images of artificial insemination" (361).

Nonetheless, when trouble arose in Gordie's life—as on the first day in Vietnam, or when he thought his youngest son might be hydrocephalic—he would find himself "almost helplessly" returning to that morning, to the scuffed suede of her ears, the white flash of her tail" (390). Similarly, in *Firestarter*, when Andy Magee and his daughter Charlie have been pursued by the C.I.A. to a point of total exhaustion, Andy sees a large Frost-like doe "looking at him thoughtfully," and "then [she] was gone into the deeper woods with a flip of her white tail." Like Gordie in the midst of his fears, Andy, too, "felt encouraged" (127). As for "The Body," what Gordie half hopes for is that the reader's memory will jog back to the time when (some thirty pages earlier) friend Richie discovered Gordie's hidden stories in a carton in a closet. Gordie expressed reluctance to have his storytelling propensities revealed to the other boys. "I want it to be a secret," Gordie said—to which friend Richie responded, "Why? It ain't pussy. You ain't no queer. I mean, it ain't *poetry*" (361).

"The Body" is constructed in a series of episodes, each emphasizing some boyish secret, until in the final paragraphs, under the not-so-subtle guise of Gordie Lachance, King tries to give symbolic expression, through the imaginary blue bucket belonging to the dead boy, to what has been bothering him throughout a lifetime. The first secret is a place, a treehouse made of scavenged planks, splintery and knotholed, the roof of corrugated tin sheets "hawked from the dump," and built by four twelve-year-old boys: the slow-witted Teddy and Vern, the quick-witted and perceptive Chris, and the narrator Gordie. This secret place contains yet another secret place, a 12 × 10 inch compartment under the floor in which the boys hide such things as ashtrays, girlie books, *Master Detective* murder magazines, and playing cards "when some kid's father decided it was time to do the we're-really-good-pals routine" (290). What the boys do in this secret treehouse is normal enough boy-stuff: complain about parents, play cards, look at spicy magazines, use off-color language, share jokes—behavior so common among teenage boys one almost wonders why secrecy is necessary.

Visible from the outside, yet hiding the activities and even thoughts of the occupants, the secret treehouse is a necessary refuge from the irrationalities of Castle Rock parents, especially fathers. The most brutal was Teddy's psychopathic father, who "shoved the side of Teddy's head down against one of the cast-iron burner plates [of the stove] . . . yanked Teddy up by the hair of the head and did the other side," Teddy being, as a consequence, half-deaf and half-blind (292). As the author of the novella words it, "the thick glasses and the hearing aid [Teddy] wore sometimes made him look like an old man" (291). Chris's father was not much better than Teddy's, for Chris was "marked up every two weeks or so, bruises on his cheeks and neck or one eye swelled up and as colorful as a sunset, and once he came into school with a big clumsy bandage on the back of his head" (302).

Considering the often callous behavior of these parents, it is not surprising that their twelve-year-old sons entangle everything they do, consciously or unconsciously, in a web of secrets and ignorances. In addition to those already mentioned, consider that the malevolent parents are not informed of the twenty-mile adventure to find a dead body (301), that hostile rival gangs are unaware of each other's plans for the trip (301), that Billy Tessio does not realize his whispered conversation with Charlie Hogan is overheard by his despised brother (299), that Gordie remains unwilling to expose his vicious attacker (427), and that (in Gordie's story) Chico's affair with Janet occurs without his parent's knowledge (312).

Secrets confront secrets when rival gangs meet over the dead body of the boy struck by a train. The temporary triumph of the younger gang over the older (406–11) and the subsequent revenge of the defeated older boys (425–28) climax the ever-developing theme of

manliness in "The Body," and are reminiscent of, though perhaps
somewhat more believeable than, the teenage confrontation between
feminine Mark Petrie and masculine Richie Boddin in 'Salem's Lot.
The tangle of boyish secrets can be summed up in Gordie's words:
"The story never did get out . . . what I meant was that none of our
parents ever found out what we'd been up to that Labor Day week-
end" (424). "Nobody knew exactly what had happened . . . a few
stories went around [in the schoolyard]; all of them wildly wrong"
(428). Secrets are interlaced in interesting ways too numerous to
catalog here, with author-to-be Gordie becoming like that "benevolent spider," the town gossip Mabel Werts of 'Salem's Lot, who sat at
her window with telephone and high-powered binoculars "in the
center of a communications web" (72)—except that here in Castle
Rock, it might be more accurate to speak of it as Gordie's noncom-
munications web.

The deepest secrets, however, are those encircling Gordie's poetic
dispositions (so shied away from in the conversation with Richie),
creating imaginative enclosures of horror from which escape is impossible. These involve not so much the discovery of the body of the
blueberry boy, although the details are graphic enough to keep one
awake for many a night, but the insidious accuracy with which
poetic Lachance reconstructs the accident. The deceased is not found
mangled on the railroad tracks, as one might have expected, but
rather some distance away. The body is "down here" (that is, at the
botton of a railroad embankment) and "relatively intact," with its
filthy low-topped Keds caught in tall blackberry brambles. Neatly
punning on "kid" and "Keds," as though he were a poet, Lachance
explains that "I could go on all day and never get it right about the
distance between his bare feet on the ground and his dirty Keds
hanging in the bushes. It was thirty-plus inches, but it was a googol
of light years. The kid was disconnected from his Keds beyond all
hope of reconciliation. He was dead" (405). Characterizing the nonexistent future of the dead boy as "*can't, don't, won't, never, shouldn't,
wouldn't, couldn't*," Gordie realizes how relentlessly the train engine
had "knocked him out of his Keds just as it had knocked the [kid]
out of his body." Full realization was "like a dirty punch below the
belt" (404).

Readers are, of course, permitted the opinion that the train's
indifference to the life of Ray Brower was less terrible than the
insensitivity of Teddy's father, when he shoved the side of the boy's

head against one of the cast-iron burner plates of the oven, a cruelty that turns Teddy's bleak future into a living parody of the dead boy's "*can't, don't, won't, never, shouldn't, wouldn't, couldn't.*" Lachance's terrifyingly plausible reconstruction of the train accident appears with a complaint about the magnetic powers of the narrator's imagination: "a little mind-movie" one can have "whenever things get dull"—the trouble being that the little mind-movie-projector "turns around and bites" with "teeth that have been filed to points like the teeth of a cannibal" (404). Five-year-old Danny Torrance in *The Shining* has similar unnerving mental projections when a hotel's emergency fire-hose (like an insidious snake) appears to hiss out the words: "What would I want to do to a nice little boy like you . . . except bite . . . and bite . . . and bite?" (173).

The cosmic entity that cruelly shapes the lives of the young preteens of "The Body" (their many beatings, mistreatments, and eventual early deaths [429–32]) behaves like "some sentient, malevolent force," some Lovecraftian cosmic horror symbolized by the "big icy hailstones" that were striking Ray Brower's face "with an awful splatting sound that reminded us of . . . [the dead boy's] terrible and unending patience" (412). Even more frightfully, the dead Brower's eyes "filled up with round white hailstones," that, melting, ran down his cheeks as if the dead boy were "weeping for his own grotesque position" (413). (Dante employs a similar ice-eyed scene in the lowest depths of his *Inferno*, the "Ptolomaea" [canto 33] where the eyes of a treacherous reprobate fill up with frozen tears, which the hell traveler callously refuses to remove.) With consummate verbal and psychological skills, King often projects such "sentient malevolent forces" into the overwrought psyches of many of his male characters—forces that in Dante's ninth circle are a "wind" from the great wings of the diabolical Dis that freezes up the infernal slush of Cocytus. High school teacher Jim Norman in "Sometimes They Come Back," senses this force as a "black noxious beast" in the empty halls of his haunted school, senses it so deeply that he "thought it could hear it almost breathing" (*NS*, 147).

Concerned with problems of masculine identity and feminine creativity, both "The Body" and the gracefully shaped *'Salem's Lot* (analyzed in the second chapter of this book) were composed at virtually the same time and, taken together, are extensive in-depth explorations—virtual confessions, as it were—of the deepest sort of personal/creative insecurities in literate and much-divided modern man. Horror and mysticism, crudity and sensitivity, inside and out-side evil—not so mutually exclusive as one might at first imagine—overlap and intermingle, in both "The Body" and *'Salem's Lot*, to create two of the most powerful self-analytical narratives in recent American fiction. In both novel and novella, the literary scalpel of Stephen King cuts deep into his own trembling flesh (his much-troubled psyche); and the "patient"—if one might be permitted to negate a famous line in T. S. Eliot's "Love Song of J. Alfred Prufrock"—lies painfully [un]etherized upon the table." As Stephen King is himself both novelist Mears (representing light) and vampire Barlow (darkness) in *'Salem's Lot*; just so he is both the novelist Lachance (living) and the train-struck Brower (dead) in "The Body." In a real sense, both novel and novella are self-elegies; and no "Orphean lute"—in the words of Robert Lowell's equally despairing "Quaker Graveyard in Nantucket—can "call life back." Considered together, these two haunting narratives of a "body" and a "lot" may eventually—without too much fuss and embarrassment—take their place beside the "succession of flights and drops," the "little seesaw[s] of the right throbs and the wrong," in Henry James's psychologically involuted "Turn of the Screw."[11]

Chapter Nine
Metaphor as Mask for Terror: A Final Estimate

Creating stories about werewolves, vampires, and things without names are only part of Stephen King's gothic paraphernalia, the more blatant part. Frequently, less substantial creatures of a phantom world—often but not always, things *with* names—weave vaporously in and about his early stories, adhering to the imagination like gothic gossamers. They are the fleshless hands of the dead that reach out toward the reader, what "Apt Pupil" calls hands with "hungry fingers," cold but insubstantial (*DS*, 267)—all the more ominously inhuman because, as "Breathing Method" observes of the terrors of the mind, one can shoot them or stab them but cannot kill them (456). Various devices may used to achieve such haunted illusions. Among the most interesting is the introduction of a series of half-suggestions to evoke the image of a famous person, preferably someone young who died suddenly. Almost imperceptible, these semisuggestions are "pressure points" that work on the imagination through what King likes to call "trace memory" (*Firestarter*, 273)—though, unfortunately, not on every reader. In these tenuous matters apparently not all gothic readers are equally susceptible.

An intriguing example occurs in the February section of poetic, calendarlike *Cycle of the Werewolf*. The dark spirit of the famous matinee idol of silent films, the Latin lover Rudolph Valentino (who died suddenly and unexpectedly in 1926 at the age of thirty-two) is evoked by the subliminal technique of using the name Randolph, that sounds much like Rudolph, and the word "Valentines" in adjacent lines—"This year Stella *Randolph*, who runs the Tarker's Mills Set 'n Sew has received twenty *Valentines*" (21)—immediately reinforcing the ghost-suggestion of a "dark lover" with the haunting names of other attractive male movie idols (Paul Newman, Robert Redford, and John Travolta), and by naming the girl who is having erotic Valentine night-dreams about these distant lovers, the Hollywoodish "Stella" (Latin for "star"). This tissuey tomfoolery turns

ominous enough when, some dozen or so lines later, a "dark [male]
shape" blocks out the dreamy moonlight of Stella's window and
seems to enter her bedroom through a "film" or "screen" of snow. But
Stella soon realizes that the "clearly masculine shape," so "wickedly
handsome," has disappeared and indeed was "never there." What
takes the place of the Valentine movie-illusion is a "beast" (the story's
werewolf) with "shaggy fur in a silvery streak," its breath "hot but
somehow not unpleasant." Despite the gross illustration that accompanies the incident, the "wolf-rape" is never graphically described in
King's poetic prose, but veiled instead in quasi-romantic images that
might have derived from John Keats's classic poem, "The Eve of St.
Agnes." When the savage sex-wolf leaps into Stella's bedroom, for
example, he is hardly more than a "cold vapor" as he softly shakes
himself "spraying a sugarpuff of snow in the darkness," as if he were
nothing more dangerous than an imaginary reindeer. Gentle romantic
breezes from the open window cause one of the silent Valentine cards,
all fictitiously sent from inaccessible male movie idols, to "fall and
seasaw lazily to the floor in big silent arcs."[1]

Yet another, and perhaps more psychologically incisive, instance of
this kind of ghost-language occurs in "Apt Pupil," where Todd Bowden's father, while reprimanding his son about low high school
grades, accidentally spells out the word *DAD*—unconsciously indicating his annoyance over his son's excessive interest in another
fatherlike figure, the Nazi commander Kurt Dussander. In enumerat-
ing his son's grades and commenting upon them, he says: "One *B*.
Four *C*'s. One *D*. A *D!*—Todd, your mother's not showing it, but
she's really upset" (*DS*, 136). What the elder Bowden is really saying
through the accidental selection of these letter grades is that one
father (that is, one "DAD") ought to be sufficient, expressing unconsciously his own hurt at being rejected by attributing his feelings to
the mother. That the grades, as enumerated, descend from B (unconsciously standing for Bowden) to D (standing for Dussander) is yet
another inadvertant symbol that betrays important but unspoken
thought.

King often produces prose of the finest quality when manipulating
nuances and innuendoes, or what in *The Shining* he considers "insubstantial shades" that grasp at the "strings of reality," or when arrang-
ing incidents that seem to overlap and interweave with few rational
connections (281, 288). The imaginative "Drinks on the House" and
"Conversations at the Party" chapters in *The Shining* are interesting

examples of extended fantasies where real and ghost worlds are divided by the "filmiest of perceptual curtains" (340); and the imagined sounds, for example, of "low, throaty female laughter" in a cocktail lounge "seem to vibrate like a fairy ring around the viscera and the genitals" of Jack Torrance (341), who had "TAKEN THE PLEDGE, GONE ON THE WAGON, SWORN OFF" (342). In a "graceful cacophony" of entwined time-frames, "talk" of the assassinated archduke of Austria (World War I) and Neville Chamberlain (World War II) blends into the imaginary martinis, wittily called "Martians" that have "landed," that an unstable Jack thinks he is drinking at the hotel bar; and "breakfast, lunch and dinner for seventy years were all being served simultaneously just behind him" in his disoriented mind (341). He imagines himself dancing erotically with a "beautiful woman" (actually the specter of the murdered rich woman in the tub of the hotel bathroom)—who, like so many of King's characters, is wearing a "mask" during her imaginary sex-dance, a "cat's eye mask" that conceals the real nature of her ghastly and decayed condition (346).

One cannot leave this discussion of King's extraordinary use of shadow language as sinister metaphor without noting how, in "Apt Pupil," the reader's sense of dread and impending disaster is heightened by sounds of "hushing," "hissing," "whispering," and "crunching" that slither in and around the narrative like a subtle serpent, just about invisible. This begins innocently enough when Todd Bowden first hears "shuffling" footsteps making a soft *"wish-wish* sound" as a slippered old Dussander approaches the front door of his house to answer an insistently ringing doorbell (110). Young Todd hears the same slippers *"wishing-wishing* on the floor" when Dussander later shuffles past him with a contemptuous gesture (114). Quiet little rasping sounds drift past almost unnoticed when Dussander ponders the implications of Todd's unusual interest in Nazi atrocities, "one hand rubbing up and down on his cheek producing a very small *sand*papery sound" (117)—the description echoing the very name Dus*sand*er (at one point mockingly even mispronounced Doo-*Zand*er" [116]). Similar sinister sounds are half-heard when young Todd thinks of pushing Dussander down the stairs to kill him. Walking around the kitchen in woolen socks that *whisper* on the "hilly linoleum" (191) and hearing with suspicious ears the presumably quiet maneuvers behind him, Dussander remarks, "I heard you, you know . . . from the moment you pushed your chair back and stood up. You are not as quiet as you imagine" (192). Thirteen-year-old Todd even has his first wet dream to the "secret sound of the rain" *whispering* through the leaves and branches of the tree outside his window; and Todd *whispers* to himself in the darkness, "Kill him and it's all over"—and to the seed-stained boy, this *whispering* made it "seem real" (188).

The word "wish"—occasionally even italicized for emphasis—is echoed dramatically, even desperately, throughout the novella as is evidenced in a sharp little exchange between the American teenager and the perverted old Nazi, each of whom has the other in "mutual deathgrips" (192):

"I *wish*—" [Todd blurted].

"You *wish*! You *wish*!" Dussander roared. Never mind your *wishes*, your *wishes* make me sick, your *wishes* are not more than little piles of dogshit in the gutter. All I want from you is to know if you understand the situation we are in!"

"I understand it," Todd muttered . . . . (174)

With typical King-like irony and unexpected reversal, this angry exchange is pathetically echoed in the final death–moments of the old Nazi. The reader is likely to be annoyed with himself for almost sympathizing with a fatherly Dussander when the latter is about to lose consciousness forever, and the perverted old Nazi "found himself *wishing*, of all absurd things, that he could leave a note for the boy. *Wishing* he could tell him to be very careful . . . . He *wished* he could tell the boy in the end he, Dussander, had come to respect him" (266).

Throughout "Apt Pupil," such sounds as *s*, *z*, *sh*, *ch*, and *sk* are endlessly echoed at dramatic points in the story in such words as "punch," "crunch," "dish," "shave," "suspicion," "puss-puss," "spiral," "escape hatch," "hush puppy," "bitch," "sheeney," and in such names as Ed French, "Sneaker Pete," Lieutenant Bozeman, Betty Task, Morris Heisel—and, ominously enough, even in the word "Prussian." One is reminded of what poet Wallace Stevens says in one of his interpretive letters about the sound-echoes that accompany his protagonist (Crispin) in "The Comedian as the Letter C": "Now as Crispin moves through the poem, the sounds of the letter C accompany him, as the sounds of the crickets must have accompanied St. Francis . . . . The sounds of the letter C include all related or derivative sounds: X, TS, and Z."[2] In much less arty fashion, and with diabolical rather than academic and scholarly overtones, King does much the same kind of "wish and whispering" word-selecting in "Apt Pupil." Results are sometimes electrifying.

It is impossible to catalog all the astute literary devices that King can dream up to deal with his gothic world divided by the "filmiest of perceptual curtains"—that is, mixtures of comedy and tragedy, autobiography and uncontrolled fantasy, or psychology and demon lore. Much of the present study has been devoted to exploration of such high points in the first decade of his fiction. However, of King's many talents two things may be stated with confidence. Certainly one must acknowledge that his range of literary skills in psychology, character, comedy, gothic symbology, and natural-sounding dialogue is easily one of the most stunning in twentieth–century American fiction. But having acknowledged this, one is compelled to point out that much of his work is entrapped in the absurd confinements, crude vulgarities, and simple-minded exaggerations of late twentieth-century gothic fiction. In a satirical poem called "A Fable for Critics," nineteenth–century Harvard professor James Russell Lowell wittily summarized similar difficulties in the work of Edgar Allan Poe—an evaluation that readily applies to many gothic writers, but most especially to Stephen King: "There comes Poe, with his raven, like Barnaby Rudge, / Three fifths of him genius, and two fifths sheer fudge." In this neat but all-too-brief evaluation, Lowell recognizes that Poe has written some things "quite the best of their kind," but goes on to complain that sometimes the "heart is all squeezed out by the mind." While one cannot complain that mind-squeezing is exactly what fudges King's work, one feels compelled to concur with a perceptive observation by reviewer Annie Gottlieb in that King sometimes "loses credibility" (especially in his longer works) and that a "recurrent flaw" is the "loss of control of, and perhaps interest in, his material after the midpoint" in all too many of his narratives.[3] Such penetrating works as *'Salem's Lot*, "Apt Pupil," "The Body," "Night Surf," "Last Rung on the Ladder," and "Reaper's Image" prove that Stephen King has the genius to overcome the too-constrictive limitations and exaggerations of the gothic imagination.

Notes and References

Chapter One

1. Biographical portions of this chapter derive from four main sources and are indentified by the indicated abbreviations: (1) "On Becoming a Brand Name," in *Fear Itself* (New York: New American Library, 1984), 15–42 [*FI*]; (2) "An Annoying Autobiographical Pause," in *Danse Macabre* (New York: Berkley Books 1983), 82–106 [*DM*]; (3) "Notes Toward a Biography," in *The Art of Darkness*, by Douglas E. Winter (New York: New American Library, 1984), 12–24 [*AD*]; and (4) "Why I Was Bachman," in *The Bachman Books* (New York: New American Library, 1985), v–x [*BB*]. "On Becoming a Brand Name" originally appeared in *Adelina* (February 1980).
2. The image of the mysterious snow globe may derive from the famous Orson Welles motion picture, *Citizen Kane* (1940) in which a snow globe falls out of the hand of the dying Kane and shatters.
3. This passage is a pastiche of literary echoes. The question that cannot be asked derives from T. S. Eliot's "Love Song of J. Alfred Prufrock" (and ultimately from Chrétien de Troyes's *Perceval*); the endless rooms and corridors from Franz Kafka's *The Castle*; the "entrances and exits" from Shakespeare's famous seven ages of man in *As You Like It*. This technique of literary echo is typical of King, for which he has received unjustified criticism. T. S. Eliot's *Waste Land*, much admired by scholars and the subject of many articles in learned journals, does exactly the same thing. The advantage of King's use of literary echo is that one does not have to plow through the original work (as in Ezra Pound's "Hugh Selwyn Mauberley" or *Cantos*) to understand the story. Oddly enough, Ezra Pound's poetry is one of the works that Mr. Adley finds in the mysterious library of mostly unknown authors (*DS*, 444–45, 458). This inclusion of Pound's name in "Breathing Method" is apparently a subtle reminder for some of King's hypercritical book reviewers of Pound's predeliction for hopelessly obscure and even sometimes inaccurate borrowings from other people's works. That Pound's obscure poetry should be found among volumes of mostly nonexistent writers is a neat little academic jest.

4. An analogy of the name and character of the protagonist with Theodore Dreiser's *Sister Carrie* (1900) should not be overlooked.

Chapter Two

1. Howard P. Lovecraft, *Supernatural Horror in Literature* (New York: Dover, 1973), 25.
2. Stephen King is not much inclined to follow the gothic tradition of using exotic foreign names, though occasionally, a significant ethnic motif manages to surface, as when the Jewish-sounding name of the vampirized Glick family in *'Salem's Lot* turns out in fact to have been originally Italian ("Gliccucchi," 214–15). King's purpose is not to make his narratives sound distant and foreign, but rather local (especially New Englandish) and immediate.
3. Ominously, the name "Chapelwaite" seems to suggest that the "chapel waits"—as in "waits on" (the devil) or "waits for" (victims).
4. This description anticipates the skeletal apparition in the bathtub of room 217 of the Overlook Hotel in *The Shining* (217).
5. Calvin ("Cal"), a name that appears in many gothic tales, suggests the reformer John Calvin (1509–64), whose grim theology of total depravity and special election dominated the thinking of the New England Puritans in the seventeenth century. Cal's murder suggests the demise of this last cold vestige of Christianity. As with such names as Naomi (in *Pet Sematary*) or Heidi (in *Thinner*), the symbolism in Cal's name does not extend much beyond the name itself; in other words, the "Cal" of Jerusalem's Lot does not preach Calvinism. The context in which Cal lives, however, is clearly demon oriented and Calvin infested. King is more frank about his treatment of certain Christian denominations in, for example, *Cycle of the Werewolf*, where he goes out of his way to brutalize the Grace Baptist Church by turning its minister into the "Beast," in other words, Antichrist (45–48, 97–127).
6. At the end of the story, the reader learns that the chapel appears never to have been desecrated (*NS*, 34). Desecrated chapel motifs in gothic tales hark back to the "chapel perilous" of medieval Arthurian romances, an interesting example of which appears in Sir Thomas Malory's fifteenth-century romance, *Le Morte d'Arthur* (6:15).
7. "Mr. Bones" was a nickname used by nineteenth-century black-faced minstrels in addressing one of their members. The name is used by poet John Berryman in his famous *Dream Songs* (cf. number 76). Addressing an "ailing abolitionist" as "Bones" (humorously and symbolically meaning "False Black Face") reveals a good deal about Charles's peculiar temperament.
8. Lovecraft, *Supernatural Horror*, 15.

9. "Usually if the vampire is male, the first victims are female, and if the vampire is female (called *lamia* after the Greek monster), then the victim is male; but there is a distinct level of homosexuality carried in the myth that is often reflected in literary treatment" (James B. Twitchell, *The Living Dead: A Study of the Vampire in Romantic Literature* [Durham, N.C.: Duke University Press, 1981], 6.
10. Noon is the exact hour when Straker visits and intimidates the usually imperturbable Lawrence Crockett in his office to negotiate the purchase of the horror-ridden Marsten House for one dollar. For the first time in his money-grubbing life Crockett "felt a nasty tremor of fear" (52–58). With respect to these hours of vampire power, one should bear in mind Leonard Wolf's warning that the "lore of the vampire is neither consistent nor dogmatic and varies from country to country," even though in *Dracula* itself (chapter 18), Van Helsing acts as if vampire lore was "fixed and systematic" (*The Annotated Dracula* [New York: Crown Publishers, 1975], 259).
11. This is a typical subtlety of King. The use of the verb "marked" for Ben's face is a kind of unconscious prophecy—or perhaps unconscious recognition—of Ben's future affection for Mark Petrie. But the implications are multiple: (1) Ben has been "marked" by Tibbets (by being knocked unconscious), (2) "marked" for death by Barlow (who would like to sink his teeth into Ben's throat), (3) "marked" by Susan's mother (by being called uncomplimentary names), and (4) ultimately will be "marked" by his quasi-amorous affection for young Mark. Other symbolic uses of "mark" occur throughout the novel (e.g. 174–75).
12. It is ironic that Mark's family name should be Petrie, since this was the name of the quintessential middle-class American television family in the *Dick Van Dyke Show* in the early 1960s.
13. Montague Summers, *The Vampire: His Kith and Kin* (1928; reprints, New Hyde Park, N.Y.: University Books, 1960), 200.

Chapter Three

1. Named after Antoinette Perry, "Tony" happens to be the popular nickname of an American theater award, annually granted to the best play of the year. Jack's drama is never going to earn such public acknowledgment of artistic and financial success. However, with his precognitive and cardiokinetic powers, precocious Danny seems to recognize this paternal anguish and realizes that this much-desired "Tony" would not be a thing of triumph or success—but terror. The ghostly "Tony" is thus a projection of a father's failure as a dramatist. Other dramatic awards are mentioned in *The Shining* in connection with Jack Torrance's worthless play, but not this one. Though perhaps only unconsciously,

King appears to be experimenting with a kind of psychic transference of the fear of failure.

2. As defined by Judith Wilt, "decreation" is the "pulling apart, laying asleep, washing away of body, soul, and consciousness—a Gothic anti-mystery . . . one that rules more strongly than the creation mystery." It is "the unbearable 'awakeness' that characterizes the citizens of the Gothic world, that makes them see and hear ghosts that we do not, gives way in the central citizen, the Gothic antihero, to a recognition, willing or unwilling, of decreation, the falling asleep" (*Ghosts of the Gothic* [Princeton: Princeton University Press, 1980], 69).

3. *The Shining*'s massive Overlook Hotel in Colorado bears considerable resemblance to the extravagant plans of Howard Hughes, in the 1960s, to build the world's largest hotel in Nevada, a $150 million 4,000-room addition to the Sands. The pleasure palace Hughes envisioned, but never built, was to be "a complete city within itself, "a resort complex so magnificently planned that any guest would have to make supreme effort to be bored"—shops open twenty-four hours a day, an entire floor for family recreation, a theater showing only first-run motion pictures, a computerized indoor golf course, etc. (see Donald L. Barrett, *Empire: The Life, Legend, and Madness of Howard Hughes* [New York: Norton, 1979], 306–7).

4. Wilt, *Ghosts of the Gothic*, 29.

5. Jack's "secret" is a pathological/psychosexual relationship with his son, a relationship with sinister implications—as when, in an early scene, Jack stands over Danny's sleeping form, takes a Spanish Llama .38 out of a shoe box from the top shelf of a closet, and sits down on the bed "looking at it for nearly an hour, fascinated by its deadly shine" (41). The pun on "shine" in this passage is an allusion to Danny's cardiokinetic talent.

6. See Samuel Noah Kramer, *Mythologies of the Ancient World* (New York: Doubleday Anchor, 1961), 38.

7. Winter, *Art of Darkness*, 80.

8. Ibid., 15.

9. James G. Frazer, *The New Golden Bough: A New Abridgment*, ed. Theodor H. Gaster (New York: Criterion Books, 1959), 309–17.

10. From "Levana and Our Ladies of Sorrow," in *Suspira de Profundis* (1845).

Chapter Four

1. One of the original titles of *'Salem's Lot* was "Second Coming," apparently named after William Butler Yeats's famous post-World War I poem, "The Second Coming," which is quoted in the beginning of *The Stand* (118).

2. The Ragnarok (Icelandic: *Ragnarokr*) is the day of the great battle be-

tween the gods and the forces of evil, culminating in the complete destruction of the universe in which the gods will perish. Though the Norse myth has its own origins, an indebtedness to the Christian apocalypse is apparent. *The Stand* is an interesting blend of the two traditions, leaning more heavily in basic mood and philosophy, however, toward Nordic traditions. A valuable discussion of the Ragnarok tradition may be found in H. R. Ellis Davidson, *Gods and Myths of Northern Europe* (Baltimore: Penguin Books, 1964), 202–23.

3. Wallace Fowlie, *Age of Surrealism* (Bloomington: Indiana University Press, 1960), 109.

4. "Captain Trips" was the nickname of Jerry Garcia of the "Grateful Dead," who recorded a rock album under the latter title in January 1967.

5. *Ka* is the ancient Egyptian term for the "double," what would be called at the present time the doppelgänger. For an explanation of the Egyptian beliefs concerning the *ka*, see E. A. Wallis Budge, ed., *The Egyptian Book of the Dead* (New York: Dover Publications, 1967), lxii–lxiv; see also R. T. Rundle Clark, *Myth and Symbol in Ancient Egypt* (New York: Grove Press, 1959), 231–34.

6. Traditional "biographies" of the Antichrist begin with the church fathers: Iraeneus, Cyril of Jerusalem, and other ancient Greek commentators on the New Testament. For a thorough summation of the ancient traditions, see Vincent P. Maceli, *The Antichrist* (West Hanover, Mass.: Christopher Publishing House, 1981), chaps. 3–6.

7. Lansing Lamont, *Day of Trinity* (New York: New American Library, 1966), 197. Lamont observes that the deception was so successful that the "decoding clerks at Potsdam thought that the seventy-seven-year-old Stimson had just become a father."

8. Ibid., 199.

9. These observations are based upon an informal three-year survey of undergraduates at Villanova University. Not unusually, upon hearing about this particular study, students volunteered their evaluation of *The Stand* as a "favorite."

Chapter Five

1. It is obvious from the beginning of *Dead Zone* that Johnny already possessed precognitive abilities, that is, "hunches": "he would know what the next record on the radio was going to be before the DJ played it, that sort of thing" (4).

2. "Rapture" is fundamentalist belief based on 2 Thessalonians 4:17, revealing that at the end of time the saved are to be taken up into the clouds "to meet the Lord." According to some fundamentalist interpretations of this passage, this "rapture" occurs while the rest of humanity (presum-

ably the inquitous ones) has to endure the inhumanities of the Antichrist.

3. Representing depression, sadness, or something unusual, blue is used in such popular expressions as "having the blues." Like all colors, blue can have positive attributes, but in King's work, negative implications dominate: coldness, cruelty, despair, destruction, inconstancy, and merciless justice. For an extended philosophical discussion of color symbolism in general, see also J. E. Cirlot, *A Dictionary of Symbols* (New York: Philosophical Library, 1962), 50–57.

4. Michael R. Collings suggests that *Dead Zone*, though published two years earlier, fits logically after *Cujo* "in a discussion of King's use of the supernatural." He argues that "Cujo leaves the question [of the supernatural] open; *Dead Zone* answers and explains" (*The Many Facets of Stephen King* [Mercer Island, Wash.: Starmount House, 1985], 50).

5. These six girls are mentioned on pages 3 and 218–24 of *Cujo* and *Dead Zone*, respectively. *Cujo* indicates the years when these sex crimes occurred (from 1970 to 1975); *Dead Zone* gives exact months and adds additional victims. It is no accident that the crimes are made to occur as a ghastly prelude to the American bicentennial, and to parallel the Vietnam War, the Watergate scandal, and especially the administrations of Nixon and Ford (1968–76). At one point in *Dead Zone*, President Nixon is referred to as the "Troll of San Clemente" (77).

6. Shana Alexander, *Anyone's Daughter* (New York: Viking, 1979, 178–79). "Cujo," a doctor's son from Pennsylvania, was the youngest and only black in the Symbionese Liberation Army. Significantly, "Cudge" or "Cudjoe" was a common name for a slave in the West Indies. The term appears in a well-known antislave poem, "To Sir Toby" (1792), by Philip Freneau, where it is associated with repulsive animals and anguished "howling."

Chapter Six

1. Lovecraft, *Supernatural Horror*, 59.
2. Known as the *Erinyes* ("angry ones"), the three furies are also known as the *Eumenides* ("gracious ones"). In their angry manifestation, they pursue and torment children guilty of impiety against their parents. For having killed his mother (Clytemnestra), Orestes, the son of Agamemnon, is one of the most famous of their victims.
3. See *Thegony*, lines 177–85, in the translation of Richmond Lattimore, *Hesiod* (Ann Arbor: University of Michigan Press, 1959), 133–34.
4. This traditional Catholic prayer of repentance is known as the Act of Contrition, and used to be recited by rote immediately after confession of one's sins. Leigh seems to have no interest in religion until her near-

death episode. By having her utter phrases of the prayer that seem to be saying the opposite of what the prayer intends—in other words, scrambling the prayer—King insinuates an unconscious yielding to diabolical influence. Other forms of satanic scramblings appear in "Jerusalem's Lot" and "Children of the Corn."

5. The plane crash here referred to occurred shortly after take-off, in snowy darkness, about five miles from the Mason City airport, Iowa, at about one on the morning of 3 February 1959. The occupants of the plane were rock stars Buddy Holly (twenty-two years old) of Lubbock, Texas; Richie Valens (seventeen) of Los Angeles; and J. P. ("Big Bopper") Richardson (twenty-four) of Beaumont, Texas. Along with *Dion & the Belmonts*, they had been on tour for General Artists Corporation. On their way to Fargo, North Dakota, after finishing an engagement in Clear Lake, Iowa, all three, and the pilot, were killed. Authorities blamed weather conditions for the crash. All three have important associations with the year 1958, the year the Plymouth Fury was manufactured. The golden oldie on Christine's car radio is "Chantilly Lace," Big Bopper's most famous song (265), released in 1958. In fact, Big Bopper's three major recordings were all made in 1958. Richie Valens's recording career was launched in 1958 when he recorded "Come on, Let's Go." In November 1958 he wrote the song "Donna," his biggest hit. The song heard on Christine's radio, "La Bamba," was recorded in 1959 (266). Buddy Holly's recording career extends from 1957 to early 1959; in May and July 1958, he recorded "Rave On" and "Early in the Morning."

6. After a successful ten-week tour of England, rock star Eddie Cochran, at the age of twenty-one, was killed in a motor accident early on the morning of 17 April 1960. In the spring 1958, Cochran developed the special sound for which he was famous in the song, "Summertime Blues," composed with fellow songwriter Jerry Capehart. Thus, he too (like Holly, Valens, and Big Bopper) has important connections with Christine's year 1958. The lyrics of one of Cochran's songs are quoted at the beginning of chapter 1, setting up death-by-car implications even before the novel begins. "Liberty" happens to be the name of Cochran's recording company, and, interestingly, "Libertyville" is the name of the imaginary Pennsylvania town where the action of *Christine* takes place.

7. For information about the "Wendigo," see Howard Norman, *Cree Windigo Tales and Journeys* (San Francisco: North Point Press, 1982). See also Algeron Blackwood's short story, "The Wendigo" (1910).

8. Frank Baum's famous *Wizard of Oz* is often considered a parable of the American "dream of success," emphasizing the wonder and joy of a fairylore without heartaches and nightmares. As with the Cinderella story in *Carrie*, King designs his *Pet Sematary* so as to reverse those cherished success-oriented values by emphasizing—one might suggest,

even overemphasizing—the heartache and nightmare of American society.

9. Howard Nemerov, "Deep Woods," in *New and Selected Poems* (Chicago: University of Chicago Press, 1960), 97–98.

10. Mispronunciations and misspellings are imaginatively interconnected in that Gage's childish sounds and Zelda's speech impediments lead directly to the misspellings on the tombstones, the latter obviously inscribed by children or illiterates. The animal tombstones with their haunted misspellings are thus a mask or symbol of the irrational universe governed by a mispronounced "Oz the Gweat and the Tewwible," of which the two-year-old's mispronunciations are a "gauge"—hence the name Gage.

11. Julia Briggs, *Night Visitors: The Rise and Fall of the English Ghost Story* (London: Faber & Faber, 1977), 212.

Chapter Seven

1. "Shudder gothics" are also known in the German tradition as *Schauerromane* and in the French as *romans noirs.* For an excellent analysis of various types of gothic tales, see Marshall B. Tymn, ed., *Horror Literature* (New York: Bowker, 1981), 3–31. Another valuable source is Eino Railo, *The Haunted Castle* (New York: Dutton, 1927), an excellent guide to English horror-romanticism with special emphasis on shudder gothic.

2. Storer's *Broadcasting / Cablecasting Yearbook 1982* lists no radio for Portsmouth, Maine, and no station under the call letters WKDM anywhere in the United States. WRKO and WBZ, however, are genuine radio stations in Boston. The only religious note in "Night Surf" is the sentimental claptrap broadcast by the "backwoods deejay" emanating from what appears to be a nonexistent radio station. The irony seems intended and is consistent with the tone of metaphysical despair that prevails throughout this story of the Latter Days: that a nonexistent radio station should broadcast sentimental religious "stuff" (52), while genuine radio stations broadcast rock music and trivia.

3. Boccaccio, *The Decameron*, trans. Frances Winwar (New York: Random House, 1955), xxvii.

4. The name "Sackheim" is another of King's cruel ethnic puns, like Glick (cf. "lick") for the first vampirized family in *'Salem's Lot* (74–104), or, more insidiously, the "gas us" in *"Pegasus,"* the code-name of the experimental nerve-gas used to exterminate Jews in a Nazi death camp ("Apt Pupil," *DS*, 135). "Sackheim," of course, is suggestively Jewish, and by burning him, the malevolent six are "sacking the hymie." His brutal burning, a kind of one-man "holocaust," is a not-so-subtle parody of the

ovens of Auschwitz and Dachau. Insidiously, the Jewish-sounding name may have suggested the mode of "execution."

5. Robert Lowell, "Quaker Graveyard in Nantucket," in *Lord Weary's Castle* (New York: Harcourt Brace, 1946), 9.

6. Lovecraft, *Supernatural Horror*, 15.

7. Without identifying it, King actually quotes Wordsworth's original line, "The child is the father of man" from "The Intimations of Immortality" in *'Salem's Lot* (138) when Mark Petrie is gluing together anatomical parts of a plastic monster in his *Aurora* set. King's purpose in using the quotation in *'Salem's Lot* may not be immediately apparent—and perhaps deliberately so. At that point in the story, the child/father phrase seems to suggest (as Mark puts together gothic pieces of "himself" to make the whole malevolent man) that the boy will grow up to be a vampire. Mark's androgynous appearance makes him a likely candidate. But, ironically, the reader's suspicions are mistaken. Mark will gain control over the town's malevolent forces. In other words, "child Petrie" will be victorious over "father Barlow"—just as the latter triumphs over the priest, Father Callahan.

8. In Robert Zelazny's *The Last Defender of Camelot* (New York: Timescape, 1980), 258. Zelazny is the author of some twenty-five books of science fiction and terror.

9. The most famous use of the medieval belief that perfect circles or spheres reflect or symbolize Divine Perfection occurs in Dante's *Paradiso*, canto 33, lines 115–20.

10. Kepler's three laws of planetary motion, taught in all elementary courses of the history of science, are generally considered the most important astronomical development between the heliocentric theory of Copernicus and the gravitional formulas of Sir Isaac Newton. The first law states that the "planets travel about the sun in orbits that are elipses with the sun at one focus." Covert images of "circles" (medieval) and "deteriorating elipses" (scientific) in "I Am the Doorway" tend to pervert traditionally held views of the advancement of knowledge since the Renaissance. Not inappropriately, King's antiintellectual symbolism is a natural consequence of literary "gothick" (hence, post–Horace Walpole) traditions.

Chapter Eight

1. "Red" makes a passing remark indicating that he too has been brutalized by gang-rapes in prison: "Am I speaking from personal experience—I only wish I weren't" (33).

2. Another interpretation is given by Winter, who claims that in "Rita Hayworth" King worked a "theme of innocence as effectively as he considered the theme of guilt in *The Shining.* . . . Red's story tells of

how the irrestible force of innocence succeeds against the seemingly immovable object of Shawshank" (*Art of Darkness*, 105–6).

3. G. B. Harrison, ed., *Shakespeare: The Complete Works* (New York: Harcourt Brace, 1952), 1431.
4. In an afterword to *Different Seasons*, King explains the order of the composition of the four novellas. Coming from the author himself, one would expect this information to be unimpeachable, but in a footnote to his chapter on *Different Seasons*, Winter explains that the sequence of compositions was not exactly as King had originally reported it (*Art of Darkness*, 207).
5. Winter, *Art of Darkness*, 207.
6. "Denker" pretends that his first name was given him by his father because of an admiration for Arthur Conan Doyle (116). This is yet another name-game: Doyle's famous Sherlock Holmes, like the crafty Dussander, is a sleuth. Ironically however, shortly after this so-called Conan Doyle explanation of the name "Arthur," Todd reveals that his mom and dad had given him a fingerprint set for Christmas, which he promptly used to discover Dussander's Nazi identity (124).
7. Richard Hanser, *Putsch* (New York: Pyramid Books 1971), 241.
8. "Stud City," *Ubris*, Fall 1969; "The Revenge of Lard Ass Hogan," *Main Review*, 1975. As samples of Gordie Lachance's story-telling abilities, the versions that appear in "The Body" have been revised.
9. Hart Crane, *Complete Poems* (New York: Anchor Books, 1966), 50.
10. Frost's line reads: "I cannot rub the strangeness from my sight / I got from looking through a pane of glass / I skimmed this morning from the drinking trough / And held against the world of hoary grass." "After Apple-Picking" is one of Frost's most frequently anthologized poems. Author Ben Mears would surely have known it.
11. From the memorable opening sentence of Henry James's *Turn of the Screw*.

Chapter Nine

1. The blatant illustrations that accompany the months in both hardback and paperback editions do nothing to enhance the subtlety and even humor of *Cycle of the Werewolf*. In fact, the graceless illustrations seem designed to deflect the reader away from any sensitivity to the nuances of good writing.
2. Holly Stevens, ed., *Letters of Wallace Stevens* (New York: Knopf, 1966), 351.
3. "Something Lurks in Ludlow," *New York Times Book Review*, 6 November 1983, 15.

Selected Bibliography

PRIMARY SOURCES

Limited to 1974–84. Special editions, magazine excerpts, abridgments of popular novels and motion pictures are not included. For detailed information on movies based on King's stories, consult Michael R. Collings, *The Films of Stephen King* (Mercer Island, Wash.: Starmount House, 1986), especially the bibliography, 167–95.

1. Novels
Carrie. Garden City, N.Y.: Doubleday, 1974; New York: Signet, 1975.
Christine. New York: Viking Press, 1983; New York: Signet, 1983.
Cujo. New York: Viking Press, 1981; New York: Signet, 1982.
Cycle of the Werewolf. Westland, Mich.: Land of Enchantment, 1983; New York: Signet, 1985. Illustrations by Bernie Wrightson.
The Dead Zone. New York: Viking Press, 1979; New York: Signet, 1980.
Firestarter. New York: Viking Press, 1980; New York: Signet, 1981.
Pet Sematary. Garden City, N.Y.: Doubleday, 1983, New York: Signet, 1984.
'Salem's Lot. Garden City, N.Y.: Doubleday, 1975; New York: Signet, 1976.
The Shining. Garden City, N.Y.: Doubleday, 1977; New York: Signet, 1978.
The Stand. Garden City, N.Y.: Doubleday, 1978; New York: Signet, 1979.
The Talisman. New York: Viking Press and Putnam, 1984; New York: Berkley, 1985. Coauthored with Peter Straub.

2. Novels under the pseudonym Richard Bachman
The Long Walk. New York: New American Library, 1979.
Rage. New York: New American Library, 1977.
Roadwork. New York: New American Library, 1981.
The Running Man. New York: New American Library, 1982.
Thinner. New York: New American Library, 1984.

3. Collections of Essays
Danse Macabre. New York: Everest House, 1981. Abridgment: *Book Digest*, September 1981. Excerpts: "Why We Crave Horror Movies" (revised), *Playboy*, January 1981; "Notes on Horror," *Quest*, June 1981; "You

Gotta Put on the Gruesome Mask and Go Booga-Booga" (revised), *TV Guide*, 5–7 December 1981.

4. Short Fiction Anthologies

Creepshow. New York: Plume Book, 1982. Comic book adaptation with Bernie Wrightson. Contains "Father's Day," "The Lonesome Death of Jordy Verrill," "The Crate," "Something to Tide You Over," and "They're Creeping up on You."

The Dark Tower: The Gunslinger. West Kingston, R.I.: Donald M. Grant, 1982 (limited edition). Illustrated by Michael Whelan. Contains five short stories and an afterword: "The Gunslinger," "The Way Station," "The Oracle and the Mountains," "The Slow Mutants," and "The Gunslinger and the Dark Man."

Different Seasons. New York: Viking Press, 1982. Contains four novellas and an afterword: "Rita Hayworth and Shawshank Redemption," "Apt Pupil," "The Body," and "The Breathing Method."

Night Shift. Garden City, N.Y.: Doubleday, 1978. Contains twenty short stories, introduction by John D. MacDonald, and foreword by King: "Jerusalem's Lot," "Graveyard Shift," "Night Surf," "I Am the Doorway," "The Mangler," "The Boogeyman," "Gray Matter," "Battleground," "Trucks," "Sometimes They Come Back," "Strawberry Spring," "The Ledge," "The Lawnmower Man," "Quitters Inc.," "I Know What You Need," "Children of the Corn," "The Last Rung on the Ladder," "The Man Who Loved Flowers," "One for the Road," and "The Woman in the Room."

5. Short Fiction in Anthologies and Popular Magazines

The frequent reprintings and/or revisions of King's short stories are too numerous to be included in the following brief listing. Also excluded are excerpts from novels, aborted novels, and self-published monographs and pamphlets. Unless retitled, each entry is limited to a single publication, usually the final version. For complete listings of all reprints, see Douglas E. Winter, *Art of Darkness* (New York: New American Library, 1984), 219–25; for plot summaries, see 159–85. Reprints in King's personal anthologies are identified with the following initials: *Creepshow* [CS], *Dark Tower* [DT], *Different Seasons* [DS], *Night Shift* [NS], *Skeleton Crew* (New York: Viking, 1985) [SK].

"The Ballad of the Flexible Bullet." *Fantasy and Science Fiction*, June 1984 [SK].

"Battleground." *Cavalier*, September 1972 [NS].

"Beach World." [SK].

"Before the Play." *Whispers*, August 1982.

"Big Wheels: A Tale of the Laundry Game (Milkman #2)." In *New Terrors 2*, edited by Ramsey Campbell. New York: Pocket Books, 1982 [SK].

"The Blue Air Compressor." *Heavy Metal*, July 1981.
"The Boogeyman." *Cavalier*, March 1983 [NS].
"Cain Rose Up." *Ubris*, Spring 1968 [SK].
"The Cat from Hell." *Cavalier*, June 1977.
"Children of the Corn." *Penthouse*, March 1977 [NS].
"The Crate." *Gallery*, July 1979. Comic book adaptation in *CS*.
"Crouch End." In *New Tales of the Cthulhu Mythos*, edited by Ramsey Campbell. Sauk City, Wis.: Arkham House, 1980.
"Do the Dead Sing?" *Yankee*, November 1981. Retitled "The Reach" in *SK*.
"The Fifth Quarter." *Cavalier*, April 1972.
"The Glass Floor." *Startling Mystery Stories*, Fall 1967.
"Gramma." *Weirdbook #19*, Spring 1984 [SK].
"Graveyard Shift." *Cavalier*, October 1970 [NS].
"Gray Matter." *Cavalier*, October 1973 [NS].
"The Gunslinger." *Fantasy and Science Fiction*, October 1978 [DT].
"The Gunslinger and the Dark Man." *Magazine of Fantasy and Science Fiction*, November 1981 [DT].
"Here There Be Tygers." *Ubris*, Spring 1968 [SK].
"I Am the Doorway." *Cavalier*, March 1971 [NS].
"I Know What You Need." *Cosmopolitan*, September 1976 [NS].
"It Grows on You." *Marshroots*, 1975.
"I Was a Teenage Grave Robber." *Comics Review*, 1965. Retitled "In a Half World of Terror." *Stories of Suspense #2*, 1966.
"The Jaunt." *Twilight Zone Magazine*, April 1981 [SK].
"Jerusalem's Lot." In *The World Fantasy Awards*, edited by Stuart David Shift and Fritz Leiber, vol. 2. Garden City, N.Y.: Doubleday, 1980 [NS].
"The Last Rung on the Ladder." [NS].
"The Lawn Mower Man." *Cavalier*, May 1975 [NS].
"The Ledge." *Penthouse*, July 1976 [NS].
"The Man Who Loved Flowers." *Gallery*, August 1977 [NS].
"The Man Who Would Not Shake Hands." In *Shadows 4*, edited by Charles L. Grant. Garden City, N.Y.: Doubleday, 1981 [SK].
"Man with a Belly." *Cavalier*, December 1972.
"The Mangler." *Cavalier*, December 1972 [NS].
"The Mist." In *Dark Forces*, edited by Kirby McCauley. New York: Viking Press, 1980; New York: Bantam, 1981 [SK].
"The Monkey." *Gallery*, November 1980 [SK]. One of King's most frequently reprinted stories.
"Morning Deliveries (Milkman #1)." [SK].
"Mrs. Todd's Shortcut." *Redbook*, May 1984 [SK].
"The Night of the Tiger." *Magazine of Fantasy and Science Fiction*, February 1978.
"Night Surf." *Cavalier*, August 1974 [NS].

"Nona." In *Shadows*, edited by Charles L. Grant. Garden City, N.Y.: Doubleday, 1978 [*SK*].

"One for the Road." *Maine*, March–April 1977 [*NS*].

"The Oracle and the Mountains." *Magazine of Fantasy and Science Fiction*, February 1981 [*DT*].

"Quitters, Inc." In *Best Detective Stories of the Year*, edited by Edward D. Hoch. New York: Dutton, 1979 [*NS*].

"The Raft." *Gallery*, November 1982 [*SK*].

"The Reaper's Image." *Startling Mystery Stories*, Spring 1969 [*SK*].

"The Revelation of 'Becka Paulson." *Rolling Stone*, 19 July–2 August 1984.

"The Revenge of Lard Ass Hogan." *The Maine Review*, July 1975. Revised version included in "The Body" as one of Gordie Lachance's original stories [*DS*].

"Slade." *The Maine Campus*, June–August 1970.

"The Slow Mutants." *Magazine of Fantasy and Science Fiction*, July 1981 [*DT*].

"Sometimes They Come Back." *Cavalier*, March 1974 [*NS*].

"Strawberry Spring." *Cavalier*, November 1975 [*NS*].

"Stud City." *Ubris*, Fall 1969. Revised version included in "The Body" as one of Gordie Lachance's original stories [*DS*].

"Suffer the Little Children." *Cavalier*, February 1972

"Survivor Type." In *Terrors*, edited by Charles L. Grant. New York: Playboy, 1982 [*SK*].

"Trucks." *Cavalier*, June 1973 [*NS*].

"Uncle Otto's Truck." *Yankee*, October 1983 [*SK*].

"The Way Station." *Magazine of Fantasy and Science Fiction*, April 1980 [*DT*].

"The Wedding Jig." *Ellery Queen's Mystery Magazine*, 1 December 1980 [*SK*].

"Weeds." *Cavalier*, May 1976. Revised as "The Lonesome Death of Jordy Verrill" in *CS*.

"The Woman in the Room" [*NS*].

"The Word Processor." *Playboy*, January 1983. Retitled "The Word Processor of the Gods" in *SK*.

6. Introductions to Novels and Anthologies

Foreword to *Night Shift*. Garden City, N.Y.: Doubleday, 1978; New York: Signet, 1979.

Foreword to *Stalking the Nightmare*, by Harlan Ellison. Huntington Woods, Mich.: Phantasia Press, 1982.

Foreword to *Tales from the Nightshade*, by Charles L. Grant. Sauk City, Wis.: Arkham House, 1981.

"The Importance of Being Forry." In *Mr. Monster's Movie Gold*, by Forrest J. Ackerman. Virginia Beach–Norfolk, Va.: Donning, 1982.

Introduction to *The Shapes of Midnight*, by Joseph Payne Brennan. New York: Berkeley, 1980.

Introduction to *When Michael Calls*, by John Ferris. New York: Pocket, 1981.
Introduction to *The Arbor House Treasury of Horror and the Supernatural*, edited by Bill Pronzini, Barry N. Malzberg, and Martin H. Greenberg. New York: Arbor House, 1981.
Introduction to *Tales by Moonlight*, edited by Jessica Amanda Salmonson. Chicago: Robert T. Garcia, 1982.
Introduction to *Frankenstein*, by Mary Shelley; *Dracula*, by Bram Stoker; and *Dr. Jekyll and Mr. Hyde*, by Robert Louis Stevenson. New York: Signet, 1978.

7. Reviews and Commentaries
The following are a representative selection of King's movie reviews, book reviews, general comments, etc., representing about a quarter of King's output.
"Between Rock and a Soft Place." *Playboy*, January 1982. Rock music.
"The Boogens." *Twilight Zone Magazine*, July 1982. Movie review.
"The Collected Stories of Ray Bradbury." *Chicago Tribune Bookworld*, 10 October 1980. Book review.
"The Evil Dead." *Twilight Zone Magazine*, November 1982. Movie review.
"The Fright Report." *Oui*, January 1978.
"Guilty Pleasures." *Film Comment*, May–June 1981.
"The Horror Market and the Ten Bears." *Writer's Digest*, November 1973.
"The Horrors of '79." *Rolling Stone*, 27 December 1979–10 January 1980.
"How to Scare a Woman to Death." In *Murderess, Ink*, edited by Dilys Winn, 173–77. New York: Workman, 1979.
"Imagery and the Third Eye." *Writer*, October 1980, 11–13. Informal essay.
"An Interview with Myself." *Writer's Digest*, January 1979.
"The Ludlum Attraction." *Washington Post Book World*, 7 March 1982.
"Not Guilty." *New York Times Book Review*, 24 October 1976.
"On Becoming a Brand Name." *Adelina*, February 1980.
"On *The Shining* and Other Perpetuations." *Whispers*, nos. 17–18, August 1982.
"Peter Straub: An Informal Appreciation." *Eighth World Fantasy Convention Program Book*, 1982. Brief informal essay.
"A Pilgrim's Progress." *American Bookseller*, January 1980. Informal essay.
"Visit with an Endangered Species." *Playboy*, January 1982. Informal essay.
"When Is TV Too Scary for Children?" *TV Guide*, 13–19 June 1981. Informal essay.

SECONDARY SOURCES

Underwood, Tim, and Miller, Chuck. *Fear Itself.* San Francisco: Underwood-Miller, 1982; New York: New American Library, 1984. Anthology of commentaries, with introduction by Peter Straub ("Meeting Stevie"), foreword by Stephen King ("On Becoming a Brand Name"), afterword by George A. Romero, and extensive bibliography by Marty Ketchum, Daniel A. H. Levack, and Jeff Levin. Includes articles by Burton Hatlen ("Beyond the Kittery Bridge: Stephen King's Maine"), Chelsea Quinn Yarbro ("Cinderella's Revenge"), Don Herron ("Horror Springs"), Fritz Leiber ("Horror Hits a High"), Bill Warren ("The Movies and Mr. King"), Deborah L. Notkin ("Horror and Humanity for Our Time"), Charles L. Grant ("Grey Arena"), Ben P. Indick ("Literary Tradition of Horror and the Supernatural"), Alan Ryan ("The Marsten House"), and Douglas E. Winter ("Night Journeys").

Winter, Douglas E. *Stephen King (Starmount Reader's Guide 16).* Mercer Island, Wash.: Starmount House, 1982. Commentary on *Carrie, 'Salem's Lot, The Shining, The Stand, The Dark Tower, The Dead Zone, Firestarter, The Mist,* and *Cujo,* with extensive chronology and primary and secondary bibliographies.

———.*Stephen King: The Art of Darkness.* New York: New American Library, 1984. Expanded version of preceding entry, with additional chapters on *Different Seasons, Creepshow, Christine, Cycle of the Werewolf, Pet Sematary,* and *The Talisman.* Valuable primary and secondary bibliographies; appendixes with complete plot summaries of all short fiction; and detailed listings of motion picture and television adaptations. In general, this is a favorable and often highly enthusiastic evaluation of King's work, much of it based on private interviews, correspondence, and generally unavailable background information. Documentation and bibliography are excellent.

Zagorski, Edward J. *Teacher's Manual: The Novels of Stephen King.* New York: New American Library, 1982. Pamphlet from publishers of paperback editions of King's novels.

Index

"Adam and Eve," 111
Adams, John Quincy, 43
Aeneas, 112
Aeschylus, 34; *Agamemnon*, 98–99
"age of favor," 111
Alice in Wonderland, 39
All-American theme, 71, 87, 121–25
American bicentennial, 146n5
American Eden, 90–91, 117, 129–30
American Everyman, 67
American slang, 122–26
anagnorsis, 101
ancestral dead, 19
Anderson, Sherwood: *Winesberg, Ohio*
androgyny, 44–46, 113, 149n7
"Anson Beach, Maine," 66, 104
aphasia, 74
apocalyptic dimension, 50–56, 109,
  115
Apollonian/Dionysian elements, 54, 75
Archduke Ferdinand of Austria (1914),
  137
Aristotle: *Poetics*, 101
Armageddon, 55
Arthurian romance/legends, 112, 118
A 6, 38, 58, 64, *106–9*
Astaire, Fred, 13
Auden, W. H.: "Musée des Beaux
  Arts," 82
Aurora horror monsters, 28
Auschwitz, 50

Babylon, 55
Bachman novels, 12
"bad news," 100, 101
Beckfordian landscape, 42
Bellow, Saul: *Herzog*, 33
Benchley, Peter: *Jaws*, 11
Ben Mears/Mark Petrie relationship,
  26–33
Beowulf, 23, 82
Berryman, John: *Dream Songs*, 142n7

"Big Bopper" (rock star), 90–91,
  147n5
bi-part soul, 67
Blake, William, 52; "The Tiger," 65
Blatty, William: *Exorcist*, 10
Block, Robert, 2; *Psycho*, 33
Bluebeard legend, 39
blue symbolism, *72–73*, 75, 129,
  130, *146n3*
Boccaccio, Giovanni: *Decameron*, 105
boogeyman, 76, 103
Booth, John Wilkes, 74
"boy called George," 38
Bradbury, Ray, 2; *Something Wicked
  This Way Comes*, 38, 90

Caesar, Julius, 74
Camelot, 112
"Captain Trips" (of *The Grateful Dead*),
  56, 145n4
Castle of Perseverance, The, 96
"Castle Rock, Maine," 66–67, 75–76
castration/impotence, 98–99
Cerberus myth, 115
Chamberlain, Neville, 137
Chaucer, Geoffrey, 96
Chrétien de Troyes: *Perceval*, 113,
  141n3
Christmas, 66, 88, 104
Churchill, Winston, 55, 65
CIA, 43–44, 61
Cibola, 61
Cinderella fairytale, 6, *13–17*, 40, 97
circles/elipses, *149n10*
cliché-ridden Americans, 122–26
Clotho/Lachesis/Atropos, mythology of,
  87, 99
Cochran, Eddie (rock star), 91, 147n6
"cold November wind," 86, 88, 92
Collings, Michael R., *146n4*
cosmology of Heliopolis, 59

Stevens, Wallace: "Comedian as the
   Letter C," 138–39; "Emperor of Ice
   Cream," 31
Stoker, Bram: *Dracula*, 18, 21, 25, 33
Straub, Peter, 12–13
Summers, Montague: *The Vampire: His
   Kith and Kin*, 143n13
surrealism, 53
symbolism, 52
Symbionese Liberation Army. *See* SLA

Tarkinton, Booth, 49
technology, 53
terror-point, 41
"Texas Tower Murderer." *See* Whitman,
   Charles
three fates, 87
thing without a name, 77, 114, 135
time: backward movement, 90–91;
   suspension of, 20
Tolstoy, Leo: *War and Peace*, 65
"Tony" (American Theater award),
   143n1
train imagery, 3–5, 72, 120, 131–32
Travolta, John, 135
Tryon, Thomas: *The Other*, 10
Twain, Mark, 127

Une Saison en Enfer (Arthur Rimbaud),
   52
unisexuality, 45
Updike, John: *Rabbit, Run*, 33

Valens, Richie (rock star), 90–91,
   147n5
Valentine movie illusion, 136
Valentino, Rudolph, 135
vampires, 77, 101, 135
Venus (goddess) 113; (planet), 50, 112–
   16
"Victoria and Albert," 110–12
Villanova University undergraduates
   (survey), 145n9

Virgil: *Aeneid*, 112, 115

Wagner, Richard: *Götterdämmerung*,
   51
Walpole, Horace, 52; *Castle of Otranto*,
   18
wasteland motif, 113
Watergate, 90
Welles, Orson: *Citizen Kane*, 141n2
Wells, H. G.: *Time Machine*, 90
werewolf, 77, *135–36*
Wheel of Fortune, 67, 70, 71, 72
Whitman, Charles ("Texas Tower
   Murderer"), 76
Whitman, Walt: "Song of Myself," 21
Wilt, Judith: *Ghosts of the Gothic*, 39,
   42, *144n2*
Winslow, Warren, 108
Winter, Douglas E.: *Art of Darkness*,
   149n2
wish/wishing sounds, 137
Wizard of Oz, The (Frank Baum),
   97–99
Wolf, Leonard: *The Annotated Dracula*,
   143n10
Wolfe, William ("Cujo"), 79, *81–83*,
   146n6
Wordsworth, William: "Intimations of
   Immortality," 109
World War I, 50
World War II, 46
Wright, Orville, 43, 48

year 1958, *147n5, n6*
year 1976. *See* American bicentennial
Yeats, William Butler: "The Second
   Coming," 64; "Leda and the Swan,"
   64

Zelanzy, Robert: "Game of Blood and
   Dust," 112, 149n8
"Z factor," 44, 49
zombie, 97